STATE BOARD FOR
TECHNICAL A
COMPREHENSIVE ED

P9-AQT-895

BEAUFORT TEC

LRC

Operating

Fire

Department

Pumpers

A Fire Officer's Guide

Operating
Fire
Department
Pumpers

by **PAUL R. LYONS**
NFPA Fire Service Editor

Published by the
NATIONAL FIRE PROTECTION ASSOCIATION
470 Atlantic Avenue, Boston, Massachusetts 02210

TH
9115
IN 28
NO FSP
13155
6A

BEAUFORT TEC

LRC

Printed in U.S.A.

Fourth Edition
September, 1974

Revised Second Printing
January, 1977

Library of Congress Card Number: 74–78802
NFPA No. FSP-6A
Standard Book Number: 87765–050–0

Copyright © 1974
National Fire Protection Association
470 Atlantic Avenue, Boston, Massachusetts 02210

Table of Contents

Foreword

For more than twenty years, the NFPA manual *Operating Fire Department Pumpers* has been widely used for the training of fire department pump operators and as an informational source for fire officers, instructors and other Fire Service members.

Developed in the late 1940s and early 1950s by a subcommittee of the NFPA Committee on Firemen's Training, the text was first published serially in *Firemen Magazine*, predecessor to *Fire Command!*, and later came out in book form. Warren Y. Kimball, at that time editor of *Firemen* and Staff Liaison on the Training Committee, expanded the texts with excerpts from his "Making a Good Job of It" series, a column he wrote during more than thirty years of staff service with NFPA.

As an indication of that book's popularity we can report that it was published in three editions during the past twenty years, with the last edition issued in six printings. Obviously, it has been an important manual among the many texts NFPA has published for the Fire Service.

In preparing this new edition we have retained much material from the old manual, but the scope and purpose of the book is different. It has been developed as a guide for chief officers and company officers who have the responsibility of commanding one or more engine companies. It presents information on the operational and tactical uses of pumpers, particularly with respect to recent changes in apparatus, equipment and manpower utilization. The book is intended as a companion to others in the Fire Officer's Guide series, particularly those covering aerial ladders and elevating platforms and aerial towers.

PAUL R. LYONS
NFPA Fire Service Editor

Acknowledgements

In preparing this book we relied upon previously published articles in *Fire Command!* and the response of manufacturers and fire chiefs who supplied information on modern trends in apparatus and fire department operations.

In particular, we want to express thanks to the following representatives of manufacturing companies who supplied illustrations and details: George R. Layden, Vice President, Peter Pirsch and Sons Company, Kenosha, Wisconsin; Andrew Ayers, American LaFrance, Division of A-T-O, Inc., Elmira, New York; H. O. Anderson, Vice President, American Fire Apparatus, Inc., Battle Creek, Michigan; R. D. Traister, Hale Fire Pump Company, Conshohocken, Pennsylvania; John Schar and Michael P. Waldoch, Waterous Company, St. Paul, Minnesota; J. S. Cussins, Advertising Manager, Mueller Company, Decatur, Illinois; H. J. Prendergast, W. S. Darley & Company, Melrose Park, Illinois; Douglas S. Ogilvie, Pierce Manufacturing, Inc., Appleton, Wisconsin; and Thomas R. Nist, Sales Manager, Ward LaFrance Corporation, Elmira, New York.

Special thanks are extended to the fire chiefs and other officers who contributed information on the operating methods and apparatus descriptions in Chapters 10 and 11 and to those who contributed pictures and related details, many of which appeared in Fire Command!

Space does not permit personal acknowledgement of all persons who provided illustrations or other details for this edition, but their assistance has been greatly appreciated and is hereby recognized.

Introduction

Without question, fire department pumpers are the most important apparatus used for the control of fire. Just as the infantry is the "queen of battles" in military operations, the personnel manning engine companies are the first line troops in fire combat. Without their skillful teamwork, without the controlled application of water and other extinguishing agents, fire losses would be far greater. Truly, no fire department can function without pumping apparatus.

During the past hundred years, as professional and volunteer fire departments in the United States were developing modern fireground tactics, the role of engine companies and pumping apparatus became obvious. Pumpers move large quantities of water at useful pressures, are operated by trained crews, are commanded by a company officer with the assistance of a driver/operator, and otherwise perform a tremendously important role in fire fighting action. Engine companies, and their apparatus are the heartbeat of fireground operation. They move extinguishing agents from source to target; they remain for the duration of the fire or emergency until control is complete, and they usually are the closest group to the most critical fire action. Without them no other apparatus can be relied upon to complete a fire extinguishing mission.

The NFPA *Fire Protection Handbook* and the grading schedule of the American Insurance Association place maximum emphasis on pumping apparatus in fire department operations. The schedule establishes travel distances for engine companies in communities requiring fire flows from 2,000 gpm to 12,000 gpm — three-quarters of a mile in the larger; 1½ miles in the smaller.

For first alarm response, the schedule calls for three engine companies to be within one and one-half miles for the larger required fire flows; two engine companies within two and one-half miles for the smaller communities. On multiple alarms, as many as fifteen engine companies may be required within a five-mile distance for the 12,000 population community; two engine companies within four miles for the community requiring less than 2,000 gpm fire flow.

Engine companies should be manned by six on-duty fire fighters, the company officer, driver and four fire fighters. In call or volunteer fire departments it is estimated that four members are needed as the equivalent to one full-paid member on duty, except at nighttime, if and when these volunteer members sleep at the fire station and are available for response at least nine hours during the night. In this role they are considered equivalent to on-duty members as far as computing fire company strength is concerned.

Pumpers, or engine companies, fill different needs in different areas. In the sandy, scrub pine lands of New England, they may operate as "brush breakers"; rugged, high-chassis apparatus capable of knocking down small trees and brush to reach static water supply. In mountainous country, such as Colorado, pumpers may need different capabilities to function in the thin, high altitude areas where atmospheric pressure is less than at sea level.

Fire departments on the U. S. west coast seem to prefer larger capacity apparatus — 1,500 to 2,000 gpm, compared to the 1,000 to 1,500 gpm sizes used in eastern and southern states.

In most city operations, pumpers are used directly from hydrants; rarely in drafting operations. In suburban and rural properties, pump operators must be skillful in using rivers, brooks and ponds for drafting, and may seldom have the backup of good hydrant supply.

Essentially, in fire fighting, the pumper must be stationed at a water source (hydrant or static supply), must be operated to take and move this water at certain pressures to supply handlines, deck monitors, ladder pipes, or other heavy streams; or perhaps to support sprinkler systems in fire extinguishment. But they must be mobile, in top functioning capability at all time, and fully equipped and manned to meet fire situations. Usually they carry secondary extinguishing agents and a variety of supplementary tools and equipment that will be used in extinguishment, mopup and related operations.

The Company Officer

The engine company officer must have thorough knowledge of the capabilities of the pumper and its operating crew, must be well acquainted with his department's procedures for drafting, hydrant supply, relay operations, and supply to ladder pipes, elevating platforms or portable monitors, and must have specific knowledge of routines for working with other fire companies within his department, and in mutual aid assignments.

The pump operator has similar responsibilities because the safety of personnel depends upon his estimate of pressures and other requirements for the fireground. The officer and operator work closely in the attack team, relying on established procedures and constant communications to assure effective operations. The role of the operator should not be diminished; in many fire departments, pump operators receive extra pay for their skills as one indication of their importance.

History of Pumpers

The forerunners of modern pumping apparatus in the United States probably were the two Newsham engines imported to New York City from London in 1731. These had long wooden "brakes" with room enough on each side for ten men to apply their strength in rocking a metal beam that operated a piston pump. According to some reports this pump could project a stream of about 150 feet. In the middle of the century (1743) the first successful pumping engine built in America was constructed by Thomas Lote of New York. This was followed by "gooseneck" hand pumpers which came in 1785.

At the turn of century, in 1806, the first pumping engine capable of taking suction was introduced in New York City, much to the distress of the volunteers. About that time a number of cities began to install cisterns in certain areas where pumpers could take draft. This was the beginning of the hydrant systems we know today.

The first steam fire engine built in America came in 1841, and in 1854 the reknowned "Uncle Joe Ross" steam fire engine, built by the Latta brothers, was activated in Cincinnati, Ohio and subsequently was used in other cities.

The first accepted performance tests on automobile pumping engines were conducted during the convention of the International Association of Fire Engineers in Milwaukee, Wisconsin in 1911. This was the parent association of today's International Association of Fire Chiefs (IAFC). In 1912, the convention held tests on seven pumping engines discharging under net pumping pressures of 120, 200 and 250 psi during operations of three to eleven minutes. By the next convention of the IAFE in New York City, (1913) a test procedure had been developed consisting of six hours pumping at full capacity at 120 psi, three hours pumping at one half capacity at 200 psi and three hours pumping at one third capacity at 250 psi. By 1912 a twelve-hour underwriters' test for automobile pumpers had become a routine procedure.

The first NFPA Standard No. 19 on automobile fire apparatus was adopted in 1914. At that time pressure-volume ratings were standardized at 120 psi net pump pressure, and this remained until the early 1950's when the present 150 psi rating was established. Today, the NFPA Committee on Fire Department Equipment includes representatives of the International Association of Fire Chiefs, manufacturing firms and associations and other representative groups. Standard No. 19 — now designated as No. 1901 — *Automotive Fire Apparatus*, is revised about every two years and is recognized nationally as a practical criterion for specifying performance of fire apparatus.

Purpose of This Book

This book is intended to provide fire company officers and pumper operators with essential information not readily available in manufacturers' manuals and other texts dealing with mechanical equipment used in pumping. It incorporates material resulting from changes in NFPA standards and other improvements in fire department pumping equipment and reflects recent experience in fireground tactical operations. The text has not been reviewed by NFPA committees, but does include information based on fire department reports and upon articles previously published in NFPA periodicals. This second printing of the fourth edition includes the new designation of Standard No. 19 to 1901, and some additional minor editorial changes.

List of Chapter Illustrations

Monitor nozzle on Chelsea, Massachusetts pumper supplied by 4-inch hose. (Photo by Charles A. Tuck, Jr.)

Chapter 1

Features of a Pumper

The function of a fire department pumper is to move large quantities of water at certain pressures so that fire extinguishment can be accomplished efficiently. In normal operations, the pumper is operated by a driver (sometimes called an engineer) with three or four other members of an engine company, all under the command of a fire company officer, who may be a lieutenant, a sergeant, or a captain. The driver operates the pump; the officer supervises and directs overall company operations; the fire fighters man the hose lines and deck gun and perform other required tasks.

The officer in charge of this group has a highly responsible command assignment. The modern engine company in a paid or volunteer fire department has to be a thoroughly trained team, with each member aware of the importance of pumper operations and his personal roles on the fireground. It is up to the company officer to lead, inspire and direct this team.

Without question, pumpers are the most essential apparatus in almost every major fire control action. Usually they operate continually from time of first alarm response until the fire has been extinguished and salvage and overhaul operations are begun. They can perform a double role: as a direct attack unit or as a source of water supply for other apparatus. In either role, pumpers and engine companies are vitally important.

It is worthwhile to review the principal components of modern fire department pumpers which will be referred to frequently in this text.   The following basic features should be apparent in walkaround examination of this apparatus:

Engine.   Most fire apparatus have gasoline or diesel engines of custom-made or commercial type, but the capability and performance of the engine is especially important for pumping because of the changing loads that must be accepted by the engine. Standard No. 19 requires an engine governor that will limit the speed of the engine under all conditions of operation to a maximum no-load governed speed established by the engine manufacturer.   The engine speed/torque ratio should be considered when purchase specifications are being developed, because road conditions and pumping operations will differ considerably in cities, towns and rural areas.

Elevation of terrain is particularly important; if a pump is going to be operated at an elevation above 2,000 feet, that should be specified.

Similarly, the requirements for power takeoff performance (pto) must be considered.   There are several possibilities: a pto driven booster pump; a pto driven hydraulic pump for an aerial ladder or elevating platform; or a pto driven electric generator, or a combination of units.   These can operate from a straight mechanical transmission or an automatic transmission, but the complete range of performance must be within the engine's designed limits.

Control Panel.   In most pumpers, this large panel is located at the left side of the vehicle just behind the step leading to the driver's cab, but at least two pumper manufacturers have placed this control panel midship, immediately behind the cab and in front of the hose body.   Regardless of the location, the control panel will include most of the following: gages, operating controls, valves, intakes, and discharge connections, all of which must be observed by the pump operator as he maintains supply for fire fighting.

Control panel of Seattle Fire Department "Big Boss" pumper has compound gage and pressure gage at upper left, gages for nitrogen pressurized sphere at right. Control for Hale relief valve is at left of operator's right hand.

Panel of 1250 gpm Mack pumper in Lexington, Massachusetts features large gages (top center), Waterous electric transfer valve and relief valve (top right), a pressure computer (center), a pump overheat indicator and water level gage (lower right center). (Raymond B. Barns photo)

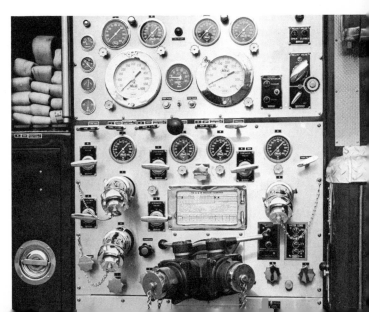

Top console panel control on W. S. Darley midship pumper. All discharge valves are controlled by mechanical linkage. Gages include relief valve, throttle, tachometer and tank level gage. Operator, standing in back of his cab, can get good view of fireground scene. Water level indicator gage at left, relief valve at right.

Primer. A device that displaces air from the main centrifugal pump or otherwise creates a negative pressure within the pump and consequently lets water into the suction hose and pump.

Throttle. Device for regulating engine speed to maintain pump operation.

Transfer Valve. A control valve for placing a pump in volume (parallel) or pressure (series) operation. May be operated manually or by electric control.

Line Valves. Devices for opening and closing supply to hose lines, the deck gun, or other parts of the pumping system.

Gages. Glass enclosed indicators of pressure, flow, engine speed, and other operating functions.

Compound Gage. Records pressures above and below atmospheric level to indicate when the pumper is accepting water under pressure from a hydrant, or is drafting water from a static source. Pressures below atmospheric are usually registered in inches of mercury when a pump is drafting. The compound gage is connected to the suction side of the pump.

Discharge Gage. Records pressure being discharged by pump. It may be a second compound gage or a simple pressure gage at each pumper outlet. Recently, flow meters have been installed on pumping apparatus to record the gpm discharge, rather than pressure. These are sometimes used in combination with self-adjusting nozzles, thus diminishing the need for calculating friction losses. If the flow meter at the pump indicates that the required gpm volume is being discharged, then the nozzle is projecting this flow at the optimum pressure for its design.

Tachometer. A device for measuring and recording engine speed (revolutions per minute). Pumps should always be operated within the engine speeds and gear ratios designated by the manufacturer.

Inlet or Intake. A water supply connection on a pumper to which suction or supply hose may be attached. Large suction intakes are usually 4½-inches to 6-inches in diameter; others may be 2½-inch diameter or larger.

The Pump. NFPA Standard No. 1901 requires modern pumpers to have a centrifugal pump of 500, 750, 1,000, 1,250, 1,500, 1,750 or 2,000 gpm capacity, designed and manufactured to give the following performance: 100 percent of rated capacity at 150 psi net pump pressure; 70 percent of rated capacity at 200 psi net pump pressure; and 50 percent of rated capacity at 250 psi net pump pressure. The pump must be able to take suction from a 10-foot lift and discharge water in not more than 30 seconds through 20 feet of suction hose of appropriate size for pumps under 1,500 gpm and not over 45 seconds for pumps of 1,500 gpm or greater capacity.

Net pump pressure is the difference between discharge pressure and the pressure on the suction side of the pump.

Standard sized pumps should not be confused with booster pumps which are defined as permanently mounted pumps rated at less than 500 gpm capacity.

Centrifugal pumps can be single-stage, or multi-stage, the difference being in the number and arrangement of impellers which move the water from the pump suction chamber to the discharge side of the pump.

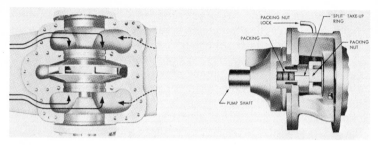

*Hale single stage QSD pump has double suction intakes on same shaft with single impeller. This view from underneath shows path of water (*arrows*) when suction feeds from both sides of pump. At right is Hale single stuffing box on low pressure (*suction*) side of pump.*

Compartments.   Standard No. 19 lists required, recommended and optional equipment and tools to be carried on each pumper. Nozzles, portable fire extinguishers, breathing apparatus and other essentials are included but it is up to the local fire department to determine where and how this equipment will be carried on the pumper. The size, location and number of compartments must be determined by the chief or the fire department apparatus purchasing committee.

Suction Hose.   Suction hose is used to supply water to a pump from a drafting source or hydrant. It ranges in size from 2½-inch to 6-inch diameter and is of two types — soft and hard suction hose. Soft suction hose is generally woven-jacketed, rubber-lined hose. Hard suction hose is usually rubber-covered, rubber-lined hose, stiff enough to prevent collapse from atmospheric pressure when a partial vacuum is created in the pump during drafting.

Relief Valve.   Not immediately visible but certainly important are the pressure controlling devices essential to safe operation. At the pump, this device is designed to prevent excessive pressure if a nozzle is shut down suddenly.

Governors and other regulators are designed to control pump pressures by changing speed of the engine, but relief valves accomplish pressure regulation by bypassing water from the discharge back to the suction side of the pump. The flow of water under pressure passes through a chamber or hydraulic cylinder in which a spring-loaded piston has been set to function at certain pressure. If a hose line closes down suddenly, or there is some other change in the discharge, the water in the cylinder forces the piston to move so that the excess water flows into the suction side of the pump and pressure in the cylinder drops to the established level.

Pressure relief valves are also available for installation on the supply side of the pump so that pressure entering the pump from another source can be discharged to the ground when the set pressure is exceeded.

Governors. The purpose of a governor on a pumper is to control the speed of the engine and the pump impellers, so there will be no surges in pressure that may endanger nozzlemen, burst hose lines, or cause other damage. Governors must be designed to function quickly and effectively and to control strong pressures in critical portions of the pumping operation.

On American LaFrance pumps, the governor is designed to throttle the engine automatically, thus varying the speed of pump impellers to maintain constant pump pressure, from 90 to 300 psi, as preset by the pump operator.

The LaFrance governor system includes a balancing cylinder that actuates the engine throttle linkage; a throttle linkage (or governor) clutch that engages the cylinder rod with the throttle linkage after the reference or control pressure has been set; a reference pressure reservoir in which air is compressed; and a water governor three-position control valve by which the entire mechanism can be set. (See sketches.) The governor should function when the volume of water is changed by opening or closing nozzles on hose lines being supplied by the pumper.

When the water supply becomes insufficient for the pump discharge lines, the governor should disengage, allowing the engine to return to idling speed so that pump cavitation will not occur. This protects the hose men from severe nozzle reaction that can occur in cavitation and protects the engine and pump from runaway damage.

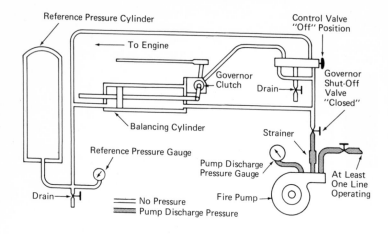

Governor control system of American LaFrance pumper.

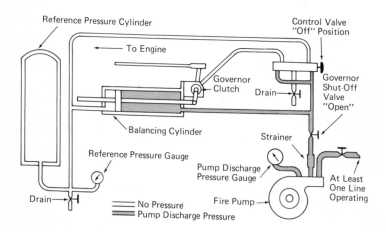

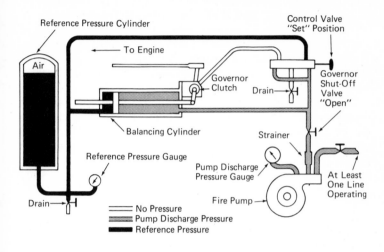

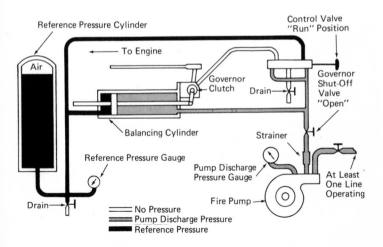

On Waterous pumps, the control of pressure is established by an engine governor that maintains constant pump pressure at any setting between 75 and 500 psig. This assembly consists of a cylinder assembly, a directional flow valve and an accumulator. The assembly includes a cylinder and two heads enclosing a hydraulically balanced piston. This assembly slides in a bracket when the throttle is adjusted manually.

The pressure actuated directional control spool valve receives pump discharge pressure at one end and acts against a spring on the other end. When discharge pressure reaches 75 psig the spring is compressed and the valve is actuated. When pump pressure drops below 30 psig the spring deactivates the valve. A needle valve controls the response rate and excessive pressure fluctuation.

The accumulator assembly is a one-gallon, two-chamber tank with a bladder separating a gas chamber from a water chamber. The gas side is factory precharged at 75 psig. When the pump is operating and the desired pressure is reached, the pressure on the water side of the accumulator will equal discharge pressure and turning the operating valve to ON activates the system for automatic pressure control.

Pierce pumper has the "New York type" gages in top center, with compound gage at left, pressure gage at right. Smaller gages are for discharge lines.

Panel on Hanover, New Hampshire Fire Department pumper has large wheel valve above top gages to control flow to turret nozzle. Compartment for "Mattydale" hose lay of 1½-inch lines is above pump at upper left. Relief valve is just below compartment. Outlets have Chiksan swivel. (Photo by S. Corpieri)

The Hale governor includes a throttle, pullout actuator and air tank. In operation the throttle is opened until desired pressure is reached, the actuator is pulled and held for three seconds, then the throttle is closed. The governor thereafter will control engine speed and pressure according to the setting, as the spring-piston arrangement regulates the carburetor and affects engine and pump impeller speeds.

Discharge Connections. Pumper outlets to which hose lines are attached. Usually these are 2½-inch couplings but may be 3- or 3½-inch. Normally a pumper has one 2½-inch outlet for each 250 gpm of its capacity. For example: a 750 gpm pumper would have at least three outlets; a 1,000 gpm pumper would have four outlets.

Other Features. In addition to these components of the control panel, the modern fire department pumper has a number of other important characteristics. Among these are: size and type of pump; amount of space in the hose bed; type and amount of hose carried; size and location of the water tank; size and placement of piping between tank, pump and discharge outlets; size and location of preconnected hose; piping and connections to the deck gun and to any other special extinguishing equipment carried on the vehicle; suction hose, lights, and special safety equipment carried on the vehicle.

Certainly of importance is the overall size — length, height, width and weight of the pumper. These factors affect its position in a fire station and response routes to emergencies. The type of chassis, transmission, axles, tires and other features should be noted. Each will be covered in subsequent portions of this text.

Waterous pressure control operation.

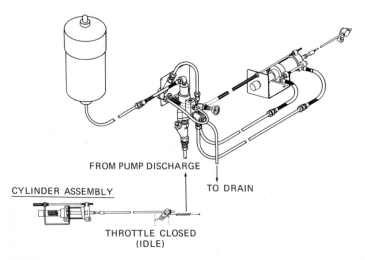

FROM PUMP DISCHARGE

CYLINDER ASSEMBLY   TO DRAIN

THROTTLE CLOSED
(IDLE)

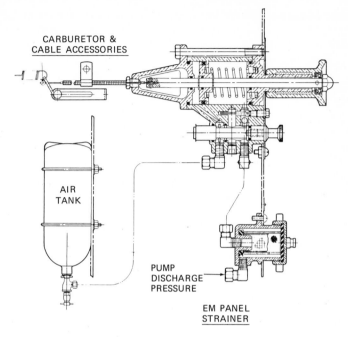

CARBURETOR &
CABLE ACCESSORIES

AIR
TANK

PUMP
DISCHARGE
PRESSURE

EM PANEL
STRAINER

Hale EM Governor system.

Hose Loads. When sizing up a pumper, a very important indication of how that pumper will be used is displayed in the arrangement, location and diameters of its hose. The loading, type, amount and connecting of the hose discloses how the fire company has anticipated and prepared for its operations — whether the crew will be ready to go into action immediately with efficient, time-saving, practical evolutions, or is unprepared for fireground operations.

The first indication is in the arrangements for preconnected hose and heavy streams. Twenty years ago, much attention was given to ¾- or 1-inch booster hose as a first attack line. When lightweight fog nozzles came into use in the early 1950's, many fire departments took pride in extinguishing small fires "with a teacup" of water, a commendable change from the bigger and slower washdowns from heavy lines and straight stream tips of earlier days, but still not a realistic preparation for the common fire emergency.

During the 1950's and early 1960's fire departments analyzed their basic response tactics and, by evaluating the combined capabilities of their pumpers, hose loads, monitor nozzles and handline nozzles, began to work toward the optimum use of each component. In the same period, apparatus and pump manufacturers were redesigning to provide more efficient use of the entire pumper. First came improved piping arrangements so that 1½- and 2½-inch lines could be preconnected for immediate supply from the tank. This resulted from fireground experience that proved that something more than booster lines were needed for first alarm fires. Development of the adjustable fog nozzle (from straight stream to 90 degree fog pattern) was an important influence in this change; so was the practicality of the monitor nozzle operating directly from the pump. The "blitz" or full attack evolution, utilizing pump and water tank while connecting to hydrant supply, was a logical outgrowth of the improved pumper components, fire hose and nozzles.

Obviously, performance of a fire department pumper will be limited by the amount and size of hose and nozzles assigned to it, and its manning. If the pumper can produce 1,250 or 1,500 gpm at standard pressures, then the combination of handlines and heavy streams using this flow must be arranged for fast and efficient distribution of water. Certain tradeoffs are necessary; if the monitor nozzle is going to deliver 750 or 1,000 gpm directly from the tank then the pumper must be close to the target fire, perhaps within 100 feet. If, however, this same flow is to be applied through 2½-inch handlines, then the pumper may be two or three hundred feet or more from the fire and the hose load might require different arrangement. Wyeing the 2½-inch lines into smaller handlines would permit extension of the water application. (Chapter 3.)

Waterous electric transfer valve.

Today, most fire departments operate with split hose beds carrying 1,000 to 2,000 feet of 2½-inch, 3- or 3½-inch hose, with perhaps a 200-foot length of preconnected 2½-inch hose, maybe the same amount of 1½-inch hose preconnected, plus 100 feet or more of booster hose on a reel.

If a modern pumper is not arranged for quick action, it probably is used as a backup piece to the principal attack forces; it certainly is not ready for the immediate requirements of today's fireground problems. The best of today's pumpers can deliver full capacity immediately, and may only be limited by the duration of tank supply, or by the speed of obtaining supply from a hydrant or other apparatus. It is up to the engine company officers and fire fighters to use this capacity quickly and efficiently.

In addition to first attack operations, the engine company must be prepared to supply other pumpers in relay, or to support heavy stream attack by the big monitor nozzles on aerial ladders, elevating platforms or mobile water towers. This may require laying multiple supply lines or a single, large-diameter line that will assure the full flow to the monitor. For these evolutions, the engine company personnel may operate in a secondary role, but still must be able to get full performance from their pumper. Much depends on how the company, or the fire department as a whole has trained and prepared for these operations.

The company officer, the engineer or pump operator, and the entire engine company crew have an obligation to use the pumper and its equipment to maximum advantage. The possibility of developing new, more efficient techniques is a continual challenge.

BEAUFORT   TEC

LRC

13459

Barton-American duplex multistage gear train.

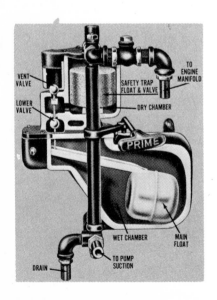

Barton-American primer.

QUESTIONS

Chapter 1

Text:

1. Name five items that are usually on a pump control panel.
2. What should be the sizes of suction intakes?
3. What is the purpose of the primer and how does it operate?
4. How does the pressure relief valve operate?
5. How does the governor operate?
6. How many outlets should a pumper have?
7. What sizes of handline hose are carried on today's pumpers?
8. Why is a tachometer needed on the control panel?

Discussion:

1. What pumper capacity is best for your fire company?
   Give three reasons why.
2. Describe what hose sizes, types of nozzles, and evolutions would produce maximum practical discharge from this pumper.
3. Describe the general design of a pumper in your fire company, then sketch and explain how you would reorganize it for better efficiency.
4. What do you think is the largest, the maximum practical capacity of a pumper? What would be some of the limiting factors?
5. What is the best hose load arrangement of 2½- and 3-inch size?

San Francisco fire fighters operating on large warehouse fire. (Photo by Chet Born)

Chapter 2

Tactical Uses of Pumpers

Among the important decisions that must be made by company officers are those concerning placement or "spotting" of pumpers on the fireground. In large cities, where fire companies usually operate within well-defined areas or districts, prefire planning and departmental orders may require specific assignment of engine companies to certain hydrants and operations. This works well for most fire emergencies. In smaller towns and in outlying suburban and rural areas, fires may require more flexible operations, particularly when mutual aid response is included.

Whatever the situation, the officer in command of a responding engine company must be prepared to order placement and operation of the pumper for maximum efficiency in direct attack or in conjunction with, or in support of other apparatus. He may not know until the last few seconds just how the company under his command will operate. His pumper may pass the nearest hydrant and go directly to the fire to start booster line or other preconnected operations directly from the tank. Or, if his company is second-in, his pumper may take the hydrant (or stop at a suction source) and supply the first-in pumper at the fire or take a reverse lay. It is likely that these operations are defined in departmental training and orders (Chapter 12) so that the fire fighters under his command will know exactly what their first operations will be. Even so, the officer has to make quick, correct decisions in these moments.

The operator of the first-in pumper will be concerned with maintaining supply to pre-connected lines or monitor nozzle, then accepting and controlling water supply from the second pumper.

The first-in pumper may not use its suction hose if quick back-up from a second pumper can be depended upon and probably will only use its main hose load as handlines or supply lines for monitor nozzles.

The second pumper may drop a man at the hydrant, then use sufficient hose to supply the first pumper in direct or reverse layout. This usually requires two or three 2½-inch or larger lines. The pumper taking the hydrant will connect with one or more lengths of hard suction, or may use its regular hose lines for supply from the hydrant.

In a rural area, or some other location where hydrant supply is not available, similar operations can be developed from a lake, pond, stream or other source of open water supply. The pumper at the source probably will be using one or more lengths of hard suction hose in a drafting operation (*Chapter* 7). For this evolution, the first-in pumper heading for the fire may drop one or more 2½-inch (or larger) hose lines at the static source to speed up relay operations when drafting begins.

Standard Layouts. NFPA Standard No. 197 defines the minimum fire fighting capability which should be expected of first-arriving pumpers on the fireground. Essentially, it requires that effective streams be delivered from two 1½-inch lines in a two-position attack, backed up by a 2½-inch line supplied by correct pressure from a pumper. In high value areas, or for target hazards, twice this attack capability may be needed.

If an engine company has adequate manpower and is well-trained, such use of effective streams should be accomplished easily. The flows required for this evolution are 75 gpm for each of the 1½-inch lines and 250 gpm for the big line, or a total of 400 gpm. Fire companies may have different methods of achieving these results and the standard allows for such variety (*see sketches*).

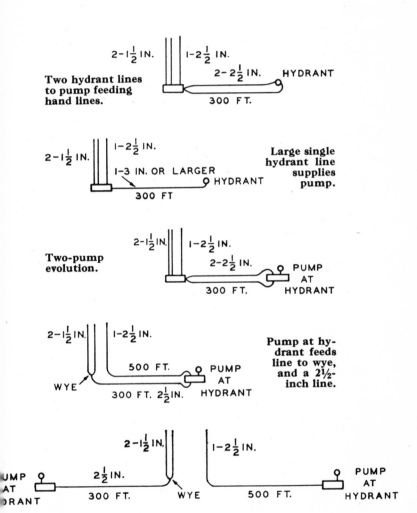

Two hydrant lines to pump feeding hand lines.

Large single hydrant line supplies pump.

Two-pump evolution.

Pump at hydrant feeds line to wye, and a 2½-inch line.

Two pumps spotted at hydrants feed line to wye and a 2½-inch hand line.

Operating from Water Tank. Full capacity of a pumper in a fast, initial attack may include operation of one or more lines of booster hose, use of a pre-connected 1½-inch or 2½-inch hose and perhaps use of a monitor nozzle, all operating simultaneously to drain the booster tank. One handicap in this type of attack is that it depends upon quick resupply from the second-due pumper, because when the tank supply is exhausted this engine company is rather helpless. But good planning, coordination and teamwork can make this attack a very effective operation if company officers and pump operators are alert to possible variables in the evolution.

The current (1974) edition of NFPA Standard No. 1901 provides for a minimum flow of 250 gpm from the water tank on a pumper when water tank capacity is 300 to 750 gallons and 500 gpm for water tanks over 750 gallons. This flow permits supply of two 1½-inch hose lines or one 2½-inch hose line from the tank for initial attack. Since most standard pumpers have a tank capacity of 300 gpm or more, this initial attack water supply would last for a little more than one minute. Depending on the fire situation, this may be adequate, if the quick blast of water can be applied directly to the fire. However, if the fire is inside a building, or otherwise shielded, the company officer may want to extend this limited water supply by using just one

All first line pumpers in Williamsport, Pennsylvania carry one 2½-inch preconnected hoseline, plus four or five preconnected 1½-inch attack lines 150 to 200 feet long. First line pumpers also have preconnected deck guns with 750 and 1,000 gpm fog nozzles. The department plans to use 6,000 feet of 3-inch hose and 1,500 feet of 5-inch hose as supply lines.

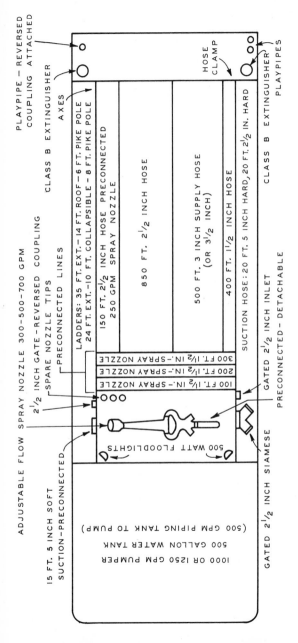

Sketch of typical attack pumper capable of various operations. Pump capacity is 1,000 to 1,250 gpm; there is a 500 gallon tank with appropriate piping to pump; fifteen feet of 5-inch soft suction hose, pre-connected; cross-bed layers of pre-connected 1½-inch lines; a pre-connected 2½-inch line; and hose load of 2½-inch and 3-inch lines. Ground ladders, play pipe, extinguishers and suction hose are standard equipment.

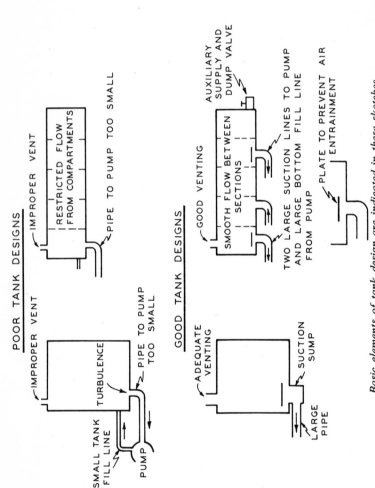

Basic elements of tank design are indicated in these sketches.

or two small lines in a holding action until secondary water supply is available.

This also applies to application of a pre-connected monitor nozzle which, if of 500 gpm capacity or greater, will use up the 300-gallon water tank supply in about a half minute. Yet, there could be occasions when this short duration of large volume discharge would solve a particular fire situation. A larger water tank, say 800 or 1,000 gallons, would permit a more sustained attack.

For each of these pre-connected operations the piping from water tank to pump and from pump to discharge outlet must be adequate to permit the flow. This is especially important when pumpers have larger tanks, such as 750 gallon capacity or more. The size and capacity of the piping from the water tank to the pump depends on the size and shape of the water tank and the location of the pump. A single 2½-inch discharge line is the minimum for supplying a pump from a vertical booster tank. For large flows, a single 3-inch or 4-inch pipe may be needed to provide enough supply to the pump. If the tank is horizontal and is of 750 gallon capacity or larger, two 2½-inch or larger discharge lines may be siamesed into the pump suction. Whatever the arrangement, each preconnected line or monitor nozzle must be assured adequate flow capacity.

Also important is the design of the water tank to permit adequate venting for rapid discharge of water by gravity. This should be stated in original pumper purchase specifications and the manufacturer must be informed when the fire department's operations require quick emptying of the water tank. The location, piping and venting of the tank should be properly designed from the start.

One- and Two-piece Engine Companies. Many fire departments have been successful in using single-piece engine companies in tactical operations but these units usually require specific tactical assignments and well-drilled evolutions. Their procedures are based on the fact that they can quickly drop sufficient hose at the hydrant, move to the fire fighting location, and thus be assured of continuous water supply for full pumper discharge capacity. In some departments these pumpers have 1,000 feet or more of large diameter supply hose and their evolutions are based on the fact that they will not receive supply from other apparatus.

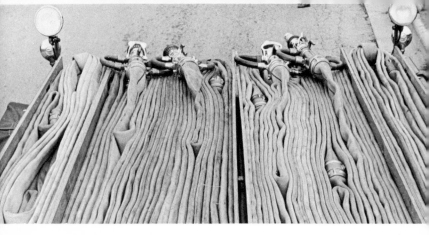

Shelby, North Carolina developed split load of 3-inch hose packed in reverse lay, (Male couplings lead off), both sides. Trays carry 2½-inch and 1½-inch hose, each 150 feet long.

Another operation requires a two-piece company. These units are usually standard-equipped pumpers and their positions on the fireground can be interchanged. The first-in pumper generally goes to the fire scene and directly applies water to the fire. The second pumper lays out the hose and supplies the first unit with water. In some departments, this second pumper is equipped as a hose wagon even though it has a standard pump. In tactical operations, its role is usually to supply other pumpers or heavy stream devices, rather than operating as a first-due pumper. Hose wagons are usually more popular in cities that have large, well-manned fire departments and consequently can be used in these manual functions rather than directly in fire fighting.

Pump and Roll. A third use of pumpers is in the pump and roll operations common in rural and forestry fire fighting. Outdoor fires, such as brush, grass, or grain fields, can be fast-moving, particularly on windy days, and small, maneuverable four-wheel drive vehicles are needed for effective flank attack on these fires.

These pumpers often utilize a power takeoff from the vehicle engine so that a small monitor nozzle or other hose streams can be operated by personnel standing on the truck. Because a large percentage of engine power must be used in moving the vehicle, there is a loss in pump efficiency but at least the small discharge of water and vehicle mobility can be effective on some of these special fires.

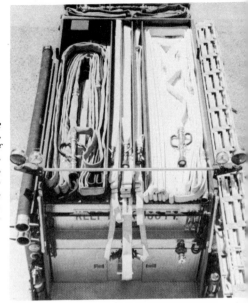

Attack pumper of Hampshire Fire Protection District in Illinois carries two (each) 750-foot lines of 2½- and 3½-inch hose, three rear 150-foot lines, two 1½- and one 2½-inch. Cross-bed compartment behind cab has two 150-foot lines of 1½-inch hose, one having an in-line foam eductor. (Photo by Gene P. Carlson.)

Another arrangement is to have a separate portable pump carried on the vehicle which can be operated at full capacity until the water tank supply is exhausted. For these pump and roll tactics, handlines are usually of booster hose size — ¾- or 1-inch-diameter, with appropriate variable pattern fog nozzles.

Supplying Elevating Streams. Another tactical use of a pumper is the supplying of water to heavy stream monitor nozzles used on ladder pipes or the baskets of elevating platforms. These nozzles may range from 500 to 1,000 gpm discharge capacity and, to produce effective streams, require at least 750 gpm intake at the siamese connection at sufficient pressure to provide 100 psig nozzle pressure while delivering the rated capacity of the nozzle. Such flows and pressures require that the supporting pumper be nearby, preferably within 100 feet, feeding at least three 2½-inch hose lines to the siamese connection of the aerial ladder truck or platform. This pumper may be stationed at a hydrant or may be accepting relay water supply from another pumper.

Pumper in Hockessin, Delaware Fire Company carries 1,000 feet of 3-inch hose in a split bed for single or double layout; a preconnected 2½-inch line (left of bed); two 2½- 1½-inch preconnects; twin booster reels; a 750 gpm Hale single stage pump; a high pressure booster pump; ground ladders and related equipment.

QUESTIONS

Chapter 2

Text:

1. What is one problem when operating from the tank?
2. What is a problem with pump and roll apparatus?
3. What is a limitation of a single-piece engine company?
4. Describe direct and reverse layouts.
5. What is the difference between "taking a hydrant" and setting up for drafting?
6. What is the minimum required tank-to-pump flow when the tank capacity is 400 gpm?

Discussion:

1. What is the difference between a hose load for direct layout and one arranged for reverse layout?
2. Is it tactically wise to equip and arrange a few pumpers for "blitz" attack and not arrange *all* pumpers this way?
3. What other practical attack pumper arrangement can you describe?
4. How should a monitor nozzle be preconnected without using hose?
5. At what speed should a pump operate for drafting?

Water Supply Officer of Philadelphia Fire Department uses hand portable two-way radio to check on pumping needs.

Chapter 3

Operating the Pumper

When the pumper has been located on the fireground to greatest advantage, the next step is to start the pump operating when it is needed. Speed is essential, so the operator must do each job in proper sequence with little lost motion.

Four general actions should be taken, the first three before leaving the driver's seat:

1. IMMOBILIZE THE VEHICLE. Make sure the emergency brake is applied to hold the vehicle against movement. (Where necessary due to terrain or other conditions, apply wheel chocks.)

2. TRANSMIT ENGINE POWER TO THE PUMP. Be certain that the transmission shift lever is in the proper position, usually in direct drive. On some makes of pumpers the lever must be in fourth gear. (Do not confuse this position with second or reverse.) Repeated practice sessions will give the operator a sense of being able to feel when the pump is engaged. This may also be determined by sound.

3. CHECK GAGES. Before leaving the driver's seat the pumper operator should glance at the oil pressure, engine temperature, gasoline supply, ammeter and tachometer gages to make certain that engine is operating correctly to begin pumping.

4. ENGAGE PUMP. In general, except for some booster pumps, the pump is engaged from the pump operator's position where the controls are grouped. This is usually at one side of the vehicle. The pump shift lever should be engaged without clashing of gears and without force. An auxiliary engine throttle is provided at the pump operator's position to control engine speed. This permits a close degree of control of engine speed and also makes it possible to slow the engine to idle almost instantly in an emergency.

If pump controls are activated from the driver's position these should be engaged before stepping out of the cab. This can be done safely for booster operation because the pump will not run dry for a relatively long period of time.

Operating from a Booster Tank

To speed delivery of water on a fire, some fire departments carry the pump and booster hose full of water at all times. However, there is the possibility of the pump freezing during winter weather, so many pumpers have all pipes, fittings and gages enclosed so they can be heated by the engine. Included are the pump, booster tank and booster lines.

Radio communication is very important for pump operation. This is a Creve Coeur Fire Protection District pumper in Missouri.

A San Francisco pumper supplies a ladder pipe, handlines and other units at apartment house fire.

The valve or valves controlling the entrance of water from the booster tank to the suction side of the pump must be wide open to assure a full flow of water. A valve only partially open may restrict the flow and result in failure of the pump to supply proper volume and pressure. This may cause excessive engine speed for the pressure produced.

Valves of several types may be used on pumpers. These vary from a type that can be opened completely by a quarter turn, to a type that takes several complete revolutions of the handle or control wheel to open. In any case the pump operator must know the type of valves on his pumper and exactly what each controls. The manufacturer's instruction manual provides this information.

As a general rule it is better to open or close valves gradually rather than instantaneously. This permits the column of water to gain momentum or cease motion gradually. Valves should not be opened or closed when water is under high pressure. Continued operation from the booster tank can be assured by adding water to the booster tank from whatever source may be available. Make sure that clean water enters the booster tank. Foreign matter (sand and other abrasive grit) will clog pipes and strainers and may do severe damage to the pump.

Some centrifugal pumps may require priming for booster operation because the force of gravity does not move the water fast enough into the pump or the pump design may leave an air space within the pump body.

Positive displacement pumps should be operated in the pressure position for booster lines. It may be necessary to crack the by-pass (churn) valve to keep the pump from laboring, to make it work smoother and to prevent overheating. In booster operation (or when supplying small pre-connected lines from another pressurized water source) relatively little engine power is required to move the small quantity of water discharged. High engine speeds are not necessary. For most work with multi-stage centrifugal pumps the transfer valve should be in the pressure position. In general, this will develop the required pressure at lower engine speed.

When a pump is supplying a stream which is in intermittent use, it often is necessary to operate the by-pass valve to circulate the water back to the tank to prevent serious overheating of the water in the pump.

Panel of Bean high pressure pump with enclosed compartment for hose-line and nozzle at top.

Connecting Suction Hose

When drafting from open water supplies it may be necessary to connect the suction hose before the pumper takes final position and wrestle the hose into position as the pumper moves forward.

Always use an adequate strainer on the immersed end of the suction hose and check the strainer in the pump intake to be sure it is unobstructed. The end of the suction hose should be kept off the bottom to avoid sucking grit and abrasive material into the pump and to avoid blocking the end of the suction hose with mud. Small stones and debris may pass through a centrifugal pump but may damage the pump because of the close fit between the impellers and pump housing and thus hinder the pump's ability to give satisfactory pressure. A rope attached to the end of the suction hose may be tied to any substantial object to keep the hose off the bottom. If the water is shallow, the strainer can be laid on a salvage cover or sheet of metal. It may be possible to use a jet of water from a booster line to keep the suction strainer clear by driving floating debris away.

All suction hose connections must be air tight. Gaskets must be new and fresh to assure perfect seat between the male and female couplings.

For large flows, the end of the suction strainer should be submerged at least eighteen inches below the water level to prevent formation of a whirlpool that permits air to enter the suction hose. Whirlpools can be prevented by placing a baffle at the water surface, or by digging a depression in the bottom of the water source so the end of the section can be submerged to a greater depth. Baffles can be improvised from metal signs, wood doors, salvage covers, or similar objects.

When drafting from a small flowing stream the depth of water can be increased by making a dam. It may be practical to use a ladder and a salvage cover for this purpose.

These same techniques will apply for drafting from a portable tank, swimming pool, or improvised basin but dirt and debris should not be a problem in this operation.

Large diameter lines from Pierce pumper supply elevating platform during IAFC demonstration.

Drafting

Operating a pumper from a source of water supply under pressure is generally done with less difficulty than drafting because the task of the pump is easier and less complicated when the water flows readily into the pump intake.

Drafting puts an added burden on the engine. It is usually undertaken when no adequate source of water under pressure is readily available, or when it is desired to conserve available hydrant supplies. It requires the same amount of horsepower for the engine to lift the water from the source of supply to the pump intake, as it does to force the water an equal distance upward.

The average city fire department does not have to draft water very frequently. As a result some pump operators may be inexperienced compared to those who draft water often. Success in drafting is assured by practice and a good preventive maintenance program.

Water obtained through draft is caused to flow through suction hose by removing air from the pump housing and all connections attached. When air is emptied from inside the pump and suction hose there is a difference in pressure between the inside of the

Adaptors are sometimes needed to connect big hose to the standard pumper fitting.

pump and the outside, so the higher outside atmospheric pressure causes water to enter the submerged end of the suction hose and flow into the pump.

The distance water can be drafted is limited partly by the ability of the pump to get the air out of the pump chamber. Normal atmospheric pressure at sea level is 14.7 pounds per square inch, and it lessens with elevation.

In theory a perfect pump could draft water 14.7 psi (the maximum pressure difference) multiplied by 2.30 (the distance in feet one pound pressure will elevate one pound of water). This equals 33.9 feet. This efficiency is never attained with fire service priming pumps or devices because no fire service pump could produce or maintain a perfect vacuum due to required operating clearances and it would not be economically practical to obtain this mechanical efficiency. NFPA Standard No. 1901 requires the priming system to be capable of producing a vacuum of 22 inches (mercury) which is the equivalent of a 25-foot lift at sea level, and calls for ability to draft full rated capacity at a 10-foot lift using appropriate size of suction hose for the required flow.

Table Showing Minimum Discharge Which Should be Expected of a Pumper in Good Condition Operating at Draft at Various Lifts.

Conditions: Operating at Net Pump Pressure of 150 psi; Altitude of 1000 feet; Water Temperature of 60° F; Barometric Pressure of 28.94 inches Hg (poor weather conditions).

(American Insurance Association, Fire Stream Tables.)

Rated Capacity Pump		500 gpm		750 gpm		1000 gpm		1250 gpm	1500 gpm		
Suction Hose Size		4″	4½″	4½″	5″	5″	6″	6″	6″	Dual 5″	Dual 6″
4	20′ Suction Hose (Two Sections)	590	660	870	945	1160	1345	1435	1735	1990	2250
6		560	630	830	905	1110	1290	1375	1660	1990	2150
8		530	595	790	860	1055	1230	1310	1575	1810	2040
10		500	560	750	820	1000	1170	1250	1500	1720	1935
12		465	520	700	770	935	1105	1175	1410	1615	1820
14		430	480	650	720	870	1045	1100	1325	1520	1710
16		390	430	585	655	790	960	1020	1225	1405	1585
18	30′ Suction Hose (Three Sections)	325	370	495	560	670	835	900	1085	1240	1420
20		270	310	425	480	590	725	790	955	1110	1270
22		195	225	340	375	485	590	660	800	950	1085
24		65	70	205	235	340	400	495	590	730	835

Lift in Feet

Notes: 1 — Net pump pressure is 150 psi. Operation at a lower pressure will result in an increased discharge; operation at a higher pressure, a decreased discharge.

2 — Data based on a pumper with ability to discharge rated capacity when drafting at not more than a 10-foot lift. Many pumpers will exceed this performance and therefore will discharge greater quantities than shown at all lifts.

Gage Behavior During Drafting

It is normal practice to measure changes in atmospheric pressure from the sea level normal of 14.7 psi with a barometer. If mercury is placed in an upright U-shaped tube that is closed at one end and open on the other in such a manner that the fluid does not run out, it will register variations in atmospheric pressure. The downward pressure of the weight of fluid in the column in pounds per square inch will balance with the pounds per square inch atmospheric pressure.

If the atmospheric pressure increases the force on the open end of the column of fluid it will cause the level to rise until the downward weight in the tube is equal to that outside. The point at which the fluid levels off in the tube will indicate the outside atmospheric pressure. If outside pressure falls, the level of the fluid will on the measuring side of the tube correspondingly fall, since less force is holding it up.

The level of fluid for various atmospheric pressures can be calibrated and the device used is a barometer. Mercury is used because it is more than thirteen times as heavy as water. Since it is compact it does not require an upright tube of over three feet. Readings from a mercury barometer are in terms of inches of mercury. One inch of mercury equals 0.491 pounds per square inch or 1.133 feet head of water. It should be easy to remember that two inches of mercury are equivalent to just under one pound per square inch.

The vacuum gage must be watched closely. A change in the reading will indicate several important possibilities: (a) the suction strainers on the end of the suction hose or in the pump intake may be clogged, and (b) the level of the water source may be falling.

When drafting with a 10-foot lift, as when testing pumps, we would have about nine inches of mercury on the suction side of our compound gage. If our pump is capable of maintaining a 22-inch vacuum we will have about thirteen inches available for useful work in moving water into the pump. This means that, considering the pump's suction capability, we will have about six psi above atmospheric pressure left to overcome all friction losses in the twenty feet of suction hose, loss in the strainer and in the pump entrance, after we have primed the pump. If we add another ten feet of suction hose we increase the friction loss in the suction line.

When it is understood that we only have eleven or twelve psi of vacuum to work with in a pump in good condition, the importance of having a large enough suction hose to reduce friction loss should be readily apparent. At high elevations the lower atmospheric pressure may make the suction problem even more difficult.

The loss of pressure in drafting (due both to elevation and friction loss) can be observed by watching the suction or compound gage on the pump inlet. At approximately 10-feet suction lift with the pump primed but with no hose stream operating it will be noted that the gage shows a suction or "vacuum" reading of about nine inches of mercury. (The suction side of the gage is graduated in inches of mercury equivalent to 0.491 psi or 1.133-foot pressure head.) This shows the loss of atmospheric pressure due to difference in elevation between the surface of the water and the pump chamber.

Next, start the discharge through a large nozzle, opening the throttle slowly. As the flow increases the pressure loss on the suction side will increase. This is due to the increase in friction loss in the suction hose and fittings on the suction side of the pump. If we have sufficient flow all of the available atmospheric pressure will be used or the point of maximum capability of the pump to maintain a vacuum will be reached. For a pump in reasonably good condition this may be a vacuum of twenty-two inches of mercury. If a pump is drafting with a lift of twenty feet it will use about eighteen inches of mercury just in overcoming elevations and will have only four or five inches left on the compound gage to overcome friction loss.

The vertical distance from the water surface to the pump intake should be as short as possible. As indicated, lifts of over ten feet seriously increase the load on the pump and engine. In some instances where the pumper cannot be placed close to the water's edge, it is possible to draft water through a long horizontal hose, but with decreased volume due to increased friction loss. In fact, some pumpers carry extra lengths of hard suction hose for this purpose. Experience gained by pumping from local sources of water supply will indicate exactly what may be expected from a pumper under the conditions existing locally.

Pumper pulls in with front wheels parallel to pier side, body at 45-degree angle. Both suction hoses are removed and placed on ground.

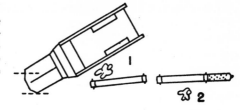

No. 2 man balances suction hose between legs, 4 feet behind coupling. No. 1 man connects hose to pumper. (If suction inlet is very high No. 2 man cannot straddle.)

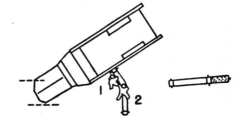

No. 1 man bends first suction hose and straddles at male end. No. 2 man straddles second suction hose 4 feet from coupling and balances it. No. 1 man makes coupling.

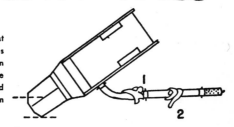

Suction hose is dropped over side. Pumper pulls ahead on pier to come close to edge if necessary, due to distance from water.

When drafting with a multistage centrifugal pump equipped with a transfer valve that gives the operator the option of pumping with pump impellers in parallel (volume) or in series (pressure), the manufacturers frequently advise that the impellers should be in parallel position before priming. This is not always a convenient operation because many times when pumping from draft it is necessary to supply hose lines under a series or pressure operation. If the pump is primed in parallel or volume, it will be necessary to use the transfer valve after water is obtained.

Many modern centrifugal pumps prime equally well in either position. When priming in series, keep the primer engaged until both impellers are filled with water. This can be determined by sound as well as by observing the discharge from the priming device under the truck. There will be a pause after the first stage is primed and then water will be discharged into the second stage impeller. Practice in priming a pump will make the operator familiar with the characteristics of his machine.

One piece of advice that is good for all pumping operations is, "don't try to hurry too much." Better results will be obtained by methodical, deliberate movements. For example, when charging lines from a pump, the discharge valves should be opened up slowly as pressure is built up, otherwise it is possible to lose the prime. Also, there is less likelihood of damaging hose or injuring hosemen when the lines are charged slowly.

Priming Pumps

A centrifugal pump is not positive in displacement. It cannot pump air because an open waterway connects the suction and discharge sides of the pump. Air must therefore be removed from the entire pump by a priming device. There are several types: a small positive displacement pump that pumps the air out; a vacuum primer that draws the air out through the intake manifold of the engine; and an exhaust primer that uses the outrushing gases of the engine to create a suction to draw air out of the pump.

The procedure for priming a centrifugal pump is as follows: Use a rubber mallet, never a metal hammer, to make all suction hose connections air tight. (A pliant rubber gasket in the suction hose is one of the least expensive items used by fire departments yet one of the most important.)

All openings to the pump such as drains, discharge gates, valves and bleeder cocks must be closed to prevent entrance of outside air. This applies equally to suction and discharge side of the centrifugal pump because air can readily go from one to the other.

Engage the pump drive gears to have the pump ready to operate.

Engage the priming device and advance the throttle to the motor speed recommended for that type of primer.

(a) The small positive displacement pump rotary gear type primer is designed to operate best at comparatively low motor speeds of about 700 to 1200 rpm.

(b) The rotary vane vacuum primer operates best at moderate motor speeds of about 1200 to 1500 rpm.

(c) The exhaust primer depends on velocity of exhaust gases discharging through a venturi for efficiency. Motor speeds of 1500 to 2000 rpm will be needed.

(d) The positive displacement rotary gear type priming pump, electric motor driven, operates at 1500–1700 rpm of the electric motor. This type primer is independent of the main fire pump and engine in its operation.

(e) If the booster tank is used for priming, a foot valve on the end of the suction hose will be needed to keep the prime and tank supply from being lost. When pumping from a small area water source such as a cistern it is important that the prime be maintained as the water level falls. It may be impossible to again prime the pump from the greater depth. A foot valve, where provided, keeps the suction hose full of water.

(f) Continue priming until water fills the entire pump. This should be accomplished within 30 to 45 seconds. A primed pump may be indicated by pressure showing on the pressure gage; a change in the sound of the pump as it fills with water; or by water being ejected from the priming device. Regulate the engine throttle until the pressure gage shows a reading of from 20 to 50 psi pressure.

As soon as the pump is primed disconnect the priming device, and connect the main pump if this has not been done. Some multistage pumps are primed with the pump in capacity or volume position.

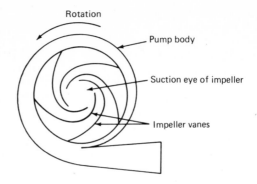

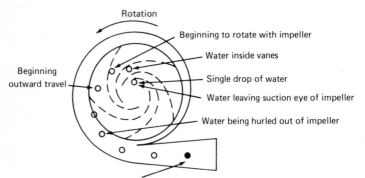

How water moves through pump impeller.

Failure to Prime

Failure to prime within 45 seconds usually indicates that air is leaking into the pump body or, that the priming pump is dry and needs lubrication. Do not run the pump dry for a longer period. Tighten all suction hose connections, close all valves and drains and try again.

A high reading on the vacuum gage with no water entering the pump within 30 to 45 seconds indicates the suction lift is too high or that the strainers are obstructed.

The vacuum required to prime a pump is the vertical height of static lift (in feet) times .88. For example, a 10-foot lift requires 8.8 inches (mercury) to prime the pump.

Priming pumps are run in a bath of oil and the oil reservoir must be refilled after each use.

Positive Displacement Pumps

Rotary gear and piston pumps achieve positive displacement, that is, they can pump air and water. There is a very close fit between the piston or gears and the pump housing that completely closes any connection between the suction and discharge sides so these positive displacement pumps are self-priming. Air from the suction side is pumped out through the discharge side of the pump. Removal of air is made easier by letting it escape through a discharge gate to which no hose is attached. This is closed as soon as water appears. The by-pass or churn valve must be closed to prevent air leak.

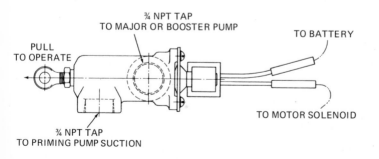

Hale priming valve.

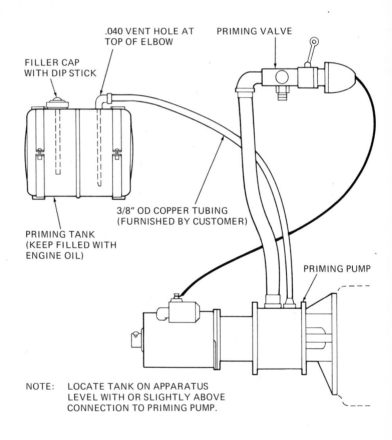

Waterous priming system.

Suction Hose

The size and length of suction hose limit the amount of water that can be drafted and the height to which it can be lifted. Minimum size recommended for 500 gpm and 750 gpm pumps is 4½-inch suction hose, and 5-inch is minimum for 1,000 gpm pumpers when drafting. Hard suction hose must be used when drafting as soft suction hose will collapse under negative pressure.

A pump of 750 gpm capacity using two lengths of 4½-inch suction hose when drafting at or near sea level should lift 500 gpm approximately 16–18 feet, but if it is necessary to use three 10-foot lengths of suction hose to reach the water with the same lift, the flow drops due to increase in friction loss. This pressure loss can be reduced by using larger diameter suction hose. In high elevations, larger suction hose must be used because there is less atmospheric pressure to overcome the lift between the surface of the water and the pump and the friction loss in the suction hose.

Operating from Hydrant

There are four general methods of supplying pumpers from hydrants. The type of operation employed may vary, depending upon the amount of water and pressure available from the hydrant, the capacity of the pump, and the number and size of hose lines desired. These factors will determine whether the pump is to be connected directly to the hydrant or will be located nearer the fire and supplied by hose lines. The type of hydrant supply may also determine whether a hard or soft "suction" will be used.

It is possible to provide full capacity for a pump, spotted near a fire yet far from a hydrant, *if enough hose lines of adequate diameter are connected to the inlet side of the pump and are supplied under sufficient pressure.* Standard pumper specifications call for at least one 2½-inch gated inlet for each pumper but most fire departments specify additional inlets. When 2½- or 3-inch hose is used to supply a pumper the friction losses will correspond to losses encountered when the same size hose supplies fire streams. Friction loss in 2½-inch hose supplying 250 gpm will be about 15 psi per hundred feet, so a hydrant having a residual pressure of 50 psi could supply this volume to a pumper through no more than 300 feet of single 2½-inch hose. At the same residual pressure, only about 175 gpm could be supplied through 600 feet of 2½-inch hose. With the same pressure and length of line the 3-inch hose would provide 440 and 300 gpm respectively. It is part of the pump operator's responsibility to see that the pump is supplied by enough hose lines.

There are two fundamentals for successful pumping from hydrants: (1) try to connect the pump to a hydrant capable of giving the desired supply, and (2) connect to the hydrant with hose large enough to provide the full capacity of the pump. If small hose is used, additional supply lines may be needed.

If a large suction hose is used the operation is speeded up if one end is carried preconnected to a pump inlet. The same advantage may be obtained by using a "squirrel tail" hard suction which is carried attached to the pump by a swivel connection. In case either of these practices is used, there should be a valve so that the pump can use water from the booster tank without filling the suction hose.

If available, the large hydrant outlet should always be used when pumping from a hydrant. Normally, a single 2½-inch outlet will not provide full capacity except to small pumps. If hydrants do not have the large steamer connection (normally 4- or 4¼-inch diameter), it is necessary to connect to both 2½-inch outlets to obtain an adequate pumper supply.

The following should be given consideration:

(1) The suction connection should be large enough in diameter to handle the desired flow.

(2) Unless a check valve is provided, the booster tank valve must be closed. Some booster tanks do not have large enough vents; consequently, an internal pressure is built up that may cause the tank to bulge or burst because air cannot empty out of the tank as fast as water can enter unless the tank valve is closed.

(3) Fire hydrants must be opened fully on every use. If a hydrant is only partially opened, the drain valve in the bottom of the barrel will not close. This permits water under pressure to escape through this valve. This escaping jet of water can wash away all the earth from around the hydrant barrel and cause it to break from the main. In addition, there is the problem of freezing in winter. Some hydrants are so constructed that they open very little the first few turns as compared to the last few

Using Hard Suction

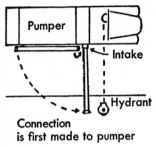

**Connection
is first made to pumper**

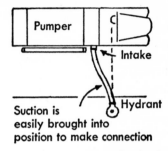

**Suction is
easily brought into
position to make connection**

One method of using hard suction hose is to spot pumper with suction intake about in line with hydrant outlet. Suction hose is connected to pumper first, then connected to hydrant. Hard suction hose connections are facilitated if the hose is slightly "wobbled" while the threads are being engaged.

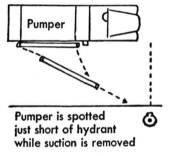

**Pumper is spotted
just short of hydrant
while suction is removed**

Another method is to spot pumper just short of hydrant. Hose is connected to hydrant first, then pumper is moved to best position for suction connection.

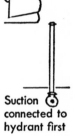

**Suction
connected to
hydrant first**

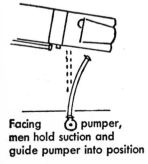

**Facing ⊙ pumper,
men hold suction and
guide pumper into position**

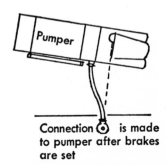

**Connection ⊙ is made
to pumper after brakes
are set**

turns. The fact that a hydrant is not fully opened may not be readily apparent until it is desired to utilize the full capacity of the pump.

(4) The supply hose between the hydrant and the pump should be kept reasonably straight with no sharp bends or kinks to restrict the flow.

(5) A practice worthy of consideration is to place a gate valve on the outlet hydrant not being used before the water is turned on. This permits connection of a second supply line to the pumper without shutting the hydrant off if the first connection is not providing sufficient water to the pump.

(6) Whenever an option exists as to which side of the pumper the suction hose will be connected to the pump intake, it is recommended that the connection be made on the side of the pump from which the controls are operated.

Charging Hose Lines

It should be standard policy that each hose line be charged only upon command from the company officer or man in charge of that hose line. Nozzle men can be seriously hurt when the hose lines they are advancing are charged unexpectedly.

Here are some precautions for the pump operator:

1. Be certain that the hose is fully coupled to the proper pump outlet.

2. Be certain that hose crew is ready and waiting for water.

3. Open discharge gate valves SLOWLY to permit the water under pressure to start movement at a low velocity and prevent loss of prime.

4. The pressure as recorded on the discharge pressure gage should preferably be 50 psi and not more than 100 psi when 2½-inch discharge valves are opened.

5. If other lines are already in service, use care in opening gates and see that the correct pressure is provided on each line. This may require partly closing gates on lines which require less pressure than that at which the pump is discharging.

6. Any significant leak or drip from gaskets or couplings should be remedied as soon as practicable.

The following suggestions cover the charging of small preconnected hose lines:

1. Pump operators should know the required pressures for small line layouts. These pressures are determined by adding the required nozzle pressure, the friction loss in small hose, and the pressure required for elevation (in general, about 50 psi nozzle pressure will be required for solid streams and about 100 psi nozzle pressure for low pressure fog nozzles). Some departments provide upwards of 100 psi pump pressure for booster lines with solid stream ties and 125 to 200 psi pressure for booster lines with fog nozzles. Friction loss for a given flow of water will vary with the diameter and length of line.

2. Control valves for small lines should be opened fully to obtain maximum flow. The quantity of water discharged by these lines may not be sufficient to indicate by pressure gage readings whether the valve is fully opened. This must be determined by position of the valve.

3. When several small lines are carried preconnected, the pump operator should know where each line is advanced at a fire in order to be certain of operating the proper control. Persons ordering water should indicate which lines are to be charged. Booster reels, however, may be charged as soon as the pump is in position at the fire.

Pounds Friction Loss per 100 Ft. in Rubber or Rubber-Lined Small Hose

Flow GPM	Hose Diameters in Inches			
	¾	1	1⅛	1½
10	13.5	3.5	—	—
15	29.0	7.2	—	—
20	50.0	12.3	—	—
25	78.0	18.5	10.4	1.9
30	104.0	26.0	14.6	2.5
40	—	—	24.8	4.3
50	—	—	37.7	7.1
80	—	—	—	15.6
100	—	—	—	25.5

Note that loss in ¾-in. hose is four times that of 1-in. hose and seven times that of 1⅛-in. hose.

GPM Discharge through Small Nozzles

Nozzle Pressure in Lbs.	Nozzle Diameter in Inches			
	¼	⅜	½	⅝
40	12	26	46	72
50	13	29	51	80
60	14	32	56	88
70	15	34	61	95
80	16	37	65	102
90	17	39	69	108
100	18	41	73	114

2½-inch Handlines

Small streams must be backed up at the earliest possible moment by one or more big lines (2½-in. diameter or larger hose). The cooling capacity provided by a large flow from big hose lines is needed to cope with fires in advanced stages. When charging big lines:

1. Open discharge gates slowly. This cannot be overemphasized. It is important for the safe handling of large size hose lines. Water turned into hose lines too quickly not only presents a hazard to nozzlemen but may burst hose or may make the line difficult to move at a time when the crew is trying to get the line into an effective position.

2. Be sure that the proper discharge gates are opened. Try to find out where each line attached to the pump is operating so that proper action may be taken in the event of an emergency. (Some departments place tags on each line to identify them by number.)

3. Hose kinks should be straightened because they may cause failure of the hose or impede the flow of water. The hoseman who signals to the pump for water should see that there are no major kinks to prevent water from reaching the nozzle. The operator should see that the line is sufficiently straightened out near the pump before opening a discharge gate. Minor kinks will be removed by the flow of water.

4. Each pump operator should observe the hose lines supplied by his pump and be alert for signals from the hose crews.

Pressure Requirements

Adjustment of pump controls so that the proper pressure will be produced for any particular hose layout is one of the most important responsibilities of the pump operator. Unlike most stationary fire pumps delivering a fixed output against a predetermined pressure or head, the fire department pumping engine is called upon to meet a variety of hose requirements from booster streams of ten to thirty gpm to master streams perhaps throwing 1,000 gpm.

Suction sources also vary, from drafts at various suction lifts from three to twenty or more feet, and flows from hydrants providing varying supplies and pressures. Pump pressures may range from 50 to almost 600 psi. High pressure boosters may increase pressure to 1,000 psi or more.

With the pump in proper pressure or volume position for the hose layout, needed pressures should be obtained by slowly increasing the motor speed with the hand throttle. (Some apparatus have a single stage pump and pressure-volume performance is regulated by engine speed and the size of nozzles supplied.)

With a multistage or pressure-volume pump, if in doubt as to whether pressure or volume operation is desirable, a good rule of thumb is to operate in pressure position for volumes under 50 percent of the rated capacity of the pump.

The charging of hose lines slowly and building up of desired pressures gradually will enable the nozzlemen to get set before the maximum working pressure reaches the nozzle. A good practice when operating from hydrants having flow pressures of less than 100 psi is first to charge the line by allowing the hydrant pressure to pass through the pump and hose when water is called for. This will get the air out of the hose and provide a stream of water at the nozzle. The operator then advances the throttle as necessary to develop the full nozzle pressure indicated or requested. High-pressure hydrants may provide more pressure than is desired and the gates and gages of the pump should be used to regulate the flow except where independent gates are attached directly to outlets of high-pressure hydrants. In the latter case the hydrant gates should be throttled to regulate the flow and thus the resultant nozzle pressure.

Pump pressures should be reasonably exact. Too little pressure results in poor fire-fighting streams and pressures that are too high are difficult for the nozzlemen to control. Excessive pressure may result in burst hose or failure of a critical part of the pumping equipment.

Using Relief Valve or Governor

The following precautions should be observed in the operation of governors and relief valves.

1. The pressure control device should be set as soon as the pressure required by the hose layout has been obtained. The control is normally set 10 psi above the pump operating pressure so that minor fluctuations in pressure will not cause the pressure control to operate unnecessarily.

2. Pressure control devices should not be relied upon to provide changes in pressure requirements. The engine throttle should be employed.

3. When a different pump pressure must be secured, the pressure control device must be reset. If the new pressure requirement is higher it will be necessary to disengage the pressure governor before increasing the engine speed. If the new pump pressure requirement is less, the procedure is to decrease the motor speed as necessary and then reset the governor.

4. A relief valve can usually be set for the pressure requirement only when water is flowing through hose lines at the desired rate. On types of relief valves that are adjustable to accommodate variations in the volume of water being by-passed, the adjustment can be made only when nozzles are shut off.

5. Where several lines are in operation, the relief valve setting must be high enough to permit adequate pressure for the line requiring the greatest pump pressure. This will mean that the automatic pressure regulation for other lines may not be as effective as might be desired. In this connection it is well to observe that although modern pressure regulators, properly set and maintained, are usually very efficient, they do not relieve the hose crews and pumper operators from the responsibility of shutting and opening both gates and nozzles slowly. It is the practice of some departments to use nozzles which cannot be closed rapidly.

There is another problem in the use of pressure relief devices which cannot always be fully solved. A pump may be supplying one or more 1½-inch leader lines equipped with fog nozzles operating at relatively high pressures and a 2½-inch solid stream nozzle requiring lower pressure. Except where a pump has separate pressure stages operated independently and with separate pressure controls, the governor setting must be sufficient to maintain effective pressure on the lines requiring the highest pressure. When pumping to open nozzles not involving the use of nozzle shutoff valves, the pressure relief devices may be disengaged.

Quite commonly in departments where apparatus maintenance is poor, pressure relief devices are found to be inoperative. This is a serious condition which can affect the safety of the men as well as causing damage to hose and pump. The relief valve or governor should be inspected and tested periodically and the manufacturer's recommendations for cleaning and lubrication should be carefully observed. It is up to the operator to see that the relief device is used when pumping and to report any failure of the device.

Failure to get the desired pressure may be due to several conditions. Here are some of the reasons:

1. Pump transmission not properly engaged. (It may be in neutral or in wrong gear, even in reverse gear.)

2. Water supply is inadequate for hose layout and nozzle sizes employed.

3. Relief valve or pressure governor setting is too low. The pressure control device should be adjusted at a slightly higher setting than will be needed and reset when the proper pump pressure is obtained.

4. Transfer (pressure-volume) valve is in wrong position. Slow down throttle and make change.

5. Control valve in gage line may be closed, or line may be clogged so that the gage is not giving a true report.

Pump operators should be careful to see that the pressures produced by the pump are not higher than the hose layout warrants. In general, it is good practice when supplying streams on relatively short hand lines to provide not much over 100 psi at the pump until the proper pressure calculations can be made and pressures adjusted accordingly. This should give a nozzle pressure in the 40 to 60 psi range for 2½-inch hose as shown in accompanying table. When fog nozzles are employed 100 psi nozzle pressure is needed and can be provided as soon as the line is safely charged. Relatively small flows in many fog nozzles result in low friction loss, and excessive pump pressures should be avoided.

Friction Loss with 100 pounds Pump Pressure
(Nozzle and Pump at Same Elevation)*

Nozzle Tip	Length of Line in Ft.	Nozzle Pressure	Friction Loss
1¼	200	50	50
1¼	300	40	60
1⅛	200	60	40
1⅛	300	50	50
1⅛	450	40	60
1	300	60	40
1	400	50	50
1	600	40	60

*For fog nozzles of equivalent flow add 50 pounds to pump pressure.

Operation of Gages

To get efficient operation from a pumper it is necessary to understand the operation of pressure gages and the meaning of their readings. All pumpers should have a gage showing pressure on the suction or the inlet side of the pump and one or more gages to show pressures on the discharge side.

The gage or gages on the discharge side register the pressure at which the pump is discharging water. When the pump is built to discharge at several pressure stages simultaneously, there will be a gage for each pressure stage. Most pumpers have individual discharge pressure gages for each outlet.

The pumper should be operated to give a discharge pressure which is the total of the desired nozzle pressure (usually 40 to 60 psi for solid streams for hand lines, 80 to 100 psi for heavy solid streams, and 70 to 100 psi for fog), plus the friction loss in the hose line, plus or minus the pressure needed to overcome the difference in elevation between the pump and nozzle.

With positive displacement pumps, such as certain booster

pumps, the discharge pressure gage usually registers only pressures greater than atmospheric and records such pressures in pounds per square inch. On centrifugal pumps the discharge gage commonly installed is a "compound gage" that registers pressures below atmospheric, sometimes called "vacuum," as well as the "positive pressure" exerted by the pump. The reason for providing a compound gage on the discharge side is that, when priming at draft with a centrifugal pump, pressures can be below atmospheric on both sides of the pump. If a compound gage is not provided, the gage must be designed so that it will not be damaged by vacuum readings.

A compound gage on the inlet or suction side of the pump registers either pressure below atmospheric, as when drafting (usually shown in inches of mercury), or a pressure above atmospheric as when connected to an adequate hydrant supply. The pump operator must be able to interpret the meaning of readings of this gage in terms of how much more can be expected from his pumper and the water supply.

Pump operators should have frequent practice sessions to be thoroughly familiar with the behavior of gages under varying conditions. Of special importance is the situation when the compound gage needle on the inlet side is near the zero mark. Generally it is true that within close limits on either side of the zero reading this gage may not be very accurate, but it is certain that the pump is taking practically all the water available from the supply hose in use.

Here are suggestions concerning the significance of readings of the pressure gage on the discharge side of the pump:

Be certain that the gage is registering. If no pressure shows on the gage when it is known that the pump is engaged and filled with water, do not advance the engine throttle past a reasonable point. Doing so may give the hose line excessive pressure. (The pipe line between gage and pump may be frozen, the passageway may be obstructed or the gage may be shut off.)

Pumps should deliver their rated capacities at draft without exceeding the maximum no-load governed speed of the engine (as shown on a certified brake horsepower curve of the engine used, without accessories). These safe motor speeds should be well known to the pump operator. Little is to be gained by racing the engine at excessive speeds which may cause early mechanical breakdown.

In some instances where a small capacity pump is on a good hydrant, it may be found that the pump is handling a volume of water considerably beyond its rated capacity but because of overload the pump and engine cannot develop the desired pressure. In such cases it may be wise to reduce the output sufficiently to bring the performance and pressures more closely in line with the design characteristics of the pump.

For example, a 500 gpm pump may be handling 850 gpm from a hydrant, but with low discharge pressures. It may be better to reduce the output to a point where the machine can function at a more efficient speed and deliver water at a pressure better related to the intended performance of the pump.

It is very important that fire ground officers know the state of the available water supply as well as the hose stream output possible from various pumpers under varying conditions. Many, many times pump operators have been blamed for poor fire ground pump performance when the error has been that the officers in charge have demanded hose streams far beyond the ability of either the pump or the water supply, or both.

To forestall such difficulties it is well that pump operators keep the fire ground officers informed regarding the water supply situation at working fires. Officers should know whether a satisfactory residual pressure is being maintained on the suction or inlet side of the pumps or whether pumps are having trouble getting enough water. In the latter case steps should be taken promptly to supplement the water supply as discussed in Chapter 7.

Lines for additional streams should not be connected to any pumper (except at draft) for which inlet pressure is less than 5 to 10 psi unless it is intended to reduce the size of nozzle tips already in service or unless additional water supply can be brought into the pump.

The only situation that justifies the attachment of additional lines to a pumper already working at capacity is when the lines are merely used to reduce pressure losses in other lines supplying the same nozzle. For example, when two 2½-inch lines from a pumper are providing 600 gpm to a 1½-inch tip the pressure loss in each 2½-inch line is 21 pounds per 100 feet of hose. By running a third line to the same nozzle the pressure loss will be cut to 10 psi per 100 feet of hose. This may be very important when it is desired to get the maximum volume from the pump at the sacrifice of high delivery pressure. With the nozzle 400 feet away the additional line would provide the same flow at a saving of 40 psi of pump pressure.

The following is a typical problem of choice between pressure and volume operation frequently encountered at fires.

A 750 gpm pump operating in pressure position is supplying two 2½-inch lines at 200 psi with 30 psi residual at the hydrant or pumper inlet. The officer in charge desires to have an additional line. The hydrant residual pressure would indicate that the hydrant can supply another line but the increased flow will cause the inlet pressure to fall somewhat. The pump is rated to give 525 gpm at 200 psi so is working close to rated capacity at that pressure.

Assuming that some help will be received from the hydrant, the discharge pressure might have to drop to about 165–170 psi to provide 750 gpm at a safe engine speed when operation is transferred to volume or parallel position rather than pressure or series operation.

In other words, a pump cannot simultaneously supply both its maximum volume and pressure. The officer will have to choose the performance he wants: for a 750 gpm pump, about 525 gpm at 200 psi or 750 gpm at about 150 psi — plus hydrant residual pressure in both cases. This decision should be based upon the pump and hydrant situation as indicated by the gages.

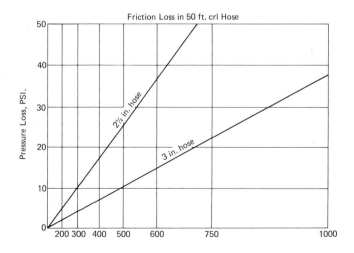

Friction Loss in 50 ft. crl Hose

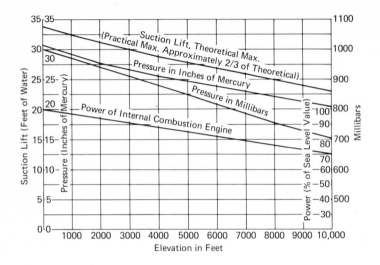

A careful study of many reports of "low water pressure" occurring at large fires reveals that in most cases the failure was not with the water system but with the fire department in attempting to use hose layouts beyond the ability of the pumpers or hydrant system or both. Water pressure may be low because the volume handled by the pump is too great to permit development of effective pressure by available pumping equipment. Volume may be low because the pump is not operated in the best position for pressure. It may be low because of excessive draft by fire department pumps beyond that contemplated when the water main system was installed.

Suction or Compound Gage

The gage on the inlet side of the pump will show "positive pressure" (pressure above atmospheric) when the supply hose or hydrant is capable of providing water at a rate greater than the demand of the pump. When the pump attempts to exceed the supply at the point registered by the intake gage, the pressure on this gage will fall below atmospheric. If a soft, rather than a hard, suction or supply line is being used this will partially collapse.

When a pumper is receiving water from a hydrant the gage reading before any hose discharge lines are opened will show the static pressure from the water system. As streams are placed in operation from the pump the inlet gage pressure will fall.

It is important that the suction hose or supply lines be large enough to supply the amount of water needed and available without excessive loss of pressure on the inlet or supply side of the pump. If these supply lines are not of sufficient size there may not be pressure enough to move the needed quantity of water into the pump. *When one soft suction or supply line will not provide enough water, run additional feeders to the pump.*

Continued operation of a fire department pumper at pressures and volumes that may be necessary to control serious fires requires that almost constant attention be given to the instruments, to give the pump operator knowledge of conditions affecting the pump, the engine, the water supply or the hose streams.

Any evidence of improper operating practices that may be disclosed by the gages or instruments should be heeded by pump operators. Improper operating practices may not result in immediate failure but rather may cause a cumulative stress or wear on critical pump parts that may cause a subsequent serious breakdown, possibly at a most inopportune time.

Flowmeter of American La-France is designed for pumper discharge lines of 1½-inch size and larger. Gage shows flows between 100 and 450 gpm.

Some pump operators are fortunate in having an instinctive "feel" for the operation of machinery and can make refinements and adjustments as a matter of course. Others may allow an abusive practice to continue because they are unable to recognize danger signals.

Do not suddenly increase or decrease engine speed while pumping. Even the quick action type of governor is intended for emergency protection of the hose crew. Engine and pump speeds should be raised or reduced moderately.

Reading Engine Control Gages

The engine temperature gage is very important in giving pump operators information concerning the proper functioning of the power plant. Other gages may be provided to record significant details concerning dependable operating conditions. The following concerns the reading of these gages.

1. A tachometer is a device for recording engine speed in revolutions per minute. Most pumpers carry a plate indicating the discharge and the engine speed at various pressures as indicated by the Underwriters' Laboratory acceptance test. When the engine speed is excessive for the work performed it is likely that the engine is not being operated in the proper gear ratio, or the transfer valve is not in the proper setting for the work being attempted, or there is some impairment of the water supply.

2. Observe the tachometer reading frequently while pumping and compare this with the pump pressure for any given layout. The tachometer might be used as an emergency substitute should the pressure gage become inoperative.

3. On some pumps a point may be reached while pumping where an increase in engine speed does not increase the pump pressure. This may indicate that the capacity of the pump or engine has been reached. Under this condition the only way to increase the pump pressure is to shut down one line or put on smaller nozzle tips. In some instances where very large volumes of water are being pumped, the engine will not be able to reach normal speeds and discharge pressures will be low. This may indicate that the volume pumped is excessive in relation to the ability of the power plant. Again nozzle sizes should be reduced to allow engine speed and discharge pressures to be built up.

4. The oil pressure gage will indicate that oil is being circulated through the engine by the oil pump. The normal oil pressure for any specific pumper must be determined by each pump operator. A frequent check of the oil gage should be made whenever the engine is running. In event of a sudden failure, steps should be taken to remedy the situation before serious damage results, causing the stopping of the engine. The gage may not indicate shortage of oil until just before serious trouble occurs. Few pumpers have oil level indicators that indicate oil level while the pump is operating. Attention should be given to the oil level between runs. Oil should be changed after every major pumping job. Don't just add more.

5. The ammeter will show the amperage delivered by the generator to the batteries and the electrical system. It is a normal and good practice to carry batteries on fire apparatus fully charged. The voltage regulator may cause a lower reading on the ammeter when batteries are fully charged than when batteries are partially discharged and are being charged by the generator. However, the ammeter should not show a discharge.

6. When a pumper has more than one ignition system the engine should be run so that all spark plugs are firing. Any spark plugs that are not burned clean with each explosion will become fouled to the point where they will not work.

Lubrication of Critical Points

Much of the success of a preventive maintenance program depends upon carefully following out the manufacturer's recommendations for both periodic and on-the-job lubrication. On some pumpers continued smooth operation depends upon oiling and greasing of critical mechanisms by the fire department. The manufacturer's manual should be carefully followed.

Controlling Engine Temperatures

The explosion of gasoline vapor in the engine driving a fire pump produces high incidental temperatures as well as the power needed to operate the pump. With older machines having an open type cooling system, the temperature should not exceed 185 degrees Fahrenheit. New engines are required to have pressurized cooling systems and may be operated up to 210 degrees

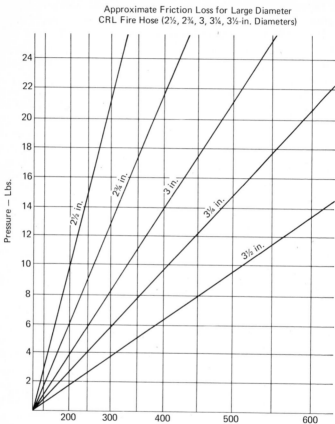

Approximate Friction Loss for Large Diameter
CRL Fire Hose (2½, 2¾, 3, 3¼, 3½-in. Diameters)

Fahrenheit. The engine manufacturer's specifications must not be exceeded.

However, the cooling of a pumper differs from an ordinary motor vehicle because the engine is called upon to operate at high speeds while the pumper is stationary. The rush of air through the radiator caused by movement of the vehicle is lacking. To compensate for this, the capacity of pumper radiators may be larger than would be necessary for road performance.

Many pumpers also require a heat exchanger to keep engine temperatures down by absorbing heat from the water circulating around the cylinders. This is accomplished by using water from the discharge side of the fire pump to cool the coolant used to cool the engine. With the use of a heat exchanger the same coolant is used over and over in the engine cooling system as the heat exchanged water is never permitted to intermix with the coolant. This permits use of an antifreeze if necessary.

The following suggestions concern the control of engine temperatures:

1. Keep engine temperature below the safe level as recorded on the temperature gage. This is done by regulating the valve controlling the amount of water circulated through the heat exchanger. Keep this valve closed until the temperature reading

Darley initial attack type unit incorporates full compartments — 18 horsepower electric start portable pump, capable of pressures to 300 psi and volumes to 150 psi — 200 gallon tank — electric reel — gated 2½-inch rear intake — and all aluminum diamond plate construction.

Mack MB series pumpers are available in two-man cab as well as five-man cab shown. The two-man cab has a manual tilt arrangement; the five-man cab is equipped with a hydraulic tilt arrangement as standard.

indicates the need for cooling. It should be tightly closed at all other times.

2. The cooling of older pumpers not having a heat exchanger simply requires adding water to the radiator from the fire pump. This valve should be opened very slowly to prevent cracking of the engine block when cold water contacts the hot metal. Remove the radiator cap to avoid building up a high pressure in the cooling system. The cap must always be tightly in place on a modern pressurized cooling system.

3. The hood of the engine may be raised to provide free circulation of air around the engine and to make points of maintenance accessible on some models.

Use of Signals   (*Pages 210–211.*)

When increasing or decreasing nozzle pressure, a change of 10 or 15 psi at the nozzle generally is satisfactory to the hose crew. However, to get this change of nozzle pressure with lines of average length it is usually necessary to adjust the pump pressure by 20 to 25 psi to make the desired change at the nozzle. This is because the change in pressure results in a change in gpm flow and a consequent change in the friction loss in the hose.

A lot of lost time and confusion on the fire ground can be avoided by simple uniform hand and lantern signals between the hose crew and pump operator. Where a pumper is stationed a considerable distance from the fire, radio communications are essential. The hand or lantern signals selected should suggest the action wanted. For example, swinging arms upward suggests an increase in pressure. Swinging the arms downward indicates that a reduction of pressure is needed. Holding the arms parallel may indicate that the pressure is satisfactory.

QUESTIONS

Chapter 3

Text:

1. When attaching suction hose, what is most important?
2. Explain five common fireground hand signals.
3. If there is a sudden loss of prime, what should the pump operator do?
4. Why is mercury used in a barometer?
5. What is the difference between series and parallel pump operation?
6. What size suction hose should be used for a 1,000 gpm pump?

Discussion:

1. Does a pumper need booster hose *and* 1½-inch preconnected hose? Which is the more practical?
2. Where should preconnected lines be loaded on a pumper?
3. Should a deck gun be permanently installed or might it also be used as a ground monitor?
4. Why not use 1¾-, 2-, or 2¼-inch hose? What are the advantages and disadvantages?
5. European fire departments supply hose at lower pressures than U.S. departments. Why? What are the good and bad results of such lower pressures?

Training session with water spray nozzle includes supply of two 1½-inch and one 2½-inch hose line.

Chapter 4

Supplying Fireground Layouts

On the fireground the engine company officer and the pump operator will be concerned with one of three means of water supply to the pumper: by drafting; by hydrant supply; or by relay from another pumper or a tanker.

Then they must consider how this water supply will be used: in direct attack on a fire; to supply a master stream device, such as the ladder pipe on an aerial or the monitor nozzle on an elevating platform or aerial tower; or merely to serve as an intermediate pumper in a relay. In the latter two assignments, the pumper and its crew may play a relatively inactive role, once the pump operator and company officer define the specific task of water use. Direct fire attack demands the greatest flexibility and output from the pumper and crew.

Depending on the fire problem, the pressure and volume discharge must be controlled according to available water supply. For some situations, pre-fire planning may determine the complete hose layout and functions of the pump for a certain fire situation — a hydrant of known capacity will be taken (connected to the pumper by hose lines), certain hose loads will be dropped, handlines with selected nozzles will be moved to attack positions, and other fundamentals will be accomplished as rehearsed in training. But there are situations which have not been planned, or when some new influence has distorted the fire company's careful preparations; in those situations the maximum effectiveness of the pumper must be developed quickly and effectively "from scratch."

Potential Layouts. The company officer and pump operator can anticipate that the pump will be used to supply one of the following operations: handlines; deck or ground monitor(s); distributor nozzle; ladder pipes, or monitor nozzles on elevating platforms; portable hydrants; pumper relays; tandem pumping; supplemental pumping; and/or special extinguishing equipment.

For each of these operations, much depends upon the amount of hose carried on the pumper, how it is loaded and arranged, the position of the pumper on the fireground and its designated role for that particular emergency. Standard procedures of the fire department usually define how hose shall be placed and supplied for these basic operations.

Handlines. Pre-connected booster, 1½-inch and 2½-inch handlines supplied directly from the tank on the pumper need to be supplemented quickly by supply from another pumper or a hydrant. This would require the normal in-line direct or reverse layout of one or more 2½-, 3-, or 3½-inch lines or even larger hose, depending upon the department's normal evolutions and hose loads.

Ground Monitor Nozzle. Usually placed at some distance from the pumper to provide heavy stream attack on a large fire. These nozzles vary in size and capacity but require two or three hose lines of 2½-inch diameter or more into the siamese connection.

Deck Gun. May be connected by pipe directly into the pump, or may be supplied by short lengths of hose, preconnected, or connected by the pump operator. These guns can deliver 500 to 1200 gpm.

Ladder Pipe or Monitor on Elevating Platform. For supplying these, the pumper should be located within 100 feet of the ladder truck or elevating platform. Two, possibly three lines of 2½-inch or larger hose are needed to supply the base siamese. These elevated nozzles should be able to deliver at least 750 gpm at a minimum of 100 psi nozzle pressure, and pumper supply at the lower siamese must be adequate for these flows.

Portable Hydrants. These may be supplied by 4- to 6-inch hose, or multiple smaller lines, perhaps 600 to 800 feet away from the pumper. Usually two or three 2½-inch lines are supplied by the portable hydrant to serve as handlines or to connect to a monitor nozzle.

Pumper Relays. In relay, the pumper may supply one, two or more lines at moderate pressure to another pumper, usually within 800 feet. Depending upon hose load, layout of these lines will be direct or reverse and, in some situations, may have to be done completely by hand.

Tandem Pumping. Connecting two pumpers to the same hydrant to gain maximum advantage of a full flow in the water main. Tandem pumping is described on page 81.

Supplemental Pumping. One pumper pumping into a hydrant and possibly into two or more other pumpers within reasonable distance. This is described on page 145.

Special Extinguishing Needs. For sprinkler systems and other special extinguishing situations the pumper crew may have to lay out one or more supply lines of 2½-inch size or larger. These situations are described in Chapter 6.

Factors that can influence the choice of pumper operation include: the volume of water needed and available; the time that will be required to obtain effective streams; and the best utilization of water, hose and pumping capacity.

The man in command when the layout is selected must balance one factor against another. The 300 or more gallons in the booster tank may quickly put out a fire that could not be put out by 500 or more gpm five minutes later when, perhaps, hose has been laid to static water sources and hard suction connected.

The correct decision of the layout to be employed depends upon the type, amount and prearrangement of apparatus available at the time, or whether additional men and apparatus are ready for action.

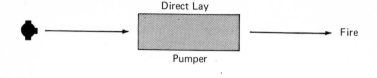

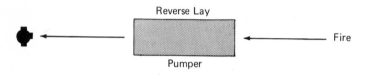

Direct and reverse layouts may be governed by hose loads.

When supplying hose lines from the booster it is desirable to have the pump located as close to the fire as is safe and convenient, yet in position to permit prompt movement if necessary.

Pump pressures necessary to supply the various lengths of hose layouts and nozzles can be calculated in advance. The chief handicap is that plans must be made for supplementing the tank supply before it is exhausted. The amount of water that a pump can discharge in this operation depends upon the adequacy of the tank-to-pump connections. NFPA standards call for a flow of at least 250 gpm from tanks of less than 800 gallons and at least 500 gpm for tanks of 800 gallons or larger.

Supplying Long Layouts

Fire departments occasionally must stretch very long lines of hose to reach a fire when only one pumping engine is available. Such departments are faced with the problem of overcoming or reducing the high friction loss in long lines without the advantage of relay pumping.

It may be possible to run two parallel hose lines siamesed into a single nozzle and thus materially reduce the friction loss. However, sometimes neither sufficient hose nor time is available for stretching double lines, especially if the pumper is equipped to lay only one line at a time.

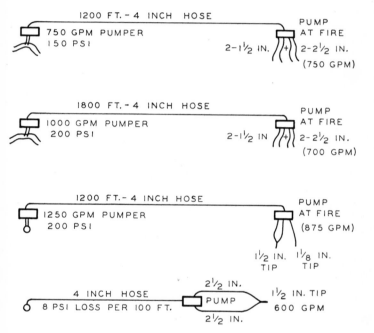

1200 FT. - 4 INCH HOSE

750 GPM PUMPER
150 PSI

2-1½ IN.

PUMP
AT FIRE
2-2½ IN.
(750 GPM)

1800 FT. - 4 INCH HOSE

1000 GPM PUMPER
200 PSI

2-1½ IN

PUMP
AT FIRE
2-2½ IN.
(700 GPM)

1200 FT.- 4 INCH HOSE

1250 GPM PUMPER
200 PSI

PUMP
AT FIRE
(875 GPM)

1½ IN.   1⅛ IN.
TIP   TIP

2½ IN.

4 INCH HOSE
8 PSI LOSS PER 100 FT.

PUMP

2½ IN.

1½ IN. TIP
600 GPM

Sketch of layout showing what can be accomplished with large diameter supply hose in normal operation.

Supplying pressure lines up to 2,000 feet long is not too great a task for a modern pumper. Formerly, with low pressure pumpers supplying long lines, it was the practice to use very small tips to reduce the friction loss in the hose so that a stream could be obtained with a low pump pressure. Unfortunately, this reduced the volume and effectiveness of the stream, making it of little use by the time the long line was placed in service. Today, even a 500 gpm pumper should have no difficulty in supplying a line of 2,000 feet of 2½-inch hose over relatively level ground. If a pump operates in series or pressure position at 250 psi, it should deliver 50 percent of its rated capacity. Approximately 200 gpm would be discharged through a 1-inch tip at about 45 pounds nozzle pressure. At about 1,500 feet from the pump a 1⅛-inch tip could be supplied with 270 psi pump pressure with a discharge of 250 gpm at 45 psi. A 500 gpm pumper at 215 psi can supply two 700 foot 2½-inch hose lines each discharging 250 gpm streams through 1⅛-inch tips. Larger pumps can handle greater volumes than smaller pumps provided sufficient lines are laid to utilize the pumping capacity at proper pump pressures. Except where it is necessary to overcome high elevations, or where it is desirable to employ high nozzle pressures, a 1-inch nozzle tip can be supplied through 2,000 feet of 2½-inch hose. Where higher nozzle pressures are wanted a fog nozzle discharging about 175 gpm can be employed.

Fog nozzles on 1½-inch hose lines can be used where it is desired to supply several small streams through a long line of 2½-inch hose. In cases where 200 pounds pump pressure is not sufficient the pump can be operated at 225 pounds or even a little higher if the hose is in good condition and care is taken to open and close nozzles slowly so as to avoid bursting hose due to pressure surges.

All these layouts are figured for relatively level ground. For every foot of elevation up which water is pumped, approximately 0.43 psi extra pressure will be needed. In other words, an extra pound of pressure will lift water a little over two feet. When pumping downhill a similar amount may be subtracted from the required engine pressure. (This refers to the relative positions of the pump and nozzle; intervening differences in elevation can generally be disregarded.)

The accompanying tables show pressures required for various flows through long lines. If 3-inch or 3½-inch hose is used the friction loss is greatly reduced. Some rural departments use light-weight 3½-inch hose (weighing approximately 60 pounds per 100 feet coupled). A single line delivers 500 gpm 1,000 feet at only 100 pounds friction loss.

Flow Data: Straight Stream Nozzles and 2½-inch Fire Hose, Single Line
(Some figures rounded out for convenience)

Length of Line in Feet	Size of Nozzle Tip in Inches	Nozzle Pressure PSI	Approximate Discharge GPM	Approximate Pressure Loss per 100 Feet	Total Pressure Loss PSI	Approximate Engine Pressure*
800	1¼	45	310	22.5	180	225
1000	1¼	36	280	19	190	225
800	1⅛	56	280	19	150	205
1000	1⅛	45	250	15	150	195
1250	1⅛	42	245	14.5	180	225
1500	1⅛	36	225	12.5	188	225
1000	1	56	225	12.5	125	180
1000	1	45	200	10	100	145
1250	1	45	200	10	125	170
1500	1	45	200	10	150	195
1750	1	45	200	10	175	220
2000	1	41	190	9.2	184	225
2000	1	36	180	8.3	166	200
2250	1	36	180	8.3	186	225

*Assumed approximately level ground.

Flow Data: 2½-inch Hose (Single Line) with Fog Nozzles
(With adjustable pattern nozzles calculated on basis of largest flow patt
to be used)

Length of Line in Feet	Flow Rating of Nozzle at 100 PSI	Nozzle Pressure PSI	Discharge GPM	Approximate Pressure Loss per 100 Feet	Total Pressure Loss PSI	Approximate Pump Pressure*
800	250	100	250	15	120	220
1000	250	81	225	12.5	125	205
1250	250	72	212	11	140	215
1500	250	64	200	10	150	215
1000	200	100	200	10	100	200
1500	200	81	180	8	120	200
2000	200	64	160	7	140	205
1000	175	100	175	8	80	180
1500	175	90	166	7	105	195
1500	175	81	157	6.5	95	175
2000	175	72	150	6	120	190
1000	150	100	150	6	60	160
1500	150	100	150	6	90	190
1500	150	81	135	5	75	155
2000	150	81	135	5	100	180
2000	150	72	128	4.5	90	160

*Approximately level ground.

After taking hydrant, Chelsea, Massachusetts pumper drops 300 feet of 4-inch hose supply line in moving toward position. Pump carries 500 feet of the big hose. (Photo by Charles A. Tuck, Jr.)

Advantages of Larger Hose

The 2½-inch nominal internal diameter fire hose (actually 2$\frac{9}{16}$ inches) was not designed with the requirements of modern fire fighting and automobile pumping engines in mind. The size is a "hand-me-down" from days of hand-drawn hose reels, hose carts or wagons. Today, fire department pumpers and other apparatus are equipped with several sizes of hose. For use inside buildings, 1½-inch hose is commonly used and the 2½-inch hose is largely reserved for outside work. Two larger sizes commonly used (other than for short lengths of "soft suction" for supplying pumpers) are the 3-inch and 3½-inch diameters. Some departments use 2¾-inch hose with 3-inch couplings in lieu of the 2½-inch hose. Most 3-inch hose is fitted with 2½-inch couplings so that reducers are not needed when connecting to pumpers or equipment carrying the threads for 2½-inch fittings.

At 10 psi loss per 100 feet the 2½-inch hose moves 200 gpm, the 3-inch hose with 2½-inch couplings moves 315 gpm, and the 3½-inch hose moves 500 gpm.

In pumping for heavy streams there are two important factors to consider. One is the amount of water the pump can be expected to deliver at a given pressure. The other is, how much pressure is left to overcome line losses including friction loss, elevation and losses in heavy stream equipment?

The accompanying table gives these factors. Part I shows the amount of water various sizes of pumpers are rated to deliver at 150 and 200 psi net pump pressure. Part II shows (at these pump pressures) how much pressure is left for line losses when providing various nozzle pressures.

I. Pumper Capacities		II. Pressures Available for Line Losses		
Gpm Flow at 150 Pounds	Gpm Flow at 200 Pounds	Nozzle Pressures (Pounds)	150 Pounds Pump Pressure	200 Pounds Pump Pressure
500	350	50	100	150
750	525	65	85	135
1000	700	80	70	120
1250	875	100	50	100
1500	1050	120	30	80

In-line Pumping

There are advantages and disadvantages in each form of pumper supply and one of the duties of fire officers is to determine which type of operation will be most advantageous in a given situation. Some advantages of in-line operation are:

1. The pumper with all its equipment may be located close to the fire and the operator will be in better position to provide pressures called for by the hose crews.

2. The fire may be attacked more quickly because it is possible to start operations with water from the tank before supply lines have been charged.

3. Lower pump discharge pressures may be possible because the pumper may have to supply only part of the pressure in the supply line to move the water from the source to the pump located part way toward the fire. For example, if 200 psi is required to overcome pressure loss in hose and supply the desired nozzle pressure, it may be possible to reduce the pump discharge pressure to 150 or 160 psi if water pressure in the hydrant is sufficient to move the required volume to the pump which is nearer to the fire.

4. Hydrant pressures may not be adequate for direct hydrant streams but the first due pumper may be needed at the fire to supply small lines.

5. More water can be placed on the fire in a given time by an average crew.

Disadvantages of in-line pumping are:

1. The full capacity of the pump cannot be utilized *unless there are enough supply lines of adequate capacity to feed the pump,* whereas one large suction hose at the hydrant should provide the full capacity of the pump or the full flow available at the hydrant.

2. There may be plenty of water at the hydrant but insufficient pressure to move a large volume through long supply lines to the pumper at the fire.

3. The pumper may not have sufficient gated inlet connections to permit an adequate supply to be brought into the pump. Some pumpers have only one 2½-inch pumper inlet while they may have two to six 2½-inch discharge connections and, unfortunately, some have no gated inlets for 2½-inch supply hose. Obviously, it is not possible to discharge more water than can be brought into the machine. Sometimes the waterways on the inlet side of the pump are not adequate to handle the desired flow from 2½-inch inlet connections. This can be corrected by attaching a gated siamese to a large pumper inlet.

Supply Lines for In-line Pumping

The officer must understand all of these factors when deciding whether in-line pumping is desirable in a given situation.

With a single 2½-inch hydrant feeder line supplying a pump, about the best that can be expected is to provide water for two 1½-inch lines, unless the feeder line is very short. Thus the single 2½-inch feeder violates one of the basic concepts of fire fighting which is: always back up the attack with heavier streams and equipment.

Basically, for any working fire not less than two 2½-inch feeder lines or one 3-inch feeder line are needed as initial supply for in-line pumping when supply is from hydrant pressure. This will provide 400 to 500 gpm in the average layout with lines not exceeding 400 feet, assuming a hydrant flowing pressure of 40 to 50 psi. If the feeder lines are under pump pressure in a relay, a single feeder may carry up to twice the flow.

The 1½-inch lines are for fast attack, but should be backed up by a big line. Normally, a 2½-inch line requires 200 to 250 gpm. Two 1½-inch lines require from 100 to 200 gpm depending upon the nozzles and pressure used. Thus, for in-line pumping we should never permit an initial supply layout that will provide less than 400 gpm. We may need more water than this from the pumper at many fires and this will mean providing supplemental supply lines to the pumper as discussed elsewhere.

Using 3-inch or 3½-inch hose permits a single feeder line to provide sufficient volume for one 2½-inch line and two 1½-inch lines. A substitute procedure is to divide the hose body and load the hose so that two 2½-inch feeders may be laid simultaneously. A third method used successfully by many departments is to operate pumpers in pairs. The first pumper may lay a single feeder and gets its 1½-inch lines in service. The second pumper lays another supply line to the first and connects to a hydrant, then operates in a relay to supply the first pumper. In some departments where two pumpers respond from the same station the relay is set up immediately in all cases where the fire appears to be beyond the size that can be readily handled by water from a booster tank.

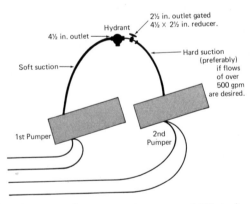

The second pumper may be connected to a gated 2½-inch outlet of a hydrant already supplying another pumper through the 4-inch or 4½-inch hydrant outlet. A 2½-inch hydrant orifice will supply 750 gpm at about 16 pounds pressure and 500 gpm at 7 pounds at the hydrant. To reduce friction, a large suction hose should be used when pumping from a single 2½-inch hydrant outlet. In most cases a pumper connected to a 2½-inch outlet cannot supply more than two lines.

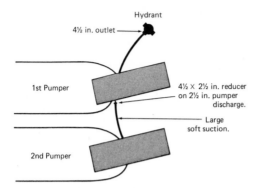

The second pumper can take suction by connecting to a large suction connection on the opposite side of the first machine away from the hydrant. This method, termed "tandem pumping," has been used where the large suction inlets are gated for this purpose. Where they are not gated the hydrant would have to be shut off to connect the second pumper. However, from a strong hydrant a single large suction hose may supply two pumpers up to 750 gpm capacity each.

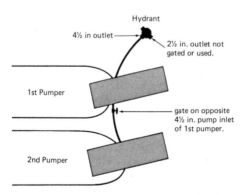

The third method, while the easiest to use, may be the least efficient. Connect a short soft suction from the second pumper to an outlet of the first pumper. The second pumper is then relaying water from the first pumper and serves as an additional pressure stage in the pumping operation. However, the volume available depends upon the ability of the first pumper to supply its own lines and spare enough water for the second pumper. A 750 pumper delivering 500 gpm at 120 lbs. from a hydrant capable of 1000 gpm at 30 lbs. should be able to deliver perhaps 500 to 600 gpm to the second machine. The machine can then use its pump to increase the pressure for heavy stream operation.

Using Large Diameter Supply Hose

The use of 4-inch hose and larger supply lines is described in Chapter 5, but here it is worthwhile to compare the flows in these larger sizes with the more usual 2½- and 3-inch diameters. Obviously, the larger diameter hose means greater water carrying capacity in the same range of pressures, so for in-line evolutions there are several advantages in using the larger hose. A typical synthetic 4-inch hose can deliver 700 gpm at only 9.6 psi loss per hundred feet; with 1,000 gpm flow, loss is only 19.2 psi per hundred feet. Compare these figures with the table below.

The following table shows flows possible with feeder lines at different losses. The hydrant or pump pressure available to supply these feeders will determine the length of line that can be served.

Approximate Flow of Feeder Lines
(Assuming adequate connections and pump capacities)

Friction Loss Pounds per 100 Feet	GPM 2½-in. Feeder	GPM 3-in. Feeder
6	150	250
8	180	300
10	200	330
12	220	370
15	250	410
20	300	480
25	330	550
30	360	600
35	390	650
40	420	700
45	450	745
50	475	790

Gated Inlets

Standard No. 1901 calls for one gated 2½-inch pumper inlet to permit in-line pump operation without shutting down lines being supplied by the tank. The standard also calls for a connection between the tank and pump on the apparatus to permit supply of 250 gpm (two 1½-inch lines or one 2½-inch line) from the tank before the hydrant connection is made.

Upon arrival at a fire the 1½-inch lines and possibly booster lines are first supplied from the tank. The pump operator can keep his foot or leg against the supply line after it has been connected to the pump inlet. When he feels water reaching the pump he should close the tank valve (unless an automatic valve is provided) and adjust to the new supply.

If the pump has only one 2½-inch gated inlet, it is a good practice to carry at least one gated 2½-inch siamese on a larger pumper intake because it is then possible to connect additional supply lines to the pump without shutting down. With a second supply line, upward of 400 gpm can be brought from a hydrant capable of providing this flow. Some departments provide as many 2½-inch gated inlets as they have 2½-inch discharge connections, making it possible to assure full volume supply with the pump operating in-line.

Littleton, Colorado pumper using 5-inch supply line 500 feet from hydrant, discharges 1200 gpm through two multiversal nozzles with hydrant residual of 40 psi. (Photo by David Brandhorst)

Range of a "Good" Fire Stream

Getting hose streams which will put out a fire is an important part of the job of fire fighting, so it is worthwhile to consider what constitutes a good fire stream.

Water should come out of the nozzle with good force and in a well-formed stream. At close range there is no question of its effectiveness. Farther away, the stream spreads, and at its farthest reach, breaks into small drops which are hardly more than a heavy mist. Such drops are ineffective on a major fire. The reach of an effective stream is, to a large extent, a matter of judgment. A stream good enough for a small fire may not be good enough for another in which more material is burning.

One of the achievements which brought fame to the late John R. Freeman as a fire protection engineer was making, in 1889, the first complete set of tests on hose streams and nozzles, then used in fire department work. In judging hose streams, he classed as "good" those which:

1. Had not lost continuity.

2. Appeared to shoot nine-tenths of the whole volume of water inside a circle 15 inches in diameter and three-fourths of it inside a 10-inch circle, as nearly as could be judged by the eye.

3. Would probably be stiff enough to attain in fair condition the height or distance named, even though a fresh breeze was blowing.

4. With no wind, the stream would enter a room through a window opening and strike the ceiling with force enough to spatter well to provide a heat-absorbing spray.

It is futile to try to set the range of a fire stream with too great accuracy, or to try and remember details about what tests have shown. Freeman cautioned that his results might have an error of 10 to 15 percent. Many tests made later show that the effect of wind tends to vary the effective range of a stream much more than differences in pressures and sizes of nozzles. Ten miles per hour is not a high wind by any means, but is enough to reduce the effective range of a stream by as much as 40 percent.

These principles can be tested. For sake of illustration, lay a 2½-inch line from a pumper and attach to it a 1⅛-inch solid stream nozzle, one of the most common sizes used in fire operations. Start up the pump until there is about 20 psi pressure at the nozzle. The nozzle is tilted up to get the maximum horizontal range. Applying Freeman's rules we can see that it is a good stream up to a point a little short of 40 feet from the nozzle (assuming there is not much wind).

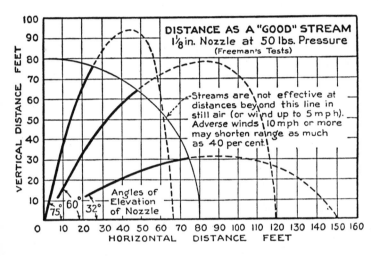

Freeman plotted the center lines of the hose streams used in his tests. The range shown on the chart was that obtained with a smooth nozzle (not a fire department shut-off type), and with substantially no wind. The practical values for the range of streams were selected with due allowance for wind conditions of moderate intensity. (See table, page 87.)

Next, the pumper pressure is stepped up until the nozzle pressure is about 40 psi. For this stream the range is about 60 feet. If the nozzle is elevated until the stream is going nearly straight up, it will be observed that the vertical range is possibly a few feet better than the horizontal but not a difference of great importance.

When the pumper pressure is stepped up so that the nozzle pressure is about 50 psi, we get a stream which is generally considered the standard for general fire fighting work. Its range will be about 70 feet. If pressures are raised more, the range can be increased, but at the higher pressures the nozzle is harder to handle and the stream is therefore less practical for fire operations. As pressure is increased, there soon appears a point at which the pressure causes the stream to break up only a short distance from the nozzle. The pressure at which this break occurs depends on the smoothness and design of the nozzle. Contrary to former theory, this break up may not be objectionable providing it does not interfere with the projecting of the water toward the fire.

The range of a fire stream can be made greater by using larger nozzle tips provided that the pumper and water supply can deliver greater flows. As a practical matter, water is often limited. If a better stream is wanted, it may be necessary to use a smaller tip that can be employed at higher pressure with the water supply available.

This can be seen by an example: a 1⅛-inch nozzle at 50 psi pressure requires 265 gallons per minute. If a 1¼-inch nozzle is substituted a slight improvement in range could be obtained, two or three feet, but 326 gallons of water would be required at the same pressure. If, however, a 1-inch nozzle is substituted for the 1⅛-inch nozzle, the pressure could be stepped up to 80 psi at the nozzle without using any more water than with the 1⅛-inch nozzle at 50 psi. This would add about ten feet to the range of the fire stream.

Other things being equal, such as the design of the nozzle, the larger orifice will project a stream farther at a given pressure and the stream will generally carry farther before it breaks.

The range of a hose stream is directly proportional to the pressure up to the point where the stream "breaks." A rule widely used in figuring range of solid streams is to take one foot of range to each pound of nozzle pressure. For the average pressures of around 50 psi this gives ranges considerably below what a stream will do with good nozzles and favorable wind conditions. Because the smoothness of the nozzles and the wind may have so much to do with performance, the use of this rule probably gives an approximately correct answer for many cases.

The best rule to remember about the effective range of a hose stream is that a 1⅛-inch nozzle at 50 psi pressure gives a range of about 70 feet. Smaller nozzles at the same pressure provide slightly less effective range and larger nozzles a little more reach. The range will be less if there is strong wind, unless the wind is blowing in the direction of the stream.

The accompanying table gives the figures arrived at by Freeman for the reach of hose streams for the pressures and nozzle sizes most commonly used. He said that very likely many persons would class a stream as "good" up to the point where he classes it as only fair, but he endeavored to allow a margin for the effect of wind.

Distance in Feet from the Nozzle at which Streams Will Do Effective Work with a Moderate Wind Blowing. With a Strong Wind the Reach is Greatly Reduced.

Pressure at Nozzle	Size of Nozzle									
	1-Inch		1⅛-Inch		1¼-Inch		1⅜-Inch		1½-inch	
	Vert. Dist. (Ft.)	Hor. Dist. (Ft.)	Vert. Dist. (Ft.)	Hor. Dist. (Ft.)	Vert. Dist. (Ft.)	Hor. Dist. (Ft.)	Vert. Dist. (Ft.)	Hor. Dist. (Ft.)	Vert. Dist. (Ft.)	Hor. Dist. Ft.()
20	35	37	36	38	36	39	36	40	37	42
40	64	55	65	59	65	62	66	64	69	66
50	73	61	75	66	75	69	77	72	79	75
60	79	67	83	72	84	75	85	77	87	80
80	89	76	92	81	94	84	95	88	96	88

Nozzle pressures are as indicated by Pitot tube. The horizontal and vertical distances are based on experiments by John R. Freeman.

Reach in Feet of Effective Solid Streams from Small Nozzle Tips

Nozzle Pressure (lbs. per sq. in.)	40	50	60	70	80
¾-in. Smooth Cone Tip:					
Effective reach of horizontal jet	50	55	60	65	70
Maximum effective reach with nozzle elevated	60	65	70	70	70
Reach of spray with nozzle elevated	90	90	100	105	105
⅝-in. solid stream from all-purpose nozzle:					
Effective reach of horizontal jet	35	45	55	60	65*
Maximum effective reach with nozzle elevated	40	50	55	60	70*
¼-in. solid stream from all-purpose nozzle:					
Effective reach of horizontal jet	30	35	35*	—	—
Maximum effective reach with nozzle elevated	30	—	—	—	—

*Stream beginning to break badly.

In Wausau, Wisconsin this portable canvas tank was used successfully on a farm building fire. Rural operations call for skillful use of supply lines, portable pumps and tanks, tank trucks and pumpers and sometimes, specialized apparatus.

QUESTIONS

Chapter 4

Text:

1. What are nine types of fireground operations that require hose layouts?
2. Monitor nozzles on elevating platforms or on ladder pipes — what flow should they be able to deliver? At what pressure?
3. What is the approximate gpm discharge of a 1¼-inch nozzle tip at 36 psi nozzle pressure?
4. In supplying water for heavy streams, what are two important factors to consider?
5. Name five advantages of in-line pumping.
6. What are some disadvantages of in-line pumping?
7. What determines the range of a good stream?

Discussion:

1. Are there situations in which you, as company officer, would ignore departmental orders for fireground hose layouts, and would try some new evolution? Explain.
2. What are some tactical advantages and disadvantages of using ground monitor nozzles versus a deck gun (same capacity) from a pumper?
3. What capacity is best for a deck gun? Why?
4. What is the best size for supply lines to pumpers: 2½-, 3-, or 3½-inch? Why?
5. What are some disadvantages of big hose?

Long hose layouts and well-planned relay operations are needed for major industrial fires such as this one in San Pedro, California. (Los Angeles City Fire Department photo)

Chapter 5

Relay Operations

Relay pumping is employed where the pressure requirement for a hose layout is too great for a single pump to supply. Relays are commonly used in rural areas and at fires in industrial and waterfront areas of large cities. Relays up to 8,000 feet in length have been operated successfully to give emergency water supplies when there has been a local water supply failure.

If we are only supplying a single line from a pump, or less than 70 percent of rated capacity, the pumping operation probably should be in series. The pump should have no difficulty in maintaining 200 or even 225 psi discharge pressure. Remember, the standard pumper ratings are 100 percent of capacity at 150 psi; 70 percent of rated capacity at 200 psi; and 50 percent of rated capacity at 250 psi.

On the other hand, if volume of water is the chief consideration, and the pump is supplying all 2½-inch outlets, it may be necessary to limit discharge pressure to about 150 psi. As a general practice, operate in series or pressure unless the volume required exceeds the following 70 percent capacities:

$$350 \text{ gpm for a } 500 \text{ gpm pump}$$
$$525 \text{ gpm for a } 750 \text{ gpm pump}$$
$$700 \text{ gpm for a } 1000 \text{ gpm pump}$$
$$875 \text{ gpm for a } 1250 \text{ gpm pump}$$
$$1050 \text{ gpm for a } 1500 \text{ gpm pump}$$

Some pumps will require volume delivery at below 70 percent rated capacity but the flows are within capability of a standard pumper.

In relays, the important function is keeping the required volume flowing between pumps so it can be moved along to reach the next pump with sufficient intake pressure, or, at the end of the relay, to provide adequate pressure for the handline nozzles or heavy streams.

The reason for the relay will have influence on the layout; a relay for fire control will be somewhat different from a relay for overhaul, for draining basements, or simply moving potable water in a flooded area. In the fire relay, the end purpose will be to apply the available water in fire attack, with adequate pressure for the nozzles.

The capacities and number of pumps make a difference; so do the size and amount of hose in the relay layout, the grade(s) of the terrain, and the kind of water source — static or a hydrant.

In relays, big hose (4 to 5 inches) usually proves to be more efficient and easier to set up than smaller sizes (2½–3½ inches). (*Chapter 12*)

Pressure Surges

With pumpers 800 or more feet apart, pumping through one or two lines of 2½-inch hose, the supply pump should maintain 200 psi discharge pressure unless greater pressure is called for. For a 750 gpm pump, this will result in about 16 psi loss per hundred feet of 2½-inch hose, for 525 gpm total flow, or a total of 128 psi for the 800 foot layout. The pumper at the fire should adjust its discharge pressure to that needed to supply the nozzles. The work of the engine at the fire is very similar to the job of pumping through soft suction from a hydrant except that the supply lines are longer.

Position in Relay

Well-trained engine companies can carry out relay operations smoothly, but their operations will differ according to position in the relay.

Obviously, the source (or supply) pumper at draft or a hydrant, is the initiator, the starter of the relay. It may be that supply lines must be stretched manually between this pump and the second pump, ladder truck, water tower, elevating platform, or other apparatus in the relay. It is also obvious that the maximum relayed flow depends on the capacity of this first pumper. A 500 gpm pumper cannot relay enough water to allow a couple of 1,000 or 1,500 gpm pumpers to operate at capacity. When possible, the largest pumper should be the source pumper.

As the second, third, or fourth pumper in a relay, the role would be to accept the incoming water flow at 10 or 20 psi, then pass it along, adding pressure as needed. If this pump is supplying handlines or monitor nozzles directly, then the operator boosts the pressure only as needed. If the output is to be delivered to another pumper through one or more supply lines, several supply lines may be utilized, and discharge pressure must be enough to move the water along to provide sufficient volume and intake pressure at the next pump.

Pumping Pressures for Relays

If 150 psi pressure is provided at the supply pump it will move 200 gpm through a single 2½-inch line a distance of 1,300 feet on approximately level ground with 20 psi incoming pressure at the second pumper. (Second pumper will supply the nozzle pressure.) This 200 gpm is the flow of a 1-inch tip at 45 psi nozzle pressure. Or, the 150 psi will move 250 gpm (the flow of a 1⅛-inch tip at 45 psi nozzle pressure, or two ¾-inch tips at 55 psi) 1,000 feet.

If sufficient hose is available, pumpers of 750 gpm or larger capacity rating can supply two lines at 200 psi and double the flow. Actually, one of the first things to determine is whether relay pumping is needed or is desirable, but, where heavy streams or substantial elevations are involved, pumper relays may be needed for hose lays exceeding 600 feet.

Using Line Relief Valve

Double-jacketed fire hose is tested to at least 400 psi when new, and hose that will not stand a 250 psi annual service test should be suspect. After all, it is not the recommended 200 psi pump pressure that is likely to burst the hose, but surges caused by opening and closing nozzles too quickly. In any pumper relay, the relief valve or engine speed governor should be set to protect the men, the pump, and the hose. (*Chapter 1.*) An alert operator will watch the gage and be prepared to open a spare gate quickly if he detects any pressure surge.

The ordinary pressure relief device operating on the discharge side does not protect the suction side of the relay pump, so some departments use a relief valve on the supply side of the receiving pump. This is set to operate at predetermined pressure and serves to prevent pressure from the supply pump from entering the receiving pump when nozzles are closed quickly. The extra relief valve in the line serves as a dump valve to protect the pump and hose. This may be important because pressure surges tend to build up and become more serious in long lines of hose. If no relay relief valve is provided, a 50-foot section of 2½-inch hose can be connected to a spare discharge gate of the relay pump which the operator can use for a bleeder if the pressure on the suction side is too high. In relay operations, the pumper relief valves or governors must be set properly and the nozzle men must open and close nozzles slowly.

This Concord, New Hampshire pumper has a 4½-inch Keystone quick dump valve and a 4½ by 2½ by 2½ gated wye suction for refilling. Rear discharge is concealed by water flow from dump valve. (Photo by Concord Monitor)

An in-line operation used in Yakima, Washington includes two 200 foot lines of 4-inch hose from a hydrant to a pumper, which then supplies two 300 foot lines of 2½-inch hose to a monitor nozzle.

What Pressure for the Supply Pumper?

The modern technique of relay pumping is to have the supply pumper maintain a good pressure on all lines between pumps. In general, for long relays relaying pumpers should build up to 200 psi as soon as the line is safely charged. If this pressure should prove to be 25 or 50 psi too high, no harm is done and the work of the operator near the fire is made easier. After all, the second pumper does not have to use all the pressure coming in any more than he would expect to pull hydrant pressure down to zero at every fire.

Contrariwise, if maximum flow is wanted, the second engine can use the supply line for increased volume as long as the hose remains firm where it enters the pump. If more water is wanted the operator of the supply engine can be directed by radio to increase pump pressure or another supply can be laid.

One large city fire department has a standard layout of two 2½-inch lines between pumps. The supply pump provides 25 psi per 100 feet plus 25 psi residual for the second pump. The pumps are located a maximum of 600 feet apart and relay relief valves are used. This evolution guarantees 600 gpm at good residual pressure at the second pump. With 750 gpm pumpers, this will supply two hand lines or a 1½-inch tip on a turret pipe or ladder pipe. If one of the lines is 3-inch hose, this relay would deliver 850 gpm at 600 feet.

For maximum volume relays with 2½-inch hose, (over 70 percent of capacity of supply pumper and with two or more lines between pumpers), and where lines do not exceed 1,000 feet between pumpers, it may be necessary to operate the supply pump at the pressure at which the pump gives rated capacity, probably at 150 psi. To this may be added the residual pressure at which the hydrant gives the desired flow.

For example, assume a 750 gpm pumper is relaying through two 600-foot lines over relatively level ground to another pumper and 30 psi residual is showing on the supply gage. The 30 psi is added to the net pump pressure giving 180 psi discharge pressure with the supply pump in parallel or volume operation. For the 600-foot distance, this would permit 30 psi friction loss per 100 feet or a flow of at least 360 gpm in each 2½-inch line. Thus the pump would be able to relay 720 gpm in volume operation.

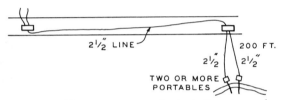

Two or more portable pumps can supply single lines to a relay pump to maintain a substantial volume of water in the relay.

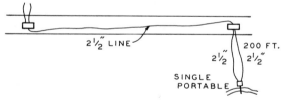

By attaching a wye to the discharge outlet of a portable pump, two 2½-inch lines can be supplied to the relay pumper. The portable should be of 500 gpm capacity for this evolution.

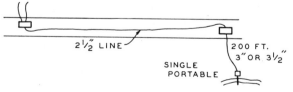

Use of a 3- or 3½-inch line from a portable pump should assure good delivery of its capacity to a relay pumper 200 feet away.

This flow would be well above the 525 gpm (70 percent) that the 750 gpm pump was designed to provide in series operation at 200 psi net pump pressure (tested at draft). However, if there was only one line between pumps, series operation at 200 psi or more would give the maximum flow for a single 2½-inch line.

This line relay valve, made of aluminum alloy with forged water turn coupling, eliminates need for shutdown when extra pumpers cut into the supply line. It can be inserted during the initial hose layout and can function as a 150 psi dump valve.

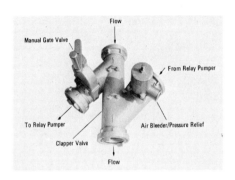

Flow

Manual Gate Valve

From Relay Pumper

To Relay Pumper

Air Bleeder/Pressure Relief

Clapper Valve

Flow

Incoming gated relief valve for use with 4-, 5- and 6-inch diameter supply lines includes relief valve with air bleeder and gate valve. It permits hookup of main water supply to suction side of pumper without having to shut down when working from booster tank supply.

This Sausalito, California attack pumper was specially designed for supply by relay and 4-inch manifold, permanently mounted on rear step has 2½-inch and 3-inch supply lines feeding siamese connection. It is also connected to pump by 3-inch line with a check valve.

Relays for Volume

Relay operations with a single line of 2½-inch hose (as used at rural fires), permit long distances between pumpers, but because of the limited capacity of this hose size, the amount of water moved is relatively small considering the total capacity of the pumpers employed. Also, with a single line the entire relay is cut off with the failure of any hose section in the layout.

With pumps 1,000 feet apart supplying dual 2½-inch lines at 200 to 225 psi, approximately 600 gpm can be relayed, provided the last pumper is not over 500 feet from the nozzle. This type of relay has been tested up to 3,400 feet using four 1,000 gpm pumps.

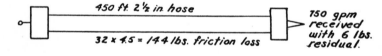

Relaying 750 gpm through two 450-foot lines to another pump. With 150 psi pump pressure at the initial supply, total friction loss for both lines is 144 psi, residual pressure at second pump is six psi. Each line carries 375 gpm at 32 psi loss per hundred feet.

A good plan is to set the supply engine immediately at the source of water without wasting time for laying hose. Hose should be laid by other companies because dual lines will be needed.

When using 750 gpm pumpers it is possible to move full capacity with adequate hose layout and pump spacing. At least two lines of hose would be required, and one should be 3-inch hose, or three 2½-inch lines will be needed between pumpers to keep down the friction loss so that the pumps may operate in parallel or volume position.

The laying of the lines will be facilitated if the pumpers have divided hose bodies carrying 2½- and 3-inch hose and pumps operating at 150 psi in parallel; approximately 750 gpm will be moved if pumps are 750 to 800 feet apart on level ground. About 675 gpm will be moved if pumps are 1,000 feet apart.

However, in a practical operation, distance between pumps should be limited to the hose carried in the divided hose bodies. Thus, the pumpers might be only 600 feet apart so that when operating at rated capacity at 150 psi there would be a good residual pressure on the inlet gage of the relay pump.

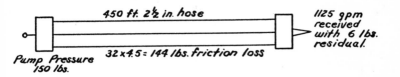

By adding a third 2½-inch line carrying 375 gpm, friction loss can be cut in half, providing 1,125 gpm at second pump.

If a single line, small volume relay is employed, pumpers can be operated in series with 225 psi discharge pressure. This will permit a pumper to move approximately 250 gpm with pumps 1,500 feet apart, or better than 200 gpm with pumps 2,000 feet apart. Thus, if relatively small flows will suffice, water can be moved relatively long distances with few pumpers.

Moving Large Flows Between Pumpers

The average fire fighter has been taught to think of the water carrying capacity of 2½-inch fire hose in the terms of 200 to 300 gpm with pressure loss per 100 feet in the 10 to 20 psi range. This is true where sufficient pressure must be retained at the nozzle to provide a good stream.

However, it is possible to move larger quantities of water through 2½-inch fire hose if we use higher pressure and provide another pump in relay near the fire to give the desired nozzle pressure.

Pressure Needed Per 100 Feet	10	15	21	28	36	45	50	55
GPM Flow 2½-Inch Hose	200	250	300	350	400	450	480	500

Different lengths of hose layouts will produce somewhat different results at a given pump discharge pressure. (It must be assumed that the pump and hydrant are capable of providing the desired flow. This will be indicated by the rated capacity of the pump and by the pump gages.) If a good residual pressure or large capacity pump is available, the pressure may be increased at the source pump.

With larger hose more water can be moved with a given pump capacity, as shown below for 3-inch hose.

Pressure Needed Per 100 Feet	10	21	30	45	50
GPM Flow 3-Inch Hose	330	500	600	750	800

Many fire departments use a line of 2½-inch hose together with a 3-inch line between pumps. Here's the flow obtainable in a relay.

Length of Line Between Pumps in Feet (Source Pump Pressure — 150 psi)	300	400	500	700	1,000
Loss Per 100 Feet	50	37.5	30	21	15
Combined Flow 2½-Inch and 3-Inch Lines	1,275	1,085	960	800	660

Obviously, if pressure at the source pump can be increased while maintaining the desired flow, the length of line between pumps can be lengthened in accordance with pressure loss at the particular flow. Average elevations and entrance pressure at the relay pump can be disregarded. Normal differences in pressure will be accommodated by operation of the second pump which will be limited by what is received.

Doubling the flow in any hose multiplies the pressure loss by 3.6, and cutting the flow in half divides the pressure loss by 3.6. For example, the flow at 18 psi pressure loss is twice that at 5 psi pressure loss ($18 = 5 \times 3.6$). The flow at 36 psi pressure loss is twice that at 10 psi pressure loss ($36 \div 3.6 = 10$). Two other relationships, while not so mathematically exact, are near enough to provide useful generalities as to flow relationships. A 50 percent increase in flow results in approximately twice the pressure loss, and a 25 percent increase in flow results in about 50 percent increase in pressure loss.

Length of Line Between Pumps in Ft. (Source Pump Pressure — 150 pounds)	Loss Per 100 Ft. 2½-in. Hose	Flow — GPM (U.S.)*			
		1 Line	2 Lines	3 Lines	4 Lines
300	50	475	950	1,425	1,900
400	37.5	405	810	1,215	1,620
500	30	360	720	1,080	1,440
700	21	300	600	900	1,200
1,000	15	250	500	750	1,000
		*Subject to hydrant and pump limitations			

Length of Line Between Pumps in Ft. (Source Pump Pressure — 150 pounds)	Loss Per 100 Ft. 3-in. Hose	Flow — GPM (U.S.)*		
		1 Line	2 Lines	3 Lines
300	50	800	1,600	2,400
400	37.5	675	1,350	2,045
500	30	600	1,200	1,800
700	21	500	1,000	1,500
1,000	15	410	820	1,230
		*Subject to hydrant and pump limitations		

The advantage of using 3-in. hose in pumper relays is clearly indicated by these two tables which show the friction loss and flow in various lengths and various numbers of lines. The key to good fire fighting is to make maximum use of the capacity of pumping apparatus.

The advantage of using 3-inch hose in pumper relays is clearly indicated by these two tables which show the friction loss and flow in various lengths and various numbers of lines. The key to good fire fighting is to make maximum use of the capacity of pumping apparatus.

The Pump in the Middle

The question is often asked "Just where should the second pump be spotted for maximum efficiency?" The answer is: Add the required nozzle pressure to the total pressure loss between the pump source and nozzle and divide by two. Each pump will be doing half the work.

For example, a 1½-inch tip is to be supplied at 80 psi through two 2½-inch lines. The nozzle is 1,000 feet from the source pump. The stream requires 600 gpm or 300 gpm per line resulting in 21 psi loss per 100 feet, or 210 psi total loss. To this we add 80 psi nozzle pressure (plus any loss due to elevation). Our total pumping requirement is 290 psi and each pump will provide approximately 145 psi. (Discharge pressure would be at least 150 psi to provide a margin of safety.) The 145 psi divided by 21 psi loss per 100 feet indicates that the pumps should be 700 feet apart.

It will not matter whether one pump is larger than the other, as long as both have the rated capacity to pump 600 gpm at 150 psi. In practice, the hose lays are usually the governing factor in a two-line relay. If a divided hose body has 1,200 feet of hose the pumps will be 600 feet apart. If it carries 1,500 feet of hose they may be up to 750 feet apart. For greater distances a single line low capacity relay would be used.

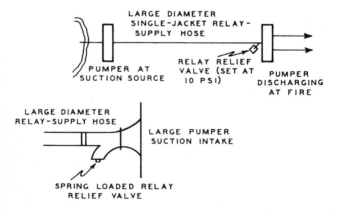

Use of relief valve in relay with large diameter hose.

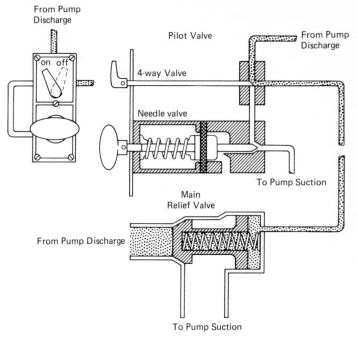

From Pump
Discharge

Pilot Valve

From Pump
Discharge

on off

4-way Valve

Needle valve

To Pump Suction

Main
Relief Valve

From Pump Discharge

To Pump Suction

Waterous relief valve system.

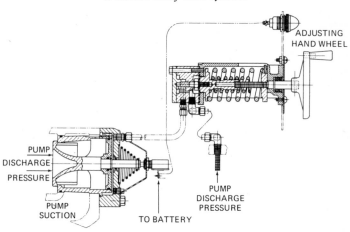

ADJUSTING
HAND WHEEL

PUMP
DISCHARGE
PRESSURE

PUMP
SUCTION

TO BATTERY

PUMP
DISCHARGE
PRESSURE

Hale relief valve.

Relaying to Elevated Streams

When the end of a relay is an aerial ladder, elevating platform or water tower with one or more monitor nozzles discharging at 50 feet or more above ground level, pressure and volume supplied to the siamese must be adequate for good monitor streams. Usually it is necessary to spot the last pumper in the relay within 100 feet of the aerial ladder, platform or water tower so it can supply at least 125 psi at the base siamese. The following tables show pressure requirements for such relays.

Pressure Loss Per 100 Feet (psi) at Different Flows in Different Hose Sizes (Single Lines)

GPM Flow	2½″	2¾″*	3″	3″**	3½″	4″	4½″	5″
250	15.3	9.3	5.9	6.2	2.7	1.4	—	0.5
300	21.2	12.7	8.2	9.0	3.7	1.9	1.1	0.7
400	36.2	21.7	14.1	16.0	6.3	3.3	1.8	1.3
500	55.1	33.1	21.2	25.0	9.5	4.9	2.8	1.9
750			45.0		20.1	11.0		
1,000					34.3	20.4		7.1

*With 3-inch couplings
**With 2½-inch couplings

Standard Pumper Capacities = No. Lines for Full Flow

Rating	2½″	2¾″*	3″	3″**	3½″	4″	4½″
500	2	1 +	1	1	1	1	1
750	3	2		1 +	1	1	
1,000	4	3	2	2	1 +	1	
1,250	5	3 +		3	1 +		
1,500	6	4	3	3	2		
1,750	7	4 +		3 +	2 +		
2,000	8	5	4	4	3	2	

*With 3-inch couplings
**With 2½-inch couplings

QUESTIONS

Chapter 5

Text:

1. In relaying through 2½-inch hose for a distance of 800 feet, what pressure should the supply pump maintain?
2. For the pump that is receiving water in a relay — what should be the incoming pressure?
3. When is a relay necessary?
4. How would you minimize the possibility of damage due to pressure surge?
5. What hydraulic change results if you double the flow in a given hose layout?
6. How do you determine where the second pump should be located in a two-pump relay? In a three-pump relay?
7. How many lines of 3-inch hose are needed to carry the capacity of a 1,000 gpm pumper?

Discussion:

1. What are the limitations of a single-line relay?
2. What is the *lowest* pressure required to keep water moving in a relay?
3. What is the highest pressure that can be allowed in the relay line between pumps?
4. What would be the best hose load arrangement to get maximum relay delivery from a 1,500 gpm pumper?
5. What is the best size hose for relay?
6. What are the advantages and limitations of portable hydrants?

The location, capacity and performance of hydrants are of special importance in municipal fire department operations.

Chapter 6

Hydrants

A fire hydrant is a well known fixture of the urban and suburban scene. In most areas it is recognized that individual properties must be within 500 feet of a hydrant to be considered under its protection. Some persons have argued that with adequate hose available this distance could safely be doubled. However, the laying of long lines takes time, requires higher pressures and might reduce the number of streams that could be placed in operation quickly. In some instances hydrants are found frozen or defective and wide spacing might mean serious delay in getting lines from the next hydrant. In general it may be said that hydrants are cheaper and more efficient than long lines of hose.

Hydrant Marking. Some cities have painted hydrant tops and caps to indicate gallons per minute supply that may be expected. The NFPA has recommended that hydrants have green tops and caps where flows of over 1,000 gpm are available, orange tops and caps for flows of 500 to 1,000 gpm, and red tops as a warning where there is less than 500 gpm. The colors should be understood to signify only the capacity of the individual hydrant and not the result to expect when a group of hydrants are employed.

While the marking of hydrants, particularly those of less than 500 gpm capacity, is highly desirable it should be remembered that each separate hydrant has a performance characteristic that is the sum total of many factors.

Where there is doubt as to the quantity of water available at any location, tests should be made. Recent test data may be available from waterworks' or underwriters' reports but where it is not, one method frequently employed by fire departments is to set up the required hose streams and take Pitot gage readings to determine the pressure and flow of the streams.

Hydrant flow tests are made by opening three or four hydrants in a given neighborhood to find available group flows at residual pressures. If water supply is seriously limited, that fact will be indicated by a marked pressure drop with two streams (400 to 500 gpm) flowing from a single hydrant.

Hydrant Distribution. The distribution and installation of fire hydrants vary from one community to the next, depending upon how much the fire chief asserts his right to influence local water supply. Even so, since hydrants are pretty well standardized today, it is up to the local chief and his department to keep continual records of hydrant capacity and performance so that dangerous or limited situations can be corrected, or noted. This is particularly important in winter when fire companies must shovel out or clear certain hydrants to assure that water will be available.

One type of hydrant evaluation is shown in the grading schedule of the Insurance Services Office, which evaluates fire departments and fire protection in cities of 25,000 and greater population. The ISO determines the need for hydrant distribution according to the fire flow required for a certain location. For example, for a flow of 1,000 gpm or less, it is estimated that the average area of coverage per hydrant would be about 160,000 square feet. For a 5,000 gpm flow the hydrant should cover an average area of 90,000 square feet. These figures are approximations, and can change from one community to the next.

One assumption a fire company officer can make is that, if hydrants are installed within a community, or at some shopping center or industrial plant, water should be available at a certain (undefined) pressure. To be certain, make a pre-fire inspection of your district or community area of fire protection. Find out which hydrants are near the end of a line; which ones have above-average water supply and pressure; and who made the last flow tests.

The local city or town water department should have maps showing water main size (*Chapter 7*) and hydrant distribution;

if not, the local insurance rating organization may be able to provide this information. Some fire departments take a great deal of responsibility in checking the installation, maintenance and capacity of fire hydrants, and perform regular flow tests and other checks of the system, especially in pre-fire planning. In Los Angeles County, California, building developers cannot proceed on new projects unless they can show the fire department plans for adequate hydrants and water supply for proposed buildings. Many other fire departments give their fire companies frequent assignments of testing and evaluating hydrant performance in their respective districts.

Types of Hydrants. All hydrants should meet requirements of the American Water Works Association and appropriate NFPA standards, but fire officers usually will be concerned with one of two types: the normal, dry-barrel type used in most communities where freezing conditions occur; and the wet-barrel, or "California" type used in that state and other warm climate areas where freezing does not occur.

Engine 1, a 750 gpm pumper of North Conway, New Hampshire, uses flexible hard suction hose to connect to hydrant steamer outlet.

There are standards for each of these types: AWWA C502 for ordinary service, and AWWA C503 for wet-barrel fire hydrants. The obvious difference is that the dry-barrel type is not supposed to retain water in the barrel when the main valve is closed; the water should drain out through an outlet at the base of the barrel. The wet-type hydrant can retain water after use.

The standards require both types of hydrants to be designed for a working pressure of 150 psi. A hydraulic test of 300 psi shall be conducted on the assembled hydrant. In the terminology of AWWA, the standards refer to hydrant discharge outlets as "nozzles," designating certain designs as "one-hose nozzle," "two-hose nozzle," "one-pumper nozzle," "one-hose and one-pumper nozzle," "three-hose nozzle," "two-hose and one-pumper nozzle," and "two-pumper nozzle." In Fire Service terminology the large outlet on a hydrant is often referred to as the "steamer" connection and the connections for smaller lines are termed "outlets."

Components of a hydrant are the bonnet, or top; the main valve, or stem; the barrel; the nozzle(s), or outlet(s), and caps; and the base inlet. Each is described in the AWWA standards, as are the lesser components, such as the nuts, threads, flanges, lugs, and waterway.

A 5-inch hose attached to 4½-inch outlet of a Mueller hydrant.

A front mount pump connects to Waterous hydrant with large diameter soft suction hose and a short length of 2½-inch into a gated outlet.

When a hydrant is placed in the ground there are two principal portions: the part aboveground, and the "bury," or portion underground. Most modern hydrants have a breakaway arrangement for the above ground portion, in case it is struck by a vehicle or otherwise needs emergency repair or replacement. If a hydrant is made of two or more sections, with a flange or joint near the ground line, this joint should be located at least two inches above grade level. The portion below ground, attached to the water main, should seldom need attention unless a leak, tuberculation or other pipe blockage occurs.

Engine company officers and pump operators should note how much effort is required to turn the main stem and open a hydrant. It is designed to be opened by one man with a 15-inch wrench; in fact, it is required to meet a 200 foot-pound opening and closing torque test at the operating nut. Use of a longer wrench or an extender, operated by one to two men, is not good practice. If a hydrant seems to need this type of force it should be put out of service until repaired.

Pressure Drops. Consider a hydrant where our gage shows we have a static or non-flowing pressure of 80 psi. If we plan to supply handlines directly from this hydrant, we may have a problem.

A number of California fire departments make frequent use of the 4-way hydrant connection as shown here in a West Covina operation.

Pressure from the waterworks pumps or the reservoir is pressing against the hydrant outlet and gage, tending to give us assurance that the water system is backing up the hydrant from which we are planning to run hose lines.

However, assume that the hydrant is supplied by 500 feet of 4-inch main connected to a larger main of the distribution grid. A fire occurs and the first engine company lays a 300-foot hose line with a 1-inch nozzle tip direct from the hydrant. When the nozzle is opened the residual pressure at the hydrant drops approximately 10 psi to 70 psi. This is due to the friction loss in the 4-inch main with some 200 gpm flowing. The nozzle pressure is 40 psi, and friction loss in the hose totals 30 psi. From these facts, the fire fighter may feel satisfied that the water pressure is good and that the hydrant can be relied on in the event of a bad fire.

Perhaps another time the company rolls out to find a brisk fire that requires several streams. It slaps two lines on the supposedly "good" hydrant with 80 psi static pressure but the nozzle pressure obtained is very poor. Even after reducing the size of the nozzle tips the hydrant pressure remains low because the greater flow from the two lines has greatly increased the friction loss in the small main. If the main has been in the ground for some time without cleaning, it is likely that incrustation has decreased the useful area of the pipe and, despite the initial high pressure, it may be impossible to supply two good streams even though a pumper is used to take all available water at close to zero residual pressure.

When possible, it is best to place a pumper at a hydrant to supply handlines, or otherwise move the water. Don't rely on hydrant pressure.

Residual Pressures at Given Flows
(disregarding hydrant efficiency)
1000 Ft. Water Main, One Direction Supply

1000 FT.	75 PSI Static at Hydrant	Residual Pressures in PSI at Given Flows in GPM				
		250	400	500	750	1000
4-in.		46	6	X	X	X
6-in.		70	65	60	44	23
8-in.		74	73	71	67	62

Officers of fire departments should order additional pumpers to draw water from the system only when they are sure the system is able to supply them at the desired location. This can usually be determined by questioning the operators already hooked up. The officer should know how much additional water he can expect by the size of the pressure drop caused by the quantity of water already being pumped.

A sudden drop in the pressure reading on the suction gage may indicate that other pumpers have connected to nearby hydrants, or that there is a break in the main or other failure of the water system.

The Intake Gage. The pumper gage customarily given greatest attention is the one showing pressure being discharged through hose lines. But, the gage on the suction or intake side is also important. An operator who can interpret this gage correctly can get maximum performance from his machine and keep out of a lot of trouble by not attempting to supply hose layouts for which there is not adequate water at the hydrant (unless the supply can be supplemented from other sources).

To make proper use of the suction or intake gage, notice the pressure on the suction side after the hydrant has been turned on but before a line is charged. This will indicate static pressure in the water system with no water flowing from the hydrant. The difference between this static pressure and the pressure with which the hydrant supplies various flows will indicate the amount of water that can be obtained from the hydrant, and the residual hydrant pressures at which various flows may be obtained.

Another convenient way of estimating available flow is on the basis of the number of streams a hydrant can supply through 1-inch tips (200 gpm) or 1⅛-inch tips (250 gpm). When supplying a 1⅛-inch tip on the first line, if the pressure drop is not over 10 percent, the hydrant should be good for three more streams or a total of at least 1,000 gpm. Or, if the pressure drop is not over 15 percent, the hydrant should supply two more streams for a total of at least 750 gpm.

Some fire departments use portable hydrants to extend or relay water supply. Here, Chelsea, Massachusetts fire fighters wheel one to position. (Photo by Charles A. Tuck, Jr.)

Portable hydrant, fed by a 4-inch hose line, supplies two 2½-inch lines, note gage at top center and gages for individual lines. (Photo by Charles A. Tuck, Jr.)

Hydrant Records

Company fire officers would be well advised to keep at least a simple record of hydrant static and residual pressures encountered each time a hose stream is placed in service. By doing this, the department will possess valuable information as to what the water supply situation may be in a given area in the event a large fire demands the maximum hydrant performance. Many departments, unfamiliar with hydrant performance under conditions of heavy draft, have been fooled because at previous fires requiring small flows the pressure remained high and direct hydrant streams were satisfactory without the use of pumps. The same hydrant might be unable to supply a second or a third stream without use of the pumper to boost the pressure. The residual pressure from the hydrant with a second line flowing could have been predicted had attention been given to the percentage of pressure drop when the first line was placed in service.

Following are charts showing typical hydrant discharge "curves" which begin with a static reading and continue to a residual pressure with 500 gpm flowing. Above the curves are the corresponding suction gage readings on the pumper.

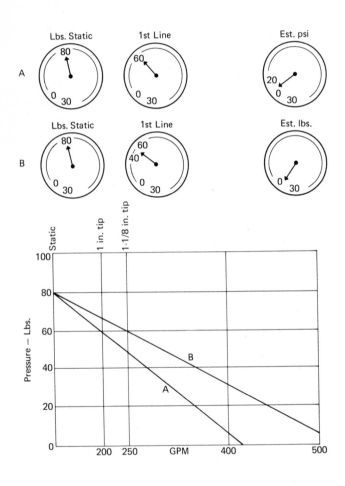

*Typical pressure drops with hydrants that showed 80 psi static pressure
(no water flowing) but which dropped to 60 psi with the first stream in
service. In the case of Hydrant A it happens that the 60 psi residual
pressure reading is obtained when the hydrant is discharging about
200 gpm through a 1-inch tip. Of course, the pumper will be discharging
at greater pressure depending on length of the hose line and elevation,
but the discharge pressure registers on the discharge gage of the pumper.
The chart is logged to record pressure loss at various flows as a straight
line. In a corresponding line above, the compound or suction gage
readings are shown. If a pumper is equipped with two compound gages,
read the gage on the intake side.*

*Line A shows a 25 percent pressure drop with a 1-inch tip in use. We
find that by running a ruled line from the 80 psi static reading to the
60 psi reading with 200 gpm, that the hydrant should be able to deliver
400 gpm at something better than 5 psi, but not much more than that.*

*Line B shows a hydrant that delivers a stream from a 1⅛-inch tip (250
gpm) with a 25 percent pressure drop. We see that this will deliver 500
gpm at better than 5 psi residual pressure on the pumper intake. It will
also deliver 400 gpm at about 30 psi residual.*

*Supposing we were using a 1⅛-inch tip on the first line from Hydrant A.
The drop of pressure to 50 psi (exceeding 30 percent) would indicate
that a second tip of the same size could not be supplied. Contrariwise,
if a 1-inch tip had been first used on Hydrant B, the slight pressure
drop with the first stream would indicate that more than twice the flow
could be obtained from that hydrant at a satisfactory residual pressure.*

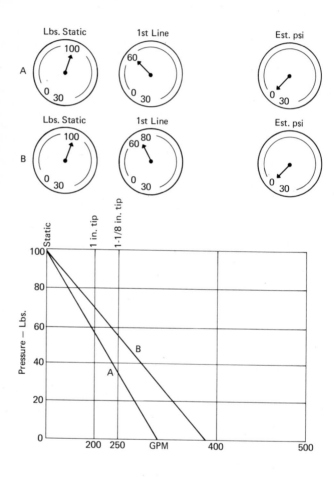

Here we have hydrants that can easily deceive the fire fighter. They show 100 psi static pressure reading. However, they probably are on 4- or 6-inch dead end mains because the pressure loss exceeds 30 percent in each case when the first line is placed in service. Take the hydrant readings shown by Line A as an example. When water is turned into the pump before a hose line is charged the pump operator notes that he has 100 psi hydrant pressure and may think that all is going well. Then a line with a 1-inch tip is placed in service. As shown by the compound gage reading (A) the pressure immediately drops to about 60 psi. This is a 40 percent drop in pressure. As the line on the chart indicates, that hydrant cannot deliver much over 300 gpm. If the first line has carried a 1⅛-inch tip the pressure on the compound gage would have dropped to nearly 30 psi showing that almost all of the full capacity of the hydrant was being utilized.

The hydrant illustrated by Line B is only slightly better. It shows a 30 percent pressure drop with the first 1-inch tip and about 45 percent pressure loss with a 1⅛-inch tip. Two streams from 1-inch tips might be "squeezed out" if the operator watched his gages closely and if the hose crew could be satisfied with nozzle pressure as low as 35 to 40 psi (which would slightly reduce the flow in each line). Usually, however, where the drop in hydrant pressure indicates that a second "big line" is not feasible, it is a good practice to use a 1½-inch leader on the second line. The pumper can provide the desired effective pressure if the flow is within the capability of the hydrant. Observe how easily an operator could be deceived by Hydrant B. He has 100 psi static and 70 psi flow pressure with a good stream with a 1-inch tip. Nevertheless, that hydrant cannot supply two good streams of that size. "Low pressure" is not to blame. A small main with resulting small volume is the real culprit.

120   *Operating Fire Department Pumpers*

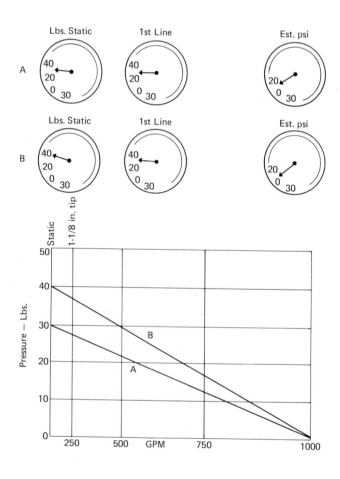

*The chart opposite shows performance of two low pressure hydrants
that would be much more satisfactory to the average pump operator
than the high pressure hydrants shown on the previous charts. Hydrant A
shows 30 psi static pressure when water is at rest but the pressure is
still close to 30 psi (27 to be exact) when a good 1⅛-inch stream is
flowing from a big line. With a pressure loss of 10 percent or less with
the first line, the pump operator knows that he can get 750 or even 1000
gpm and still have a satisfactory pressure on the suction side of his
pump. This means that although the initial static or starting pressure
was relatively low, the hydrant is on a big main, well looped or gridded
and is able to supply all of the water that a 750 or 1000 gpm pumper
might want. As long as the pumper can get enough water it can deliver
its capacity at 150 psi pressure. Of course, if very high pressure is
needed the pump can deliver 70 percent of its volume at 200 psi. Thus
a 750 gpm centrifugal pump working at Hydrant A will get 525 gpm
with 20 psi residual at the hydrant and can, if necessary, deliver this
quantity at 220 psi on the discharge gage.*

*Hydrant B has a higher static pressure and the same percentage of
pressure loss but its actual pressure drops a little faster with increased
flow. It still shows a superiority in pressure at 500 gpm but with 1000
gpm flowing its performance is much the same as that of Hydrant A.*

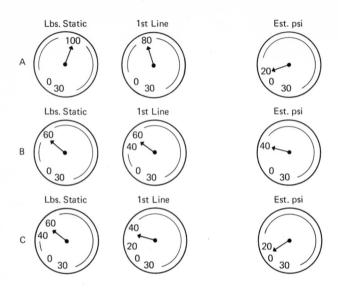

Pressures at which 500 gpm centrifugal pump may deliver rated capacity from hydrants may be calculated by observing static pressure and pressure drop with the initial line. See chart below.

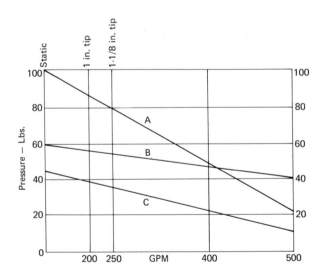

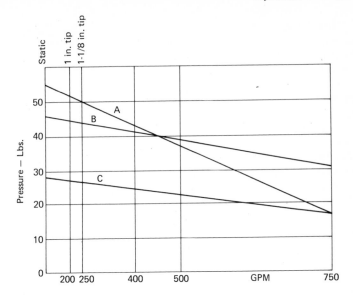

Typical hydrant residual pressures with 750 gpm flowing.

The chart above shows residual pressures from three typical low-pressure hydrants with flows up to 750 gpm. Suppose a fire department wishes to know at which pressure Hydrant A will supply a 750 gpm pumper operating at capacity. This hydrant has a static (non-flow) pressure reading of 55 pounds. The suction or compound gage pressure falls to 50 psi when 250 gpm is being discharged through a 1⅛-inch tip. A ruled line (A) extended from the static and first line gage readings shows that the hydrant should give 750 gpm at about 16 psi residual. Of course, the hydrant may give somewhat more than this if the municipality's water works pumps are arranged to increase the pressure. In any event, the 16 psi can be added to the 150 psi at which the 750 gpm centrifugal pumper can deliver its 750 gpm so that capacity may be obtained at about 166 psi pump pressure.

Hydrant B, although starting with 45 psi static pressure gives 750 gpm at 30 psi because it has a much flatter "curve" as indicated by the small pressure drop when the first line is placed in operation. Hydrant C, although having a relatively low static pressure, gives 750 gpm at the same flow pressure as Hydrant A.

Now let us suppose that a 750 gpm pumper is called upon to supply two 265 gpm streams at 230 psi pressure (1⅛-inch tips at 50 psi). Can this be done at the hydrants shown on the 750 gpm chart?

The total required flow is 530 gpm. A 750 gpm Class A pumper delivers 525 gpm from 10-foot draft at 200 psi. As shown by the chart, Hydrants A and B give better than 500 gpm at well in excess of 30 psi. This pressure added to the pump output indicates that a 750 gpm pumper operating from these hydrants should readily deliver the 530 gpm at 230 psi (200 psi pump pressure + 30 psi hydrant flow pressure).

Hydrant C, on the other hand, would give 530 gpm at only a little more than 20 psi so that the pump might be exceeding its rated performance in attempting to supply the desired flow from this hydrant. However, knowing the maximum performance of the pump and hydrant, reasonably satisfactory results might be obtained by accepting slightly less nozzle pressure. This would reduce the flow and the friction loss in the hose. Two 45 psi streams with the same tips would total 500 gpm, and the drop in NP and FL would bring that hose layout within the performance of the 750 gpm centrifugal pumper receiving 500 gpm at 20 psi and discharging at 220 psi.

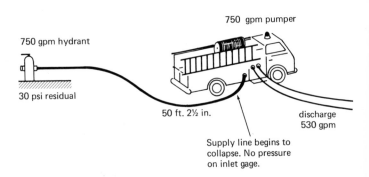

With a 2½-inch hose the 30 psi hydrant pressure is used completely when 530 gpm is flowing from this pumper. A larger hose, or a second line, could be used.

Some persons will say that fire pumps are built with a reserve and can exceed their rated capacities. This may be true just as it is true that the human heart (a pump) has a reserve that can exceed normal demand. However, it is poor practice to exceed the rating for which a machine is built because impairment or failure may result at a critical time due to needless and protracted overload. It is important that company officers and pump operators know the gpm at which pumpers will deliver rated capacities at 150, 200 and 250 psi. Then, assuming that the pump is operating in the desired pressure or volume position, it will be possible to run the machine at its safe rated capacity at the appropriate engine speed, taking advantage of whatever additional pressure that the hydrant may be able to provide.

Flow from Hydrant to Pumper

Assume a pump capable of 750 gpm output connected in-line to a hydrant providing 750 gpm at 30 psi flowing pressure. If the supply hose between hydrant and pump is too small, too much pressure will be expended in friction loss and there will not be sufficient pressure to take the full 750 gpm flow to the pump inlet.

Let's say a 50-foot length of 2½-inch hose is used between this hydrant and pump. When 530 gpm is reached the friction loss in the line will have used all 30 psi from the hydrant. On the other hand, 50 feet of 3-inch hose would use only 23 psi of hydrant pressure with 750 gpm flowing.

If accurate, the pump inlet gage would show only about 7 or 8 psi, even though a gage placed on an unused outlet of the hydrant would show 30 psi residual pressure with the 750 gpm flowing.

With very large flows there may be pressure losses of over 10 psi between the hydrant and the inlet gage on the pumper even if large diameter suction hose is used.

The reading on the suction gage shows the pressure under which water is being supplied to the pump. It may also be used to give an indication of the quantity of water available for use.

Identical readings will appear on both gages on a centrifugal pump (or on a positive displacement pump when the by-pass valve is open). This reading should be noted and remembered. As soon as a discharge valve is open and a line is in operation, the suction gage should be read again to observe the amount of drop in incoming pressure. If the difference in these two readings is slight, or does not exceed about 25 percent of the initial static pressure, this indicates that there is additional water available for another hose line. On the other hand, a major drop in the incoming pressure indicates that the water supply is limited and there may not be enough water from that hydrant for another stream of the same volume.

For example, suppose the suction gage shows a reading of 50 psi pressure with the hydrant open, but no water leaving the pump. If this drops to 40 psi when water is turned into a 2½-inch hose line it is safe to assume that the amount of water still available at the hydrant is at least equal to that being discharged. However, if the pressure drops from 50 to 30 psi there is not much more water available from the hydrant.

During practice sessions operators should connect their pumpers to hydrants of different capacities, preferably those having more and less flow potential than the capacity of the pump. In this way they can get personal experience with how much water is available from hydrants in different parts of town, how the pumpers can use the water, and the various gage and engine speed readings. Performance of different pumpers with the same hydrant may vary.

Assume that a 750 gpm pumper connects to a hydrant having a 50 psi static pressure (no water flowing) but capable of discharging only 375 gpm at 5 psi residual pressure. With the operation of the first 250 gpm stream, the residual pressure would drop to about 30 psi. When the pump has "pulled the hydrant down" to 5 psi it would only obtain about 375 gpm. A 750 gpm pumper rated at 150 psi can discharge that 375 gpm at 250 psi pressure without help from the hydrant. On the other hand, a 500 gpm pumper is designed to pump 350 gpm at only 200 psi net pump pressure but to discharge only 250 gpm at 250 psi.

Next, assume that a 500 gpm centrifugal pumper rated at 150 psi connects to a 50 psi hydrant which drops only 3 psi, or say, 6 percent, when the first 250 gpm line is opened. It is evident immediately that the hydrant can give 750 gpm at 30 psi residual.

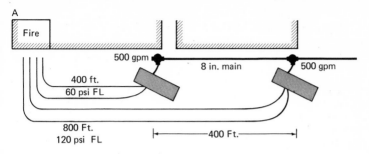

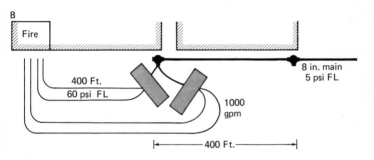

By taking full advantage of a large capacity hydrant output friction loss can be minimized. As shown above, two pumpers connecting to a good hydrant nearest to the fire (as in B) offer greater efficiency than two pumpers connecting to separate hydrants (as in A) which sometimes necessitates long lines and large friction loss. One city has marked all hydrants flowing over 1,200 gallons at 25 psi for possible two-pumps use.

PRE-FIRE PLAN FIRE FLOW ESTIMATE
OF LINCOLN, NEBRASKA FIRE DEPARTMENT

Address.. .... Zone No.............
Description of Block or Complex:
Type of Construction:...................................... Occupancy....................
Ground Floor Area, Sq. Ft.........No. of Stories....Total Floor Area.......
                                                        (if needed)
Fire Flow from Table... G.P.M......................
Automatic Sprinklers........Standpipes.......Fire Detection System.......

Exposures	*Distance*	*Hazard*
1. Front		
2. Left		
3. Rear		
4. Right		

WATER AVAILABLE — (Color Coded)

Size of Main..................................... Location of Hydrants..................
Hydrants..................... Static-psi.................... Residual-psi..................
1 2 & 3

FIRE DEPARTMENT EQUIPMENT RESPONSE

First Alarm: Truck Co's......... Engine Co's....... Dist. Chief.........
Second Alarm: Truck Co's......... Engine Co's....... Dist. Chief.........
F.C................ Ass't. Chief............... Inspectors........... Mechanic ....
Special Equipment..

Third Alarm:

AERIAL PHOTO

Show streets, access, mains, hydrants and siamese connections. Gas
and Electric shutoffs, P.I.V. and System.

SCHEMATIC DRAWING OF BLOCK BUILDING
OR COMPLEX

---

*Typical prefire plan of sprinklered building or target hazard should be
kept up to date by engine company responsible for protecting that location.*

"Pacer" hydrant of Waterous Company.

Thus, the limiting factor may be the water horsepower output of the pumper.

A modern 500 gpm centrifugal pump might take the 750 gpm available at about 30 psi and perhaps add 100 psi discharge pressure and discharge the 750 gpm at 130 psi without danger of an overload.

A 750 gpm centrifugal pumper would have been able to take the 750 gpm at 30 psi and discharge at 180 psi or better because it is capable of delivering 50 percent more water horsepower than the smaller pumper. A 1,000 gpm pumper can handle 750 gpm from a hydrant at about 200 psi net pump pressure.

Incoming Pressure

When a pumper is connected to a hydrant or other source of water supply under pressure, it is desirable to maintain 10 psi or more pressure on the suction gage. However, with large flows, the friction in the hydrant and suction hose may be 5 to 10 psi or more. When using a soft suction, the point at which maximum volume is being received can be detected by feeling the suction hose at the point it enters the pump intake. If the soft suction or incoming hose is soft and flabby when squeezed, it indicates

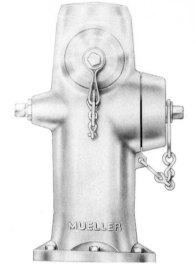

Mueller/109 wet barrel fire hydrant can be used in areas not subject to freezing conditions.

Dry barrel hydrant showing "bury" section below flange near ground level.

that the pump is beginning to "run away from water," since there is no pressure left to keep the suction hose solid. Retard the throttle until the supply lines are reasonably firm where they enter the pump. This will prevent damage to the pump from "cavitation" which can occur when a pump runs away from water. Cavitation can be detected by a chattering sound from the pump.

To attempt to get more water without additional supply lines is futile and may result in poor hose streams as well as possible damage to the pump due to "cavitation" which means that air cavities are formed in the pump which can set up water hammer and cause serious damage. Cavitation can also occur during drafting if the operator runs the pump faster than the suction hose can deliver water. The reliability of the suction gage readings at pressures near the zero mark may be determined approximately by observing the gage when the pump is taking all available water.

Using Available Hydrant Supply

In one type of in-line pumping, when we have a single feeder line 300 feet long between hydrant and pump with water flowing at only 18 psi we divide 18 by 3 and find that when utilizing all available hydrant pressure we have a possible 6 psi loss per 100 feet. Using 2½-inch hose the approximate maximum flow would be 150 gpm with the line almost collapsing at the pump inlet. With 3-inch hose the maximum flow would be 250 gpm. If, instead of a low pressure hydrant supplying the 300-foot feeder line, we have a high pressure hydrant or pumper capable of flowing the desired quantity at 150 psi we divide the 150 by 3 and find that we can expend approximately 50 psi per 100 feet. This will provide about 475 gpm through a single 2½-inch line and up to 790 gpm through a 3-inch line. However, we must be sure that the pump inlet is of adequate capacity to carry the full flow. If the line was 400 feet long, we would divide the available hydrant pressure by 4 to find the allowable friction loss per 100 feet (on approximately level ground). If the hydrant flow pressure is 40 psi we would be able to use about 10 psi per 100 feet which would provide 200 gpm through each 2½-inch feeder or 330 gpm through a 3-inch feeder. Remember that static pressure at the hydrant when no water is flowing does not count. More important is the ability of the hydrant or supply pump to give the desired flow at an effective pressure. When additional pumpers are placed in service, residual pressure at the hydrant may be further reduced, and the pumper may then be unable to obtain enough water to supply the laid out hose lines.

It is not possible to obtain more water than the hydrant can supply. Some hydrants on small dead-end mains are poorly supplied, and should be marked to indicate their limitations. If a certain hydrant will flow only 100 gpm at 15 psi it will then be able to feed a pumper 500 feet away through 2½-inch hose if the pumper output is limited to 100 gpm, or one good 1½-inch line. This is because, with only 100 gpm flowing, the friction loss in the 2½-inch line will be only 2½ psi per 100 feet. The pumper will then provide the pressure for one usable line. In such situations an acceptable practice might be to lay out two 1½-inch lines and to operate them in turn or intermittently to avoid exceeding the available hydrant supply.

If the pumper has a large tank, the 1½-inch lines might be supplied from the tank, with the 2½-inch hydrant line used to keep the tank full. Care must be taken not to turn strong hydrant pressure into a tank that is not adequately vented or damage may result.

Collapsing Supply Line

A good pumper operator will have little difficulty in making the most of the water available to his pump from a hydrant supply line. Compound gage readings may be somewhat inaccurate, particularly at low pressure. The operator can observe the supply line where it enters the inlet of the pump. As long as that line is hard or firm the pump is getting enough water to meet the demands of the hose lines. When the line or lines begin to get soft, the limit of the supply available from the feeder lines in use has been reached.

If the operator reduces the pumper discharge pressure slightly he can usually correct the situation with a slight reduction in nozzle pressure. A decrease of 10 gpm in each of two leader lines will reduce friction loss in the supply line to the pumper by about 2 psi per 100 feet. A decrease of 5 gpm in each leader line will reduce the friction loss in the 2½-inch supply line by about 1 psi per 100 feet.

Interior view of dry barrel hydrant.

Triangular shaped hydrant of Clow Corporation's Eddy-Iowa Division.

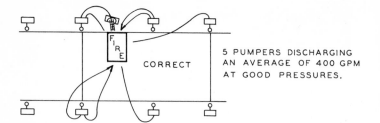

CORRECT

5 PUMPERS DISCHARGING
AN AVERAGE OF 400 GPM
AT GOOD PRESSURES.

Here is a situation where hydrants near the fire building provide a total 2,000 gpm flow. Pumpers stationed properly supply eight 2½-inch lines averaging 250 gpm. Hydrant residual pressures and nozzle pressures are good.

In the same locality as above the massing of seven pumpers is too much for the available flow. Fourteen 2½- inch lines each average 143 gpm. Hydrant residual pressures are dragged down and nozzle pressures are weak, even for small tips. The lines shown actually would require 3,500 gpm (14 times 250 gpm).

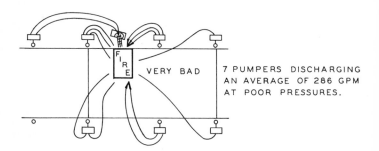

VERY BAD

7 PUMPERS DISCHARGING
AN AVERAGE OF 286 GPM
AT POOR PRESSURES.

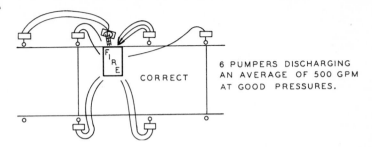

6 PUMPERS DISCHARGING
AN AVERAGE OF 500 GPM
AT GOOD PRESSURES.

In a hydrant layout providing 3,000 gpm total flow six pumpers feeding a reasonable number of lines (twelve) can operate with good hydrant residuals and good nozzle pressures.

In the same location, the 3,000 gpm flow can be overwhelmed when eight pumpers try to supply eighteen 2½-inch lines, which would actually require a total fire flow of 4,500 gpm. Fire officers through experience learn to estimate the entire hydrant supply when they are spotting pumpers and other apparatus.

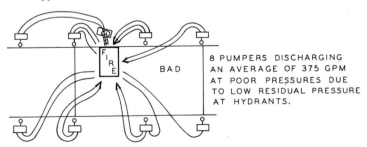

8 PUMPERS DISCHARGING
AN AVERAGE OF 375 GPM
AT POOR PRESSURES DUE
TO LOW RESIDUAL PRESSURE
AT HYDRANTS.

Sketches of fireground situations showing how tactical placement of pumpers should be adjusted to hydrant supply.

When the fire department wants to obtain large flows, it should seek to take advantage of the carrying capacity of the big mains under the street and avoid long lines of hose. This can be done by making maximum use of the hydrants nearest to the fire which have the best water supply. It is poor practice, generally, to have a number of pumpers working at different hydrants each supplying a single line, unless the nearest hydrants are incapable of supplying the required flow.

But let us assume that 1,400 gpm is available from a hydrant near the fire and that a 500 or 750 gpm pumper is connected to the hydrant and supplying several lines. Two more lines are needed from another pumper and the next nearest hydrant is 400 or 500 feet away. The suction or intake gage on the first pumper shows a good residual pressure indicating that ample water is still available at the first hydrant. It is assumed the pumper already there is working at near its capacity and is unable to supply more lines at the desired pressure. It then may be advisable to connect a second pumper to this hydrant rather than to lay several long lines which would require a pump pressure of 200 to 250 psi and reduce the output of the second machine by 50 per cent or more.

Normally, if pumpers are of 1,000 gpm rated capacity or larger, one pumper can utilize the full output of a hydrant. No two-pump operation should be attempted from a hydrant unless tests have shown that the hydrant can supply the necessary flow.

Operating from Hydrant

There are four general methods of supplying pumpers from hydrants. The type of operation employed may vary, depending upon the amount of water and pressure available from the hydrant, the capacity of the pump, and the number and size of hose lines desired. These factors will determine whether the pump is to be connected directly to the hydrant or will be located nearer the fire and supplied by hose lines. The type of hydrant supply may also determine whether a hard or soft "suction" will be used.

It is possible to provide full capacity for a pump, spotted near a fire yet far from a hydrant, *if enough hose lines of adequate diameter are connected to the inlet side of the pump and are supplied under sufficient pressure.* Standard pumper specifications call for at least one 2½-inch gated inlet for each pumper but most fire departments specify additional inlets. When 2½- or 3-inch hose is used to supply a pumper, the friction losses will correspond to losses encountered when the same size hose supplies hose streams. Friction loss in 2½-inch hose supplying 250 gpm will be about 15 psi per hundred feet, so a hydrant having a residual pressure of 50 psi could supply this volume to a pumper through no more than 300 feet of single 2½-inch hose. At the same residual pressure, only about 175 gpm could be supplied through 600 feet of 2½-inch hose. With the same pressure and length of line the 3-inch hose would provide 435 and 300 gpm respectively. It is part of the pumper operator's responsibility to see that the pump is supplied by enough hose lines.

There are two fundamentals for successful pumping from hydrants: (1) try to connect the pump to a hydrant capable of giving the desired supply, and (2) connect to the hydrant with hose large enough to provide the full capacity of the pump. If small hose is used, additional supply lines may be needed.

If a large soft suction hose is used the operation is speeded up if one end is carried preconnected to a pump inlet. The same advantage may be obtained by using a "squirrel tail" hard suction which is carried attached to the pump by a swivel connection. In case either of these practices is used, there should be a valve so that the pump can use water from the booster tank without filling the suction hose.

If available, the large hydrant outlet should always be used. Normally, a single 2½-inch outlet will not provide full capacity except to small pumps. If hydrants do not have the large steamer connection (normally 4- or 4¼-inch diameter), it is necessary to connect to two 2½-inch outlets to obtain an adequate pumper supply.

Supplying Two Pumpers from a Hydrant

In high value districts of large cities 3- and 3½-inch hose is generally used to supply heavy streams. However, some fire departments have little or no hose larger than 2½-inch diameter. Except for very short lines, or where pumpers are used in relay, this limits the flow in each hose to about 250 gpm because at higher flows the friction loss in the hose is excessive.

To utilize full output of a 750 or 1,000 gpm pumper, three or four lines of hose may be needed. Few pumpers carry enough hose for the rated capacity except for comparatively short layouts, but some fire departments use auxiliary trucks that carry 5,000 to 6,000 feet of extra hose.

For large fires it is desirable and often necessary to concentrate large flows. This may require substantially the full capacities of available pumpers. There is little difficulty with first alarm pumpers which can take advantage of the hydrants close to the fire, but pumpers arriving on multiple alarms or mutual aid may be so far from the fire that much of their pumping energy is used to overcome friction loss rather than in delivering large quantities of water.

QUESTIONS

Chapter 6

Text:

1. What are the NFPA recommended color markings for hydrants?
2. What is an indication of a limited hydrant supply?
3. What is residual pressure? Static pressure?
4. What is the difference between wet barrel and dry barrel hydrants?
5. What are the principal parts of a hydrant?
6. What would be a serious pressure drop after a pumper starts taking water from a hydrant?
7. How does a pump operator know when he is "running away" from the hydrant?

Discussion:

1. Who should be responsible for testing hydrant capability — the Fire Department? The Water Department? The local insurance rating bureau? Explain why.
2. Why do some hydrants have a big (4½-inch) outlet and others have only small 2½-inch outlets?
3. If you were to design a hydrant to be attached to a 10-inch main and to be used only for fire fighting, what features would you include?
4. Should a fire company rely on handlines from a hydrant or should a pumper *always* take the hydrant and supply the handlines?
5. How much authority does the local fire chief have in requiring hydrants at certain locations?

In small communities and in rural areas portable water tanks can be used successfully to supply pumpers and hose streams. (Photos by Ben's Foto Shop)

Chapter 7

Water Supply

When an engine company is going into action one consideration of the company officer and pump operator should be: where is the water supply and how much is available? Without water, a pumping engine is useless, although its crew or fire company may be used for other emergency tasks. In most urban and suburban areas fire fighters will have some knowledge of the water supply in their districts but in rural, or other less developed areas, the responding fire company may not know what kind of supply is available until it reaches the scene of emergency. In mutual aid operations and in similar assignments the engine company may even have to improvise some form of supply.

In one respect, a static water source such as a lake, pond or stream may be more dependable than a city hydrant system, because at least the amount of water is clearly defined and the drafting routine is obvious. In contrast to this, a municipal water system with undersized or dead-end mains and inadequate hydrants may create severe operational problems. (*Chapter 6.*) Obviously, every fire company should be familiar with the type of water supply in its area of operation, yet be ready to follow a secondary course of action if this supply suddenly becomes inadequate.

Water Main Systems. Modern systems of supplying water for municipal fire protection include (A) a reservoir or other source of stored water; (B) one or more pumping stations; (C) underground water mains with appropriate layout for balanced distribution; and (D) a quantity of hydrants spaced to provide efficient supply for fire department pumpers.

In the typical system there are three classes of distribution mains: primary feeders, secondary feeders and distributors.

Primary feeders are large diameter pipes used to carry large quantities of water to certain points for local distribution to small mains. These feeders are usually eighteen to twenty-four inches in diameter, or larger.

Secondary feeders, which form a network of intermediate size pipes to reinforce to distributor, are twelve inches in diameter, or larger.

Distributors, usually a grid arrangement of small mains, may run from twelve inches down to six inches in diameter. In high value districts, it is recommended that distributors be no less than eight inches in diameter and interconnected every 600 feet.

A very important feature of a water system layout is that mains be looped and interconnected so that failure at any point will not interrupt the supply. There are requirements for valves to be installed at certain intervals to permit closing off portions of the system for repairs and other work. The local water department should have maps and other documents explaining the complete layout and capacity of every portion of the system.

Three problems that often plague fire departments are: dead-end water mains, weak hydrants and unexpected pressure drops. Actually, each of these should be identified before a fire emergency through normal inspection and evaluation of the hydrant and water system. Dead-end mains, those at the end of a street or other single main layout, with water supply coming from only one direction, may be identified at a glance, but it would be best to check the actual water department data on the installation. There are still some towns and other localities where a single main of 4-inch or 6-inch size leads to a hydrant which may be a critical, but useless source of water for firefighting.

Weak hydrants (*Chapter 6*) may be on such mains, may have small outlets, or may be attached to an old, tuberculated or otherwise blocked main system that produces inadequate flow.

Pressure drop in water supply can result when too many

1250 gpm pumper of Littleton, Colorado Fire Department has 5-inch supply line hooked to hydrant and discharges through two 2½-inch lines.

pumpers hook up to hydrants in one area, or when water in the system is suddenly shut off, or otherwise diverted from the fire locality. There is always a reason for pressure drops, but the engine company officer and pump operator should know what action to take immediately if the sudden change in pressure is critical.

Each of these deficiencies should be corrected promptly in co-operation with the water department, otherwise the fire department must alter its operations.

Flow Test. The best way for a fire company to understand its available hydrant supply is to conduct flow tests, or to observe them being conducted by insurance rating bureau representatives or other qualified personnel. Flow tests are not difficult, but they do require certain equipment and an understanding of hydraulic calculation. Items needed include: a Pitot gage; a hydrant cap with pressure gage; a ruler or scale marked down to at least ⅟₁₆ of an inch; hydrant wrenches; and a smooth bore nozzle or play pipe. Purpose of the flow test is to determine static and residual pressures in the hydrant, Pitot pressure of the flowing hydrant stream, diameter of the hydrant flow opening, and the hydrant co-efficient.

Often outlying areas of communities are supplied with water through comparatively long runs of 6- or 8-inch main, fed from only one direction. In such cases there may be very high pressure loss if required flows exceed 500 gpm, based upon losses in only 1,000 feet of pipe. For example, a mile long 6-inch main fed from one direction will have 76 psi loss with 500 gpm flowing and an 8-inch main of the same length and not part of a loop system can lose 68 psi with 1,000 gpm flowing (four 1⅛-inch tips). Even with a pumper operating at very low residual pressure at the hydrant it may be impossible to get the required flow.

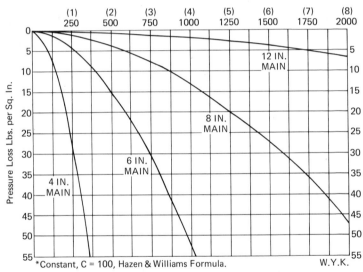

PRESSURE DROP PER 1000 FT. WATER MAIN OF VARIOUS SIZES*
Flow in Gallons Per Minute — No. Standard Hose Streams in Parentheses

Comparison of pressure drops in different size mains. If hydrants are spaced properly, such main losses are minimized, but obviously the 4-inch main would be of little use for today's fire problems.

The test procedure requires at least two hydrants, one to be tested for pressure, the other for flow. The cap is removed from the pressure hydrant and replaced by a hydrant cap with pressure gage. Then the hydrant is opened and static pressure is recorded.

Next a cap is removed from the flow hydrant, the inside diameter of the open hydrant butt is measured and examined to record the hydrant coefficient, then the playpipe or nozzle is attached and the hydrant is opened completely. When the stream is stabilized its flow is measured by the Pitot gage and, simultaneously, the residual pressure is measured back at the pressure hydrant.

The complete procedures are more extensive, but are described in the NFPA Fire Protection Handbook and other reference sources. Any fire department planning to conduct a flow of hydrants should obtain the cooperation of the local water and health departments and prior advice from the insurance rating bureau.

Supplemental Pumping

It is often feasible to supplement the supply coming to the pump. If more water is available from the hydrant but the supply hose is being used to full capacity, it may be advantageous to run an additional supply line or lines between the pump and the hydrant. If an unused hydrant outlet is gated the problem is simple because an added feeder can be run from the hydrant to a pumper inlet without shutting down.

If the unused hydrant outlet is not gated the added supply line should first be connected to a pump inlet and the officer informed that there will be a slight interruption to the stream while a hydrant outlet cap is removed and the line attached. This takes but a few seconds. However, if another hydrant is available it is often more convenient and efficient to run the supplementary feeder from a second hydrant assuming that the pump is using most of the supply from the first hydrant. The operator can easily do this unaided by pulling off enough hose to reach the second hydrant and connecting it to the pump. In some cases, he may find it desirable to run two supplementary feeder lines.

It should be obvious that the best method of assuring that the delivery of water will not be restricted by the capacity of the supply connection is to connect the pumper to the hydrant with the same size and length of suction hose required to supply capacity of the pumper at draft. This does not necessarily require use of hard suction hose. If hydrants have only 2½-inch outlets, reducing adapters and a soft supply line can be used.

However, a 2½-inch hydrant outlet flows only 30 percent as

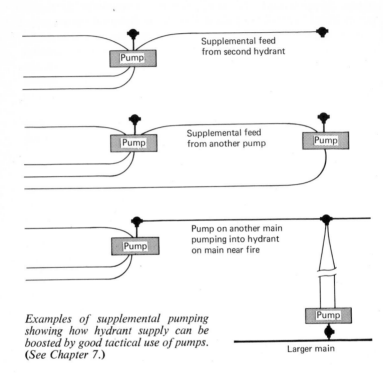

Examples of supplemental pumping showing how hydrant supply can be boosted by good tactical use of pumps. (See Chapter 7.)

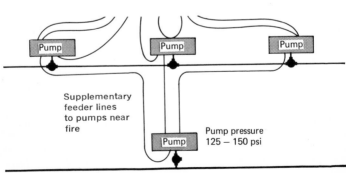

much water as a 4½-inch hydrant outlet. With a single 2½-inch outlet, 29 psi residual pressure is needed to supply a 1,000 gpm pump and 17 psi residual is required for a 750 gpm pump.

In some cases where serious fires occur in areas served by small mains, some or all of the pumpers near the fire will be troubled by inadequate supply and very low residual pressure from the hydrant. Generally, this condition can be corrected by one of the following means:

1. Supplemental pumping can be employed with a pumper supplied by a distant main not affected by the low pressure being used to pump into each of the pumps having supply trouble at the fire.

2. Another very good way of supplementing a pump is to run a line from another pumper which has an adequate supply and is not working at full capacity. One line will usually provide ample supplement to water supply the pump is receiving from a hydrant.

3. The pump on the other main can pump into a hydrant in the fire area to boost the pressure in the main near the fire. This has the effect of providing the equivalent of another main into the fire area.

4. In some cases, the water department can be requested to open valves or raise pressure to increase the supply. However, in many instances this may not be possible.

Tanker Shuttle. In rural areas, fire companies often have to rely upon water supply by tank trucks and this type of operation requires good planning and coordination of apparatus and manpower assignments. Some years ago a number of volunteer fire departments in the state of Connecticut developed a practical sequenced tanker evolution with water being dumped into portable canvas tanks from which pumpers drafted to supply handlines or monitor nozzles.

The evolution was rather simple: the first apparatus was an 800 gallon tank truck with a 500 gpm pump. At the rear of this truck was a 3-way siamese connection with 2½-inch clappered intake that led to 3-inch piping so the tank could be filled at the rate of 500 gpm. The suction line from pump to tank was also 3-inch size.

The second piece of apparatus was a 500 gpm pumper with a divided hose body. This piece was designed to drop two parallel lines of 1100 feet or a single 2200-foot hose line. One third of the load was 3½-inch hose. A third, supplementary truck, was a small service vehicle carrying emergency equipment such as breathing apparatus, resuscitator, portable pumps, generator and salvage covers.

The usual procedure on the fireground was for the 800 gallon tanker to take a position near the fire and put two preconnected 1½-inch lines into operation. If the 500 gpm pumper could obtain water at a source within 2,000 feet of the tank truck, one or two hose lines would be used for this relay. However, if no water was available for such drafting, then other incoming tank trucks would discharge water into the clappered siamese connection at the rear of the tanker, then move off quickly for water. Depending upon the fire location, these trucks had to fill at a hydrant, or they might be supplied by portable pumps spotted at some static source. If more water was being delivered to the fireground than could be used by the tank truck, the excess was dumped into a 3,000 gallon portable canvas tank, used as a standby source. This supply operation can be effective on fires of long duration, but much depends upon the ability of portable pumps and other sources to keep the tankers filled.

Relays

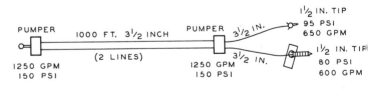

CITY RELAY OPERATION FROM HYDRANT

Comparison of relay operations in city and rural areas. In these sketches, city operation requires supply of monitor nozzle and ladder pipe after relay through twin lines of 3½-inch hose.

RURAL RELAY OPERATION FROM DRAFT

Rural operation involves use of handline after 2000 foot relay through single 3½-inch line.

Hydrant Hookups

FIG. I — SOFT SUCTION ON 4½ INCH HYDRANT OUTLET

FLOW (GPM)	HYDRANT PRESS.(PSI)	PUMP SUPPLY PRESS.(PSI)
500	66	63
750	64	60
1000	55	51

Comparative flows of soft suction hose on 4½-inch hydrant outlet and hard suction hose on 2½-inch outlet using reducer.

FIG. 2 – HARD   SUCTION   ON   2½ INCH   HYDRANT
OUTLET (USING   2½ INCH GATE AND
4½ x 2½ INCH DOUBLE   FEMALE
REDUCER)

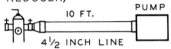

FLOW (GPM)	HYDRANT PRESS. (PSI)	PUMP SUPPLY PRESS. (PSI)
500	65	57
750	62	41
958 *	56	0

* MAXIMUM FLOW WITH NO RESIDUAL AT PUMP

FIG. 3 – 50 FEET OF 2½ INCH HOSE TO 2½ INCH
GATED PUMPER INTAKE

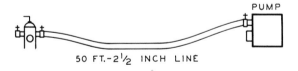

FLOW (GPM)	HYDRANT PRESS. (PSI)	PUMP SUPPLY PRESS. (PSI)
500	65	10
560 *	65	0

* MAXIMUM FLOW WITH 0 RESIDUAL ON PUMP GAGE, BUT
HOSE FIRM AT INTAKE GATE

Comparative in-line pumping flows from hydrant using 2½-inch supply line. In Figure 3 a 2½-inch gated pumper intake is used; in Figure 4 the 4½-inch intake is used.

FIG. 4 – 50 FEET OF 2½ INCH HOSE TO 4½ INCH
        PUMPER INTAKE (USING 4½ x 2½
        INCH DOUBLE FEMALE REDUCER)

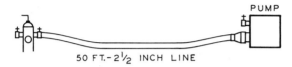

50 FT. - 2½ INCH LINE

FLOW (GPM) HYDRANT PRESS. (PSI) PUMP SUPPLY PRESS. (PSI)
    626 ✳   65   5
✳ HOSE GETTING SOFT AT POINT OF CONNECTION TO PUMP

FIG. 5 – PUMP SUPPLIED BY TWO 50 FOOT LENGTHS
        OF 2½ INCH HOSE (ONE LINE TO 2½ INCH
        GATED INTAKE, THE OTHER TO REDUCER
        ON 4½ INCH INTAKE)

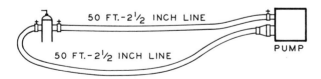

50 FT. - 2½ INCH LINE

50 FT. - 2½ INCH LINE

FLOW (GPM)   HYDRANT PRESS. (PSI) PUMP SUPPLY PRESS. (PSI)
    500   65   53
    750   62   33
   1036 ✳   53   0

   ✳ MAXIMUM FLOW OBTAINED

FIG. 6 – TANDEM PUMPING FROM SINGLE 4¹/₂ INCH
HYDRANT OUTLET

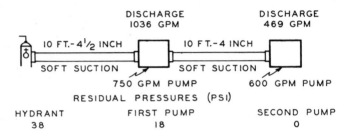

*Pumps operating in tandem from single 4½-inch hydrant outlet; and
single pump supplied by two 50-foot lengths of 2½-inch hose.*

QUESTIONS

Chapter 7

Text:

1. Why should a static water supply prove more reliable than a city hydrant system? Give three reasons.
2. Describe primary feeders, secondary feeders and distributors.
3. What is a weak hydrant?
4. How would you determine a dead-end main?
5. How do you use a Pitot gage?
6. Why should two hydrants be used in a water flow test?
7. Sketch and describe three examples of supplemental pumping.

Discussion:

1. Explain how poor placement of pumpers can overburden a water supply system.
2. Are water tank trucks, say 1500 to 2000 gallon capacity, a reasonable equivalent to water main supply because of their mobility?
3. Even though a municipality has a good hydrant and water main system, should fire department pumpers have booster tanks filled with water? Of what capacity?
4. How much water would you expect from a good hydrant on a 4-inch main? On a 6-inch main?

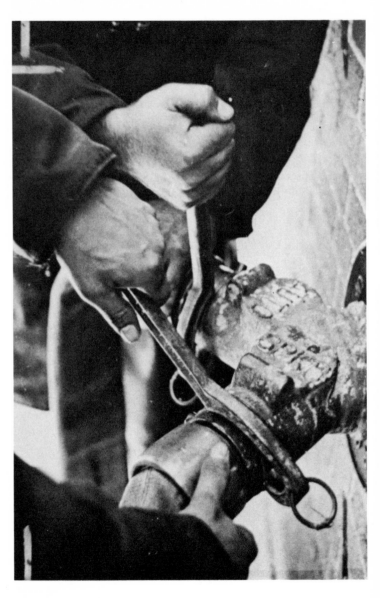

At least two 2½-inch hose lines must be hooked up to the fire depart-ment connection supplying a sprinkler system.

Chapter 8

Sprinkler Systems and Other Operations

On many occasions the average engine company finds itself involved in operations somewhat different from the normal routine of laying out hoselines and moving water. These situations call for special knowledge and equipment, so the company officer, the pump operator and the fire fighters must be ready to adjust to the circumstances.

Special engine company operations would include the following: supplying sprinklers and standpipes in a building; using the pumper for exceptional drafting or relay; dewatering; and long distance relays for purposes other than fire fighting. Even though such incidents may be infrequent, every fire officer must be ready to direct his company for successful performance.

Supplying Sprinklers. Because automatic sprinklers are being installed in most modern industrial plants, apartment buildings and other occupancies, just about every fire company has received instruction and training in fireground operations at sprinklered properties. While these evolutions are fundamental, quite a few fire situations occur in which sprinklers are shut down prematurely or are diminished because too many pumpers hook up to inadequate water supply on plant property. One serious problem is that modern industrial buildings can be very large in ground floor area and this not only hampers communications between chiefs and other officers in a fire emergency, but also can increase confusion concerning the location and use of local water supply. Much of this can be avoided through pre-fire inspections; even so, large fires in these huge sprinklered properties can still be very difficult to control.

The fire officer and his company personnel need to know certain fundamentals: the complete layout and functioning of the sprinkler and standpipe systems; location of certain valves, pumps and hydrants; availability of private and public water supply; fire department connections for sprinklers and standpipes; amount of volume and pressure that has to be supplied from the pumper; correct method of shutting down the sprinkler system and putting it back in service; and finally, the command and operational procedures that will apply for this particular property.

NFPA Standard No. 13E — *Fire Department Operations in Properties Protected by Sprinklers and Standpipe Systems* — contains many helpful recommendations. It diagrams and explains the layout and components of typical sprinkler and standpipe systems and presents practical operational routines for fire departments or fire companies that respond to such properties.

This W. S. Darley & Company in-plant truck has a four stage centrifugal PTO pump, 200 gallon tank, electric booster reel and other specialized features for plant fire protection.

It stresses the fact that fire companies should develop standard operating procedures for these buildings, because simple oversights or errors can turn a reasonably successful operation into a disaster. Here are some suggestions from the standard:

When responding to a fire involved in sprinklered property,
   (1) Immediately send a fire fighter to the proper control valve to:

(a) Determine that the valve is fully open. (Valves are designed to show open or closed positions.)

(b) Open the valve if it has been closed. (One possible exception would be where valve is "tagged for repairs.")

(c) Shut the valve only when ordered to do so by the officer in charge.

(d) Remain at the valve (after closing it) so that in the event of rekindling or any detected extension of fire, the valve can be reopened immediately.

NOTE: The man assigned to the valve should take a light and portable radio so that no time will be lost in transmitting orders to open or close the valve. He should remain at the valve until orders are given for the companies to pick up and return to quarters.

   (2) One of the first alarm pumper companies on arriving at the fire should immediately connect two lines to the proper sprinkler siamese connection and start pumping at about 150 pounds per square inch. If there is more than one sprinkler system in the fire area, pumpers should be connected to provide adequate pressure and volume to each sprinkler system that may be in operation.

NOTE: Pumpers should not be connected to hydrants on private water systems unless such systems are designed to maintain the flow needed by fire department pumpers in addition to that required by sprinklers or other private fire protection facilities. Use of pumpers on private hydrants has on a number of occasions deprived private fire protection facilities, including sprinklers, of their water supply, resulting in heavy damage or total losses.

   Other needed information:

   Location of the gravity water supply tank and the suction tank for stationary pumps; location of public water mains and underground mains on plant property; location of fire department connections for sprinkler and standpipe systems and any wall hydrants that may be available; location and arrangement of main post indicator valve, check valves and city water supply valve; location of tank control valves and pump valves that may be shut off or otherwise controlled according to the fire situation.

In addition, pre-fire inspections should have resulted in scale-drawn maps of the complete sprinkler system, showing location of shutoff valves, number and arrangement of sprinklers, alarm bells and other components of the fire protection system.

Initial Response Actions. In the ordinary fire situation, when the first or second responding engine company connects to supply the sprinkler system, usually two 2½-inch pumper lines can supply twenty to twenty-five sprinkler heads. If more sprinkler heads are already operating, higher pressure at the siamese may be necessary, perhaps 175 or 200 psi if the hydrant flow and pumper capacity permit this. If 3-inch or larger hose is available, it would make a better supply line.

Types of Systems. Basically, the fire officer and the engine company will be concerned with one of four types of systems: the wet type or the dry pipe sprinkler system, or a standpipe system, which also may be wet or dry. Operating principles of these systems are generally well understood by fire department members, but may vary in detail according to the individual plant or locality. If each system is supplied with adequate water, it may be more effective than a number of hose streams. Fixed systems are engineered to be adequate for anticipated fire loads within the structure. Standard sprinkler heads are designed to discharge at least 8 gpm at about 15 psi. Standpipes, on the other hand, should be supplied with 500 to 1,000 gpm. If placed into operation they will produce a substantial flow, depending upon the size of nozzle and hose attached to the standpipe line. Flows from both systems will be localized to certain floors and areas in the building.

Outside Sprinklers. Some buildings have outside sprinkler protection in addition to interior systems. Usually these protect severely exposed property. Sprinkler heads for outside systems are designed to produce a water curtain and may have small or large orifices, depending on the type of hazard; otherwise they should be treated like inside systems.

These systems may be manually or automatically operated and the responding fire company officer should know the type of system, where control valves are, what water supply exists, and where the fire department connection is located. If the fire has activated the outside sprinklers, one man should be sent to the appropriate control valve with orders to close it when the sprinklers are no longer needed, because it may be necessary to conserve the water for other fire fighting.

At the same time, the engine company should be hooking up to the siamese connection for supplying these outside sprinklers. If the system is manually operated, the man at the valve should have it open by the time this supplementary water comes into the system. Two 2½-inch hose lines should be attached to the siamese, supplying 150 psi pressure, or more, as needed.

After the fire is extinguished, the system is shut down, hose lines are disconnected, mopup is completed, then the system is restored to service according to its type.

Standpipe Systems. Standpipe systems are usually considered in three classes of service: Class I provides 2½-inch hose connections on each floor and on the roofs of structures with combustible roofs or having special exposure problems; Class II provides 1½-inch hose connections on each floor; and Class III service provides 2½-, and 1½-inch connections on each floor with appropriate roof or exposure protection outlets. The number of hose stations will vary but in Class I and Class III service all portions of each story of a building are supposed to be within thirty feet of a nozzle attached to not more than 100 feet of hose. At least one fire department connection should be provided for each Class I or Class III standpipe system and in high-rise buildings having two or more zones a fire department connection must be provided for each zone.

Shutting Down System. After the fire has been extinguished, water supply to the sprinkler systems can be shut down and preparations can be made for putting the system back in service. Fire departments have different procedures for performing this service, sometimes simply inserting sprinkler stoppers or wedges in heads that have been used, and sometimes replacing all fused sprinkler heads. The tools and equipment for this purpose are usually carried on salvage trucks, ladder trucks, or other designated units. NFPA Standard No. 1901 designates the following equipment: twelve standard sprinkler heads (assorted temperatures and types); six sprinkler stoppers or wedges; one set of sprinkler head wrenches for the type of heads carried.

When replacing sprinkler heads, sprinklers of the proper temperature rating should be used and the following table identifies the classification:

TEMPERATURE RATINGS, CLASSIFICATIONS
AND COLOR CODINGS

Maximum Ceiling Temperature - F	Temperature Rating - F	Temperature Classification	Color Code
100	135 to 170	Ordinary	Uncolored
150	175 to 225	Intermediate	White
225	250 to 300	High	Blue
300	325 to 375	Extra High	Red
375	400 to 475	Very Extra High	Green
475	500 to 575	Ultra High	Orange

Off/On Sprinkler Head. A recent development has been the automatic sprinkler heads which activate at a certain temperature, then shut off when the temperature is reduced below a certain level. One approved type operates at 100 degrees F. and shuts off when temperature cools to 100 degrees F. All fire officers should know how to recognize these sprinklers and how such a system should be restored after the fire emergency.

Pumper Suction at High Lifts

It is important to know the proper sequence for drafting with a particular pump or type of pump. All pumps that pass acceptance tests are capable of providing rated capacity at 150 pounds net pump pressure through 20 feet of suction hose at not more than a 10-foot lift from the surface of the water to the pump. The pump may be able to do better than this at a hydrant or at a lower lift. In addition, it has been required in a short spurt test to give rated capacity at 165 pounds net pump pressure to demonstrate power reserve.

So, if the operator can reach water 10 feet below the pump with 20 feet of suction hose (properly immersed) there should be no difficulty in pumping rated capacity, if the pump is in good condition.

If water cannot be reached with 20 feet of suction hose, either because of the vertical lift or horizontal distance, we have a different problem. First, we know that with a given flow we will have about 50 percent more friction loss through 30 feet of suction hose of the same size. This can be observed by watching the suction gage while drafting. The increase in friction loss may not be a major factor where the lift is below 8 or 10 feet because there will still be better than 10 pounds of atmospheric pressure left (near sea level) to overcome losses in the hose and the increased friction loss in the extra 10 feet of suction hose on the level will ordinarily not exceed one pound.

However, when the height of lift exceeds 10 feet the amount of water that a pump can lift is cut drastically. Accordingly, if the lift is above 10 feet and it is necessary to use 30 feet of suction hose it is best to conclude that the pump may not be able to deliver its rated capacity. While ability to lift water to heights will vary with different pumps, it will be reasonable to expect that we will have to be content with smaller flows. There is no convenient way to determine what this flow will be other than a test with a given pump at a particular location. Accordingly, the safe procedure is to figure on supplying one less line or using smaller nozzle tips when it is necessary to use 30 feet of suction hose at lifts above 10 feet.

This can be important at high lifts as well as at high elevations above sea level. Actually, suction hose may be less efficient as a conductor than its nominal diameter would indicate, because of roughness and corrugations. Also, pumper suction capability may be much less than the theoretical maximum which only takes into account atmospheric pressure and line losses.

The ability of a pump to draft water decreases at higher altitudes and a larger suction hose may be needed. In addition, the power generated by internal combustion engines decreases about 3.5 percent for each 1,000-foot elevation above sea level.

The loss in the suction line can be observed by watching the compound gage on the suction side of the pump. After the suction hose has been connected and immersed the vertical lift can be measured. Each 2.31 feet of lift requires one psi. Prime the pump and observe the reading on the suction side of the compound gage (which incidentally is calibrated in inches of mercury and not in pounds per square inch). Run lines to a large nozzle at which flow can be measured with a Pitot gage. With little or no water flowing the compound gage will show the loss due to the lift. As the discharge is increased the reading on the compound gage will increase until all of the atmospheric pressure is being used and no more water can be made to flow into the pump. If the suction hose is not large enough, and the lift is high, the limit of the suction capability may be reached before the rated capacity of the pump is obtained.

At a 10-foot lift 4.34 psi of the atmospheric pressure are used which at sea level leaves a little over ten psi to overcome friction and other losses on the suction side of the pump. At a 20-foot lift 8.68 psi are lost due to lift, leaving only six psi to overcome other losses. This may be expected to reduce the volume that can be handled unless a larger diameter suction hose is employed.

Let us assume that a rural pumper is lifting water eight feet through thirty feet of 4-inch suction hose. Can this hose supply 500 gpm at sea level?

The 8-foot lift costs us 3.5 psi, leaving 11.2 pounds for overcoming line losses. The loss per 100 feet with 500 gpm through 2½-inch hose is 55 psi ÷ 11 (factor for 4-inch hose) or five psi per 100 feet. As we have 30 feet of hose the actual friction loss is only in the order of 1.5 psi so theoretically we will have no trouble in supplying capacity at the pump *provided we do not exceed the capability of the pump to develop vacuum.* However, with 750 gpm flowing, the loss with 4-inch suction hose increases to at least 10 psi per 100 feet and 4½-inch suction hose is required at sea level. This would reduce the friction loss to approxi-

Los Angeles City pumper in lower left foreground has two lines supplying outside standpipe at corner of building. This is a Task Force response to a downtown building. Note elevating platform, two aerial ladders and three pumpers. (Los Angeles Fire Department photo)

mately six psi per 100 feet saving over 35 percent of the available atmospheric pressure.

Another fact to be remembered is that pump capacity is calculated in terms of 150 psi net pump pressure. This means that pressure used on the suction side of the pump is deducted from the discharge pressure. For example, if a pump is using 5 pounds on the suction side to get water (as determined by a formula in the standard specification), it is only expected to deliver its rated capacity at 145 pounds on the discharge gage.

Friction losses in the suction side of the pump are not the only considerations in efficient pump operation at draft. If a pump is operated so that it "runs away from water," that is, at an excessive speed for the capabilities of the suction arrangement, damage may result due to cavitation. This is a turbulence or hammering effect during which air cavities are formed about the impellers resulting in vibrations, loss of efficiency and damage to the pump. Obviously, sufficient pressure is needed at the pump inlet to provide the required velocity of flow for the volume.

In general, when drafting it is desirable to have some reserve on the suction side although there may be times when it will be desirable to draft all the water the pump can handle without damage to the pump or engine.

Pounds of Water Lifted Vertically with Suction Hose

(Weight of water content of hose from water level to pump inlet disregarding horizontal travel.)

Height of Lift in Feet	4-inch Suction	4½-inch Suction	5-inch Suction	6-inch Suction
5	27.17	34.43	42.51	61.23
10	54.35	68.86	85.02	122.46
15	81.52	103.29	127.53	183.69
20	108.70	137.71	170.05	244.92

Note: The total weight lifted in figuring work load would take into account the flow in gallons per minute as related to foot-pounds of water being lifted.

Atmospheric Pressure Available to Overcome Suction Losses (at Sea Level)

Feet of Suction Lift	Pounds Required for Suction Lift (No Water Flowing)	Maximum Theoretical Pressure Residual for Losses in Suction Hose and Strainers*
2	0.9	13.8
4	1.7	13.0
6	2.6	12.1
8	3.5	11.2
10	4.3	10.3
12	5.2	9.5
15	6.5	8.2
20	8.7	6.0
25	10.8	3.9
30	13.0	1.4
33.9	14.7	0.0

*This assumes the ability of the pump to utilize all available atmospheric pressure, which is never the case.

Pressures Required for Suction Lift

Feet of Suction Lift	Pounds Required for Lift	Pressure Residual for Friction and Other Losses
32.3	14	0.7
30.0	13	1.7
27.7	12	2.7
25.4	11	3.7
23.1	10	4.7
20.8	9	5.7
18.5	8	6.7
16.2	7	7.7
13.9	6	8.7
11.6	5	9.7
9.2	4	10.7
6.9	3	11.7
4.6	2	12.7
2.3	1	13.7

Relative Capacities of Pumper Suction Hose
(Based upon normal 20-foot line)

Size of Suction Hose (Internal Diameter)	Cross Section Area of Hose in Inches	Volume of Hose in Cubic Inches	Gallons Content of 20 Feet of Suction Hose	Pounds of Water in 20 Feet of Suction Hose
4	12.566	3016.04	13.05	108.78
4½	15.904	3816.96	16.52	137.71
5	19.635	4712.40	20.40	170.05
6	28.274	6785.76	29.38	244.91

The 4½-inch suction has 26 percent more waterway area than the 4-inch; the 5-inch has 56 percent more area than the 4-inch and 17 percent more than the 4½-inch. Atmospheric pressure is measured in pounds per square inch. Thus, other things being equal, at given atmospheric pressure, the 4½-inch suction hose provides 26 percent more area for the atmospheric pressure than with the 4-inch suction hose. The 5-inch hose provides almost as much again. Thus, while we cannot increase the atmospheric pressure, it can be made to work over a larger area through a bigger suction hose that holds more water so we have a lower velocity and reduce the friction loss with a given flow.

The 4-inch suction hose is not recommended although it is sometimes found on 500 gpm pumps in rural service because it is a little cheaper than the recommended 4½-inch minimum size. Yet rural fire departments normally must draft to supply their pumps at capacity, so 30 feet of 4½- or 5-inch suction hose is an essential item of equipment.

Injection or Eduction Pumping. For some emergencies it may be possible to raise water beyond normal suction lifts through injection, or eduction. This is a procedure of pumping a stream to a device in the water so that the pump pressure takes (or educts) additional water and brings this flow up to the position where it can be used for fire fighting supply. The method can be applied with a portable pump or with a standard pumper. It is more likely to be used in rural or forestry fire control but has also been applied for some urban situations, such as dewatering.

Dewatering. Engine companies and other fire department personnel sometimes are called upon to remove water from building basements and other localities, particularly after a flood, storm, or other natural disaster. If the fire and emergency frequencies permit such non-fire action, the department can render some excellent public service with its portable pumping equipment.

Large quantities of water can be moved through normal drafting and relay operations, perhaps using local utility and commercial tank vehicles to haul away the unwanted water and debris. Portable pumps, particularly the low pressure, low volume units designed specifically for dewatering, are very useful for small accumulations of water. One caution: when working in basements with electrical pumps, think about the shock hazard, particularly if electrical power is being interrupted periodically. Avoid using gasoline-driven engines in basements unless the exhaust is vented to the outside.

QUESTIONS

Chapter 8

Text:

1. When an engine company responds to a fire-involved sprinklered building, what are three essential elements of information the company officer must know?
2. How much pressure and flow should be supplied to a fire department sprinkler connection?
3. How much area should be covered by a 1½-inch standpipe
hose stream?
4. Do standpipes need more water supply than sprinkler systems?
Explain.
5. Which would give better coverage of a fire-involved floor area:
a system of automatic sprinklers, or well-planned and directed
hose streams? Explain why.

Discussion:

1. Describe an on/off sprinkler system. Should it be supplied
through the fire department connection like a regular sprinkler system?
2. Exactly when should a sprinkler system be shut down during
a fire?
3. To what extent should a fire department place a sprinkler
system back in service? Give details.
4. What would be the maximum length of 5-inch suction hose
hookup that could be used in a tidal slope totaling 15 feet
vertical lift? Sketch and explain.
5. How do you determine the capacity of an industrial plant
hydrant system?
6. Suppose that a home for the aged is protected by an automatic sprinkler system supplied by a pressurized tank. Explain how your fire company should be prepared to operate
if fire involved this building. What would be the good and
bad factors?

High expansion foam was used to control a flammable liquid tank truck fire that severely damaged this bridge overpass in Glen Burnie, Maryland.

Chapter 9

Extinguishing Agents
and Equipment

Fire department pumpers use two means of applying extinguishing agents — by portable fire extinguishers, or by hose lines with large or specially designed nozzles. Either means of extinguishment must be coordinated with any simultaneous use of water applied by other members of the pumper crew.

Standard No. 19 recommends that each pumper carry two approved portable extinguishers for Class A, B, and C fires with minimum rating of 20 BC in dry chemical, 10 BC in CO_2 and 2A in water-type extinguishers.

Obviously, each fire fighter who uses an extinguisher other than a hose stream must understand what to expect in capability and duration of the extinguishing agent; it is dangerous for any untrained person to try and control a fire without prior knowledge of what results to expect from attempts at extinguishment.

A number of NFPA standards describe the classification of extinguishers, the characteristics and capabilities of extinguishing agents, and the use of appropriate equipment. Training of engine company members in use of this equipment should include reference to these standards.

169

For example, NFPA Standard No. 10 covers the installation of portable extinguishers, primarily in business or industrial properties, but includes information that is important in fire fighting. It defines the basic types of fires in four classes as follows: Class A fires involve ordinary combustibles, such as wood, cloth, paper, rubber and many plastics. Class B fires involve flammable liquids, gases and greases. Class C fires involve energized electrical equipment, and Class D fires involve combustible metals such as magnesium, zirconium, sodium and potassium.

Underwriters' Laboratories, Inc., uses a classification and rating system to test portable extinguisher capability against these types of fires. Extinguishers for Class A or B fires are designated by a letter and numeral to indicate the relative extinguishing effectiveness. Thus, 1-A, 2-A, 3-A, 4-A, 6-A, 10-A, 20-A, 30-A, and 40-A are the ratings for extinguishers for Class A fires; 1-B, 2-B, 5-B, 10-B, 20-B, 30-B, 40-B, 60-B, 80-B, 120-B, 160-B, 240-B, 320-B, 480-B, and 640-B for Class B fires.

For extinguishers classified for use on Class C and Class D fires, no numeral is used, because Class C fires are essentially Class A or B fires involving energized electrical wiring and equipment, and the relative effectiveness of extinguishers for combustible metal fires is designated on the extinguisher nameplate. On Class C fires involving energized electrical equipment, a non-conductive extinguishing agent is needed.

Fire fighters must be informed of the possible health and safety hazards that may develop when extinguishers are used on certain types of burning materials or in confined areas, such as: thermal decomposition of halogenated extinguishing agents can be hazardous; carbon dioxide as an extinguishing agent can dilute the oxygen supply in an unventilated space; extinguishers not rated for electrical fires can present a shock hazard if used on energized electrical equipment; dry chemical in a confined space can hamper visibility. These and other safety lessons must be clearly understood by engine company personnel who are likely to use extinguishing agents.

Foam. The foam used for fire control creates a blanket of air-filled bubbles, formed by mixing the foaming agent with water. Foam is intended to float on burning flammable and combustible liquids, to exclude air and cool the fuel, to prevent reignition, and to cling to surrounding surfaces. Types include: air or mechanical foam; chemical foam; protein foam, fluoroprotein foam and synthetic foam concentrates. The latter include aqueous film forming foam (AFFF), high expansion and other synthetic foam concentrates. Special alcohol type foam concentrates are used on fires in flammable or combustible liquids that are destructive to regular foams. Foam is a conductor of electricity and should not be used on fires involving energized electrical equipment.

Air Foam. Air foam is applied by using a foam nozzle inductor, a venturi pickup tube that draws foam concentrate from a container and inducts it into a hose stream, mixing automatically in correct proportion.

An in-line inductor can also be used in the water supply line, using single or multiple lines to the source of foam concentrate.

Foam concentrate can also be induced by venturi in a by-pass between the pump suction and pump discharge; by metered proportioning, inducing foam concentrate through appropriate orifices or venturis, with manual or automatic adjustment of the concentrate injection; by a proportioning tank; or by a small, positive displacement foam pump.

Chemical Foam. Chemical foam is no longer in general use but is the oldest type of foam for fire control. It is made by mixing dry chemical powder with water at or near the location where the foam is going to be used. It can be mixed in a continuous foam generator, or used as a stored solution in which the alkaline and acidic salts are premixed with water in separate containers, then are piped to the point where foam is generated by their mixing and interaction.

High Expansion Foam. High expansion foam is generated by passing an aqueous solution of surface active foaming agents through a net, a screen, or other porous medium. Expansion ratio can be from 100 up to 1,000 to 1. When generated in sufficient volume, this foam can blanket a fire, preventing air from reaching the involved material. In addition, the heat of the fire can convert the foam to steam, diluting the air and reducing the oxygen content. This foam can be quite effective on basement fires and other fires in confined areas, but fire fighters must be careful not to get trapped in deep amounts of foam in which they can slip and be injured, or lose visibility completely. Company officers must be alert to prevent such accidents. A coarse water spray from a handline can cut a path through a foam-filled area but the footing will be slippery.

Like other foam extinguishing agents, high expansion foam is electrically conductive and is not compatible with some other extinguishing agents, but application of this foam can be accomplished easily by one man using the appropriate nozzle. Standard lined fire hose is used to connect the generator to the water or solution supply. The proportioned solution is impinged on the mesh or screens at certain velocity and the film formed on the screen is distended by an aspirated or blown air stream to expand into a mass of bubbles or foam, with the foam volume expanding 100 to 1,000 times the liquid volume, depending on design of the generator.

High expansion foam unit of Las Vegas Fire Department is powered by 7 horse power engine which drives a 30-inch propeller fan. Foam generator produces 37,000 gpm of detergent foam at 1,000 to 1 ratio, using 45 gpm at minimum pressure of 45 psi. It is supplied by a 1½-inch hose line.

National Foam System, Inc., foam pumper has 800 gallon water tank, 200 gallon foam liquid tank, preconnected hose line and booster reel, demountable 500 gpm foam and water turret, side compartment, 1,000 gpm Hale pump and full complements of foam nozzles.

Aqueous Film Forming Foam. The concentrate of this agent is a fluorinated surfactant with a foam stabilizer, diluted with fresh or sea water to three or six percent proportion. The foam develops a film that floats on the surface of a flammable fuel and blankets, or suppresses the evolution of fuel vapors. It is not compatible with protein and fluoroprotein foam concentrates, but is compatible with dry chemical. AFFF is applied with hose streams, similar to other foam concentrates, at specified rates, such as 0.10 gpm/square foot of fuel surface, with appropriate duration of discharge, at least ten minutes. AFFF can also be used in combination with dry chemical with a discharge time of at least one minute for each agent. The rates of discharge of these two extinguishing agents should be from 0.6 up to 5 pounds of dry chemical per second for each pound of AFFF solution per second when used in combination.

Carbon Dioxide. Carbon dioxide, often referred to by its chemical symbol, CO_2, is an odorless, colorless gas with a density about 50 percent greater than the density of air. It can be liquefied easily by compression and cooling, and can be further cooled into the solid state. At 87.8 degrees Fahrenheit the liquid and vapor have the same density and at this critical temperature the liquid disappears. At the point of 60 psi gage pressure (75 psi absolute) carbon dioxide may be a solid, liquid, or vapor, depending on the temperature. At 60 psi (75 psi absolute) it freezes into dry ice at a temperature of —69 degrees F. and if the pressure continues to reduce to atmospheric, it will lower the temperature of the dry ice to —110 degrees F.

Fire fighters should understand that atmospheres containing only three to four percent of CO_2 will cause a person to breathe rapidly, but a nine percent concentration can cause a person to lose consciousness after a few minutes. A twenty percent concentration can cause death within twenty to thirty minutes unless the victim is removed to fresh air. CO_2 in lesser concentrations can hinder a person's ability to think clearly and take proper action. It is most effective when applied in still air, as within a building. It is noncorrosive and leaves no residue but if fire fighters are going to be present during prolonged discharge of CO_2, they should wear self-contained breathing apparatus.

In addition to being used in portable fire extinguishers, CO_2 is also applied by wheeled extinguishers, by standpipe systems and by fixed systems. It is effective on electrical fires, grease and flammable liquid fires, ordinary combustibles and hazardous solids.

Dry Chemical. The extinguishing agent used in dry chemical portable fire extinguishers is a powder comprised of very small particles, usually of sodium carbonate, potassium bicarbonate, urea-based potassium bicarbonate, potassium chloride, or monammonium phosphate with added particulate material supplemented by special treatment to provide resistance to packing, resistance to moisture absorption (caking) and proper flow qualities.

Multipurpose dry chemical is usually monammonium phosphate-base and is effective on fires in ordinary combustibles, such as wood and paper, and flammable liquids.

When dry chemical is used in combination with foam, the two agents must be compatible. There are listed foam compatible dry chemicals and appropriate foam liquid concentrates.

In using this agent outdoors, fire fighters must realize that the supply is limited, that wind can bend or destroy the discharging stream of chemical, that visibility will be hampered, and that the extinguisher will not provide the cooling protection of a hose stream.

Crash truck of Minneapolis-St. Paul International Airport directs foam nozzle on flammable liquids fire. (Minneapolis photo)

Wet Water. A wetting agent can be added to plain water to alter its extinguishing characteristics. The agent reduces the surface tension of the water, thus increasing the penetrating, spreading and emulsifying characteristics and permitting the water to flow and spread uniformly over solid surfaces.

Wetting agents that have foaming characteristics can be used as additives to plain water to produce a foam that has the same wetting and penetrating characteristics of the wetting agent. Such foam can be used on Class A and Class B fires or as a liquid for insulation against fire exposure. This foam breaks down at about 175 degrees F. and returns to its liquid state.

Wet water and wet water foam have the same limitations as plain water in application to energized electrical equipment — each can be a shock hazard and company officers should be alert to this possibility.

Seattle fire fighter uses handline while dry chemical attack from "Big Boss" pumper is supplied from right.

Fire departments have used wet water from pumpers in different ways. Some years ago it was common practice to drop the wetting agent into a booster tank and apply the mixture through small handlines. However, wet water is very corrosive and this practice became less popular when the corrosion began to affect the booster tanks. Wetting agents have a cleansing capability and will remove grease, oil, mill scale, dirt and galvanized protective coatings from tanks and may cause pitting on other metals.

Current practice of fire departments is to use wetting agents with corrosion inhibitors, such as sodium chromate, so that the booster tank will not be any more affected than it would by plain water. Underwriters' Laboratories, Inc., lists wetting agents that have these properties. Another pumper installation is a separate container or tank for the wetting agent which is proportioned as needed into the discharge side of the pump.

Wetting agents and wet water are considered non-toxic but may cause skin irritation. They are considered to be food contaminants, and like other detergents, are considered harmful when discharged into lakes, streams and other outdoor water sources.

QUESTIONS

Chapter 9

Text:

1. What portable fire extinguishers should be carried on a pumper?
2. Can a Class A extinguisher be used on a fire involving electrical equipment?
3. How can carbon dioxide be hazardous to fire fighters?
4. Describe the types and characteristics of foams mentioned in this chapter.
5. What are the extinguishing properties of wet water?
6. What are some of the potentially harmful effects of wet water?

Discussion:

1. Which is better on a flammable liquids tank truck fire, plain water or foam? Why?
2. Which is better on a *small* flammable liquids fire, dry chemical or foam?
3. What would be a good quantity of (a) regular foam, (b) pressurized dry chemical, (c) high expansion foam, or (d) wet water to carry on a pumper?
4. How would you apply high expansion foam on an underground fire involving electrical insulation?
5. Foam extinguishing agents may not be compatible with other extinguishing agents. Which ones? Why?
6. Describe some other practical extinguishing agents in addition to those mentioned in this chapter.

One of two 1-inch handlines discharging ten pounds of dry chemical per second from 1750 gpm pumper of Seattle Fire Department. Effective range of chemical stream is 65 feet. Truck carries 1500 pounds of the extinguishing agent. (Seattle Fire Department photo)

Chapter 10

Operating Procedures in Major Departments

The fireground operations of principal fire departments in the United States underscore the importance of pumpers and some of the modern trends in fire fighting. The following information, developed from a recent survey, indicates the operating similarities and differences, but some of these departments already are changing pumper specifications, using different size hose and different layouts and otherwise making operational improvements.

For example, the fire department in Birmingham, Alabama has specific operations for its high value district. Engine companies coming in on first and second alarms have predetermined layouts. Tactics call for two engines and a ladder company or elevating platform in front of the building and the same amount of apparatus at the rear. Initial attack is made with 2½- or 3-inch hand-lines, with supply coming from 3-inch hose or 5-inch suction hose at the hydrant.

In the Mobile fire department, pumpers carry split hose beds of 2½- and 3-inch hose and are supplied by two 12-foot lengths of 2½-inch soft suction hose. The department plans to change this to 3-inch and 4½-inch size for hydrant work. Drafting operations are performed with 4½- or 5-inch suction hose using 2½- or 3-inch hose for supply lines. In fire attack, first-due engine companies use 1½-inch preconnected lines or 2½-inch handlines backed up with 2½-inch lines from the second-due pumper.

The Montgomery Fire Department has a detailed pre-fire planning program for its downtown area and special target hazards such as schools, hospitals, shopping centers, nursing homes and college campuses. For the buildings designated, the department has detailed maps with supplementary data and assigned operations for the responding companies. The department is planning to split hose beds on all pumpers to use 1½-inch preconnects for initial attack after 2½-inch supply lines are placed by the second-due company, which will also attack the fire with a 2½-inch preconnected line from the first truck. If three companies respond, the last-in will lay supply lines and attack with 2½-inch handlines.

In Arizona, the Tucson Fire Department varies its response to first alarm fires depending on the building or area involved. Residential buildings bring a district chief, two engine companies and a ladder company with fourteen firefighters; mercantile buildings bring an assistant chief, a district chief, three engine companies and a ladder company with eighteen fire fighters; target hazards, such as high-rise buildings, hospitals and nursing homes bring an assistant chief, district chief, three engine companies, two ladder companies and twenty-six fire fighters.

Second alarm response includes two additional engine companies, one more ladder company and a district chief. Normally the department will use preconnected 1½-inch handlines for initial attack, when appropriate; otherwise they use the bigger 2½-inch handline. For supplying pumpers, suction hose is 4-½inch size, but longer supply lines may be 3-inch or 5-inch size, depending upon the operation.

The Phoenix Fire Department has to deal with outdoor fires in the desert area as well as the usual building fires within the city. For structural fires, normal attack might be with preconnected 1½-inch lines backed up by 2½-inch lines from the second-due and other fire companies. The department has two four-wheel drive brush trucks, each carrying a pto pump and 250 gallons of water which can be applied from 1-inch booster lines.

Pumper of Talleyville Fire Company in Pennsylvania supplies 100 foot aerial ladder with support of Claymont pumper in center foreground. (Photo by Donald Pile)

The well-known fire department in Los Angeles City, California has flexible guidelines concerning operations of first- and second-in companies. In normal situations the first-in company must assume command, give a radio size-up report to the signal or dispatching office, request additional companies and equipment as needed, and retain command until relieved. Actions of second-in companies are dictated by commands of the officer in charge. The department uses three different sizes of handlines for initial attack: 1-, 1½- and 2½-inch. For drafting, 4-inch soft and hard suction hose are used and supply lines for pumpers are 2½- and 3½-inches in size. The fire department has a variety of heavy duty apparatus including aerial ladders, elevating platforms and water towers, all of which are triple-combination units with pump, tank, hose and ground ladders and operate according to specific response plans.

In San Francisco, first-arriving engine companies drop a supply line of 2¾- or 3-inch hose, hydrant to fire and the second engine coming in drops two lines, fire to hydrant (one for itself and one to supplement the first engine company). The third arriving engine stops nearby and the officer and crew report for orders. For interior attack most work is with 1½-inch handlines, preconnected or wyed from a 2¾-inch line. In drafting operations, 5-inch or 6-inch suction hose is used but for hydrant supply to pumpers 3½-inch hose may be used.

In San Diego, the department uses 1½- and 2½-inch handlines for initial attack, 2½- and 3-inch hose with 2½-inch couplings as supply lines, and 4- and 4½-inch suction hose at hydrant.

In normal response to a structural fire the Anaheim, California Fire Department sends two engine companies, an aerial ladder, a rescue unit, a battalion chief and sixteen fire fighters, but for the high value district, another engine company and four more fire fighters are assigned. Second alarms bring in another engine company and additional equipment as required. The first-in engine company usually starts fire attack with preconnected 1½-inch lines supplied by water from the tank on the pumper. The second-in company lays 2½-inch lines for heavy streams or as supply lines to the first engine. These evolutions are usually reverse lays — fire to hydrant. Suction hose, hard or soft, of 5-

During Maplewood, Minnesota department store fire tank truck at left supplied pumper which in turn feeds handlines for fire action. (Photo by Lowell Ludford)

This 1500 gpm Ward LaFrance pumper with 500 gallon tank and deck gun was designed for city and suburban service in Monroeville, Pennsylvania.

inch diameter is used for hydrant supply or drafting. Present supply lines are 2½-inch size but the department expects to go to 3-inch lines with 2½-inch couplings. Hose loads are arranged so that four 2½-inch lines can be laid simultaneously for distances up to 500 feet. This allows better volume and flexibility for supplying master streams, ladder pipes or other apparatus. As an alternative a single line of hose can be laid for a distance of 2,000 feet.

Long Beach engine companies carry 700 feet of 3-inch hose, used primarily to supply ladder pipes and ground monitor nozzles. The split hose beds on pumpers also carry 700 feet of 2½-inch hose, used for handlines or supplementing supply to heavy stream appliances. For hydrant supply, 4-inch soft suction hose is used and 5-inch hard suction hose is used for drafting.

In New Haven, Connecticut, the fire department has standardized on using 1½-inch preconnected lines for initial attack, if the fire is small enough for this evolution. In about 90 percent of the operations, the first-in company drops a 2½-inch feeder line hydrant to fire. This is connected to the pump and initial attack is made with the preconnects. The second-due company drops a second 2½-inch feeder line parallel to the first, then backs up the first company with one or more 1½-inch lines. The third company coming in supplies the first pump with a 2½-inch line.

There might be changes in these operations, such as: if the first company arrives at the fire before taking a hydrant it makes a reverse lay, using a gated wye at the fire building. If the length of the feeder line is more than 300 feet, the company officer directs a line to be laid from the fire to the nearest hydrant. However, if the fire situation is very serious, the company is supposed to develop an attack with heavy lines (2½-inch) or monitor nozzles. The pumper must be connected to the nearest hydrant using 4½,- 5-, or 6-inch suction hose, depending upon the size of the pumper.

In Stamford, Connecticut, the first-in engine company drops a 3-inch feeder line hydrant to pumper, and works with 2½- or 1½-inch handlines. The second-due company brings in another 3-inch feeder line, making a reverse layout fire to hydrant. Divided hose bed on pumpers includes 700 feet of 2½-inch and 700 feet of 3-inch hose. Suction hose used by the department is 5½-inches in diameter and supply lines are 3-inch size. Pumpers lay a double reverse line from heavy stream appliances to hydrants.

In Atlanta, Georgia, the fire department might use booster handlines on small fires, backed up by 1½- or 2½-inch line. Pumpers use 4½-inch suction hose for major fires but otherwise might use 2½-inch lines for pumper supply. The first-in aerial ladder acts as a support to first-due pumper company.

Portable pump on rear step of North Conway, New Hampshire pumper can receive water from tank and pump while truck is moving.

1750 gpm pumper of Seattle Fire Department is on a Kenworth chassis and has 1500 pounds of dry chemical stored in a 41-inch diameter sphere behind the cab. Sphere is pressurized by three nitrogen cylinders each having 275 cubic foot capacity. Dry chemical is discharged from permanently mounted turret nozzle or from two 150 foot 1-inch hand lines.

In Hawaii, the fire department in the City and County of Honolulu uses standard first alarm response of two engine companies and a ladder company, followed by two engine companies, a ladder company and a rescue squad for second alarms. The first-due engine uses two 1½-inch and one 2½-inch preconnected lines in initial attack, backed up by two 2½-inch supply lines. The second-due company lays two 2½-inch lines fire to hydrant. Suction hose is of 4½-inch size but supply lines to pumpers might be of 2½-inch size. For heavy streams, two 2½-inch lines are laid from the appliance to the hydrant, then two more lines are stretched back to the appliance.

In South Bend, Indiana, first-due engine companies lay out one line of 2½-inch hose hydrant to fire and start fire attack using booster lines and preconnected 1½-inch lines from the tank on the pumper, until the supply line is connected. The second-due company follows the same procedure, while the first-due ladder company and rescue squad perform their operations as needed. The first-due engine company also has the responsibility of supplying the standpipe or sprinkler system in the high value district. This pumper lays two 2½-inch lines from the hydrant to the fire department siamese connection, then the pumper returns and hooks up to the hydrant with a 5-inch soft suction hose. The second-due engine company responds to the rear of the building, lays two 2½-inch lines hydrant to fire, using one line directly from the hydrant until the engine returns to hook up. The third-due engine company lays two 2½-inch lines to the front of the involved building, following the same procedure as the second engine.

The department uses 1-inch booster lines for initial attack on residential fires but, if the fire has broken through the roof, 1½-inch preconnected lines are used, backed up by 2½-inch hand-lines.

In Columbus, Indiana, the fire department has been a strong supporter of high pressure water fog (500–900 psi). They use small nozzles and booster lines for this attack, followed by 1½-inch and 2½-inch handlines. Each pumper carries two 10-foot sections of 5-inch hard suction hose and two 20-foot sections of 3-inch soft suction hose preconnected.

1,000 gpm Darley pumper of Melrose Park, Illinois Fire Department has stainless steel panel, relief valve with pilot light, flush valve, manual relief valve shutoff, lighted tank level gage, hose layout calculator, individual gages for each 2½-inch outlet, pilot light for pump control, push-pull controls for all valves including rear 2½-inch discharge line.

Mack pumper of Lexington, Massachusetts Fire Department has 1½-inch preconnected lines in Mattydale compartment preconnected to 2½-inch line, large New York style gages, booster reel, and 1250 gpm pump.

In Kansas, the fire department in the City of Hutchinson has a routine for first-due engine companies at resident fires, requiring a direct lay hydrant to fire, followed by a reverse lay by the second-in company. In the high value district both companies lay double lines hydrant to fire and the incoming ladder company will be ready to set up for ladder pipe operation, if needed. Hutchinson uses 1½- and 2½-inch handlines for initial attack; 2½- and 3½-inch supply line; and 4½- and 5-inch suction hose.

In New Orleans, Louisiana, the fire department uses preconnected 1½-inch handlines, followed by 2½-inch handlines with 3-inch supply lines and 6-inch soft and hard suction hose for hydrant supply and drafting.

Bangor, Maine has two preconnected 1½-inch lines on each pumper as well as a booster line. The first-in company attacks the fire with the 1½-inch or 2½-inch handline, while the second-in company lays additional lines. If a water tower or deluge set is brought into action, an additional pumper will be used to supply them.

In Battle Creek, Michigan, the first engine into the fire drops hand lines for the fire fighting and the second engine drops 2½-inch supply lines straight off the first lay out. The initial attack is 200 feet of 1½-inch preconnected hand line and suction hose at 4½-inch size.

The fire department in Hamtramck, Michigan has some interesting evolutions, with two triple combination pumpers and a quad unit. The latter has a one thousand gallon tank. Initial attack is made with a high pressure booster line, or a 1½- or 2½-inch preconnected line or a 3-inch preconnected line with a 500 gpm fog nozzle. A 4-inch soft suction hose is used for hydrant supply to provide a 500 gpm supply. A 3-inch hose with a 2- to 2½-inch gated reducer is connected at the hydrant but if greater supply is needed, the first-in pumper drops a 2½-inch hand line and a 3-inch supply line. This provides 1,000 gpm or more in a two pumper operation.

The Detroit Fire Department, in residential areas, has the first-in engine drop a line fire to hydrant, then use 1½-inch attack lines reduced on a 2½-inch supply line. The second engine helps the first or makes another layout hydrant to fire. In January, 1972 the department began using tactical mobile squads (TMS), highly flexible fire fighting units with four-man assignments. These squads respond to all structural fires and to other alarms where additional manpower is needed. One of these TMS units is assigned to each of the department's eleven fire fighting battalions.

In Great Falls, Montana, the fire department has the standard initial attack using the 1-, 1½-, and 2½-inch hand lines. Normally, the first engine company drops a straight layout, using 1½-inch or 2½-inch preconnected lines. The second company makes a reverse layout using two 2½-inch lines with 1½-inch handlines wyed from one of them, and two 3-inch supply lines. This permits use of both pumpers at capacity from the hydrant. A 5-inch preconnected soft suction hose is used at the hydrant for reverse lays; 3-inch hose is used for forward layout. Great Falls also has small pickup trucks with monitor nozzles mounted. These trucks carry their own 3-inch hose loads or supply line. The elevating platform used by the department also carries its own 3-inch hose load supplied from a pumper spotted at a hydrant.

In Lincoln, Nebraska, the standard operating procedure for first-due engine companies is to lay two 2½-inch lines, then use preconnected 1½-inch lines for initial attack. The second-due pumper drops a 4-inch supply line and otherwise supplies the first pumper. The third arriving engine company holds at the hydrant for instructions. All pumpers carry soft suction hose but one engine is equipped with 400 feet of the 4-inch hose.

In Baltimore, Maryland, booster lines and 1½-inch preconnects are used in initial attack on small building fires. These are backed up by 2½-inch handlines with adjustable fog nozzles. Hard suction hose is 4½-, 5-, or 6-inch size and supply lines are usually 2½- or 3-inches in size.

The Springfield, Massachusetts Fire Department has the first-in engine company lay a 2½-inch line from the hydrant. Then, upon reaching the front of the building, depending on conditions, will use the first line or connect a water thief to the 2½-inch line in with 1½-inch lines. If conditions are bad enough, the company may just use 2½-inch lines or heavy stream appliances — three 2½-inch lines are laid from a pumper to the siamese at the deck gun, ground monitor, water tower or aerial ladder. Pumpers use two 2½-inch suction lines ten feet long when connecting to hydrants.

The Omaha, Nebraska Fire Department carries 300 feet of 1½-inch and 150 feet of 2½-inch lines preconnected on each pumper. Suction hose is 5 inches in diameter and supply lines vary from 5 inches down to 2½ inches. Most pumpers have a 350–700 gpm turret nozzle mounted directly in the rear of the driver's compartment and a 500 gallon booster tank. On fully involved structures, the first-due pumper blasts the fire with a turret stream for as long as the tank supply lasts, and this has proven to be a successful operation. Aerial ladders and elevating platforms carry split loads of 3-inch supply lines.

Design sketch for preconnected deck gun of Canonsburg, Pennsylvania Fire Department pumper.

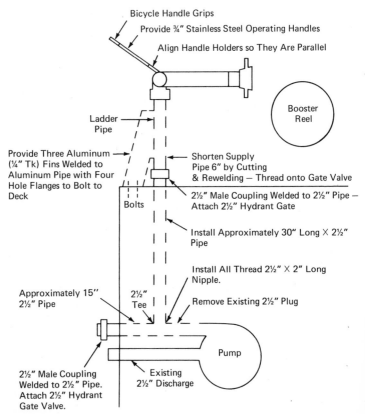

Bicycle Handle Grips

Provide ¾" Stainless Steel Operating Handles

Align Handle Holders so They Are Parallel

Booster Reel

Ladder Pipe

Provide Three Aluminum (¼" Tk) Fins Welded to Aluminum Pipe with Four Hole Flanges to Bolt to Deck

Shorten Supply Pipe 6" by Cutting & Rewelding — Thread onto Gate Valve

2½" Male Coupling Welded to 2½" Pipe — Attach 2½" Hydrant Gate

Bolts

Install Approximately 30" Long × 2½" Pipe

Install All Thread 2½" × 2" Long Nipple.

Approximately 15" 2½" Pipe

2½" Tee

Remove Existing 2½" Plug

Pump

2½" Male Coupling Welded to 2½" Pipe. Attach 2½" Hydrant Gate Valve.

Existing 2½" Discharge

QUESTIONS

Chapter 10

Text:

1. Considering what you have read in this chapter, how would you set up the best engine company procedures for initial attack?

2. What has this chapter told you about the use of (1) booster line operation, (2) preconnects, (3) deck guns?

3. Descriptions of operating methods in these cities have been simplified in this chapter, but even so, which seems the most practical? Why?

4. What seems unusual in the use of suction hose by some departments mentioned in this chapter?

Discussion:

1. If you had complete authority to set up your engine company's fireground procedures, how would you equip a pumper with hose, preconnects, suction hose, deck guns and other essentials?

2. What would be your choices concerning booster hose reels and sizes of handlines?

3. What size tank would you want on the pumper for these evolutions? Why?

4. Is a single-piece engine company, well-designed and equipped, better than a pumper and hose wagon combination? What are the advantages and disadvantages of each?

5. How many efficient methods of laying out and picking up hose can you describe?

College Campus building fire in Great Barrington, Massachusetts brought pumpers, aerial ladder, and tank trucks and required difficult operations in winter snow. (Berkshire Courier photo)

Chapter 11

Specialized Pumper Design and Operations

Most fire departments can develop effective operations using standard pumping apparatus because local fire problems, water supply, terrain, community development, manpower availability and other important factors permit normal levels of fire protection. However, there are cities and towns whose special needs require unusual fire apparatus and fireground tactics and often these communities influence the national trends in apparatus. Most frequently, such changes begin in small communities, perhaps in volunteer fire departments, but sometimes the major city fire departments depart from the usual standards.

The most unusual fire department apparatus of the Twentieth Century probably was the "Super Pumper" of the New York City Fire Department, placed in service in late 1965. Built by Mack Fire Apparatus Company of Allentown, Pennsylvania to meet unusual performance requirements, this was a combination of five pieces of apparatus — a pumper, hose wagon and three satellite pumpers, all of which were to function as a system or team to deliver a mammoth quantity of water for major fires in the dock area of the city. As the following data shows, the design and per-

Triple combination Crown pumpers of Los Angeles Fire Department. Manifold wagon at left has 334 horsepower engine, 2,000 gpm Waterous pump, fourteen outlets with 2½-inch individual control valves and gages, Stang monitor nozzle, 1200 feet of 3½-inch hose, 1500 feet of 2½-inch hose, 600 feet of 1½-inch hose and 500 feet of 1-inch hose in transfer hose beds. There is also a 400 gallon tank.

Pump at right has similar engine and 2,000 gpm Waterous pump with four 6-inch intakes, front and rear 4-inch rear intakes and two 2½-inch gated intakes. There is a 400 gallon tank, six 1½-inch manifold outlets, a monitor nozzle supplied directly by the pump or by four 2½-inch outside inlets; 600 feet of 3½-inch hose, 800 feet of 2½-inch hose, 300 feet of 1½-inch hose and 500 feet of 1-inch hose. There are four 3-inch main outlets.

formance of this combination has been unequaled in the history of the Fire Service.

The Super Pumper is powered by a Mack 255 diesel engine, has an Allison transmission and power takeoff arrangement. The vehicle is 43 feet long, 11 feet 10 inches high, and 8 feet wide. It has a six-stage De Laval pump that weighs more than 3½ tons, and eight 3½-inch intakes at the rear which are supplied by hydrants. The pump is rated at 8,000 gpm at 350 psi; 4,400 gpm at 700 psi. Four discharge gates on each side of the pump supply water to the tender and satellites.

The hose wagon accompanying this pump has a special monitor nozzle that was tested discharging 10,000 gpm at 900 psi with 2½-, 3-, 3½-, 4-, 4½-, and 5-inch tips, each weighing eighty-five pounds.

The satellite tenders each have four 4½-inch intakes and carry 3,000 feet of 4½-inch hose. Altogether, the tender and satellites carry 10,000 feet of the lightweight 4½-inch hose. Drafting for the pumper is accomplished with 12-inch hard suction hose.

Obviously, a powerful pumping combination of this capacity needs tremendous water supply, and, in the years since the apparatus was accepted, it has been used in the dock and warehouse areas and throughout the city where massive fires require such heavy attack.

But New York is not the only city to develop unusual apparatus. Others, in previous years, tried their own methods of coping with fires peculiar to their locale.

Back in the 1950's the Memphis, Tennessee Fire Department created its "Multi-Master," a 2,500 gpm monitor nozzle on a special salvage wagon. This had ten gated 3-inch inlets which were supplied by a group of pumpers when a large warehouse or other industrial fire required a huge barrage of water. The department also made effective use of a large caliber combination nozzle mounted on a salvage truck and supplied by four 2½-inch lines. At times this truck was driven into buildings to accomplish fire knockdown with spray or straight stream.

Evolution of Shelby, North Carolina Fire Department includes using 2½-inch lines wyed from 3-inch line, or larger. Hose clamps permit quick shutoff for changing operations.

For many years the Los Angeles City Fire Department used "manifold" companies, a combination of hose wagon and pumper capable of delivering 4,000 gpm stream or more at 150 psi. The pumper was of 2,000 gpm capacity and the manifold on the hose wagon had eight 2½-inch inlets, four at the rear, two on each side, and five 2½-inch outlets on each side, each with pressure control for 1¾-, 2¼-, and 2¾-inch tips. The wagon usually would lay out 3½-inch lines, hydrant to fire, to supply 2½-inch couplings on the pumper. The turret nozzle was capable of 2,000 gpm and 250 gpm was supplied for each of the ten outlets.

During the 1940's and the fifties, Chicago developed its squad wagons, eventually thirteen of them, averaging 5,000 runs annually. These carried hose and a powerful turret nozzle, capable of 1200 gpm at 130 psi. They were used for rescue as well as fire fighting and carried appropriate equipment for these tasks.

Wyoming, Michigan Fire Department uses 4-inch synthetic hose to supply 1250 gpm deluge gun. The big hose is also used for hydrant drafting of water for relays, and for supplying two or more 2½-inch lines at the fire building.

A different type of operation was developed by the Phoenix, Arizona Fire Department which, in the early sixties experienced rapid municipal growth and absorption of outlying areas at a pace beyond the capability of existing municipal water supply. The fire department began using combination pumper-tankers as first attack or "holding" apparatus until large caliber streams could be developed from other apparatus and water sources. These trucks had tanks of 1,000 to 1,500 gallon capacity and 500 gpm pumps and could operate from ponds, pools, or streams to maintain first attack through 1½-inch handlines. Phoenix had six of these combination pumper-tankers with 1,000 to 1,500 plus two that had tanks of 2,000 gallon capacity. As the city's hydrant system developed, these trucks were reassigned or gradually eliminated.

Perhaps the most important change in fire department operations in recent years has been the use of large diameter hose for supply lines. Fire departments have been using lightweight, synthetic hose for this purpose, in 4-, 4½-, 5- and 6-inch size, perhaps 2,000 to 4,000 feet or more on a pumper. The basic evolution is to drop this hose in straight lay, hydrant to fire, and use the hydrant flow to supply the pumper. Or, the hose may be used in relay, or to supply other apparatus or monitor nozzles.

Among the first fire departments to use such evolutions were those in Wenatchee and Yakima, Washington, back in the early sixties before lightweight synthetic hose became generally available. Wenatchee, for example, carried 1,800 feet of 4-inch hose on a 1,000 gpm pumper, with 800 feet of 2½-inch handlines and two 4-inch to 2½-inch manifolds. In one operation, the department was able to supply fourteen good handline streams, using four hydrants.

Wenatchee also developed a preconnected combination deck gun and ground monitor which could be fed directly from the pump, or detached and set up on the ground to be fed by the 4-inch hose or by a three-way siamese supplied by the 2½-inch hose.

The Yakima Fire Department carried 600 to 800 feet of 4-inch cotton and dacron jacketed hose on pumpers, plus 1,000 feet or more of 2½-inch hose and 300 feet of preconnected 1½-inch handlines. Altogether, the department had 4,200 feet of the big hose in service. A pumper would drop one or two lines of the big hose at the hydrant, lay out for the required distance, then attach the hose to the big suction intake at the rear manifold, or, by using a reducer, attach to a 2½-inch intake. In a typical operation, two 750 gpm pumpers could maintain four 2½-inch handlines in a 1,200 foot relay with the pumps operating at rated capacity. (*See sketches.*)

The Littleton, Colorado Fire Department was another that went to large diameter hose as a means of developing a strong fire-ground attack with limited manpower. Back in 1969 the department obtained 700 feet of 5-inch synthetic hose with ½-turn quick-connect couplings and adapters for standard thread. Using a 750 gpm pumper, the department developed an evolution for moving 1,100 gpm 500 feet from a hydrant to produce a good stream from a 2-inch tip at 85 psi nozzle pressure. At 1,000 gpm flow, pressure loss in this hose was only 6 psi per hundred feet; at 1,500 gpm, 14 psi per hundred feet; comparably, 2½-inch hose has a loss of 10 psi per hundred feet. With these results, the department eventually bought 1,500 additional feet of the 5-inch hose so that its four engine companies each would carry 500 feet of the big hose, 1,200 feet of 2½-inch hose, two 200-foot lines of preconnected 1½-inch hose and preconnected multiversal nozzles.

The Mack Super Pumper of New York City prior to its acceptance tests in 1965. It was supported by a specially designed hose wagon and three satellite pumpers.

Chicago's "Big John" was built on surplus 6 by 6 chassis, has ten 3-way siamese intakes and rear manifold that is raised hydraulically. Two Eastman monitor nozzles are mounted in front for placing streams in lower portions of fire building. Large floodlights are used for night work. (Chief C. Jimmy Johnson photo.)

The companies developed evolutions for producing 1,200 gpm flow within three minutes of arriving on the fireground; 2,400 gpm within six minutes.

More recently, the Wyoming, Michigan Fire Department developed its evolutions with 4-inch lines. In one arrangement, this big hose supplies a 1,250 gpm deck gun rather than using three 2½-inch lines into the siamese. In another, the hose supplies three 1,250 gpm pumpers and a deck gun fed by 25 feet of the 4-inch hose.

A typical hose load includes 1,400 feet of the lightweight 4-inch hose, and 1,500 feet of 2½-inch hose for additional supply or handlines. The department used this hose on four new 1,250 gpm Mack diesel pumpers, each with a 1,250 gpm deck gun, three preconnected 1½-inch lines and a preconnected 2½-inch line.

Chicago Fire Department developed two massive nozzle arrangements on government surplus trucks for use in dangerous areas. This is "Big Mo" which has ten 3-way siamese intakes each with a plastic window for observing gate position. It uses tips up to 4- and 5-inch size. (Chief C. Jimmy Johnson photo.)

A number of fire departments in the State of New Hampshire went to the use of big hose, because they had to handle fire problems in areas remote from hydrant supply. In Laconia, the fire department purchased a new 1,500 gpm pumper and added two hydraulically powered hose reels, each capable of holding 1,000 feet of the 4-inch synthetic hose. A deluge gun with self-adjusting nozzle capable of 200 to 2,000 gpm discharge was semi-fixed so the operator could direct it from the console. The hose reels were arranged to lay out single or double lines and, with two men, retrieve or pick up 2,000 feet of this line in about ten minutes. With this supply hose, the deck gun could discharge 1,500 gpm at draft, 2,000 gpm from a hydrant. All valves on the pump were remote-controlled from the console and the two 4-inch outlets could discharge total capacity of the pump.

In the same state, the Meadowood, Jaffrey and Kingston Fire Departments used 3- and 4-inch hose for supply to distributors, attack pumpers, tankers and monitor nozzles, adjusting evolutions for most efficient movement of water. Jaffrey built a power-operated reel designed to hold 6,000 feet of 4-inch synthetic hose, using it to supply a deck gun and ground monitors as well as pumpers.

Kingston used 3-inch lightweight hose in 100-foot lengths with 2½-inch couplings; and Meadowood used 3½-inch hose with 3-inch couplings feeding a portable hydrant from which two 2½- and four 1½-inch handlines could be supplied.

More recently, the Chelsea, Massachusetts Fire Department was one of the major municipal departments to try large supply lines. The department used 4-inch and 4½-inch synthetic hose equipped with snap couplings and laid out by pumpers for initial attack. The hose was loaded accordian-style in 100 foot lengths in the center of each pumper hose bed, dropped at a hydrant, then paid out as the pumper moved to its fireground position. Each pumper carried 500 to 600 feet of this hose and had appropriate color coding for couplings and adaptors for quick identification when companies were working together.

Monitor nozzle on pickup truck of Cheyenne, Wyoming Fire Department directs stream on lumber yard fire as ladder pipe works in background. (Photo by W. B. Akerlund)

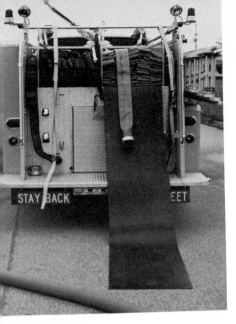

Typical hose load in Wyoming, Michigan includes 1500 feet of 2½-inch hose, with preconnected line at left; 1400 feet of lightweight 4-inch hose with quarter-turn snap couplings. Rubber mat is used to protect couplings as hose drops to ground.

As another innovation, the department used a portable hydrant, fed by the big hose and supplying 2½-inch lines or more big hose in relay. Flow characteristics of the 4-inch hose were impressive: with 700 gpm flowing it had only 9.6 psi loss per hundred feet; with 1,000 gpm flowing, loss was only 19.2 psi per hundred feet. When necessary, the department siamesed three 2½-inch lines into the 4-inch line, when not using hydrant supply.

These were some highlights of innovations in pumping operations during the past decade. As mentioned in other chapters, there were changes in pump design and performance which helped to increase mechanical performance and fire fighting efficiency, but the most noticeable changes were in the major appliances and size of fire hose.

1250 gpm deluge gun supplied by 4-inch line.

QUESTIONS

Chapter 11

Text:

1. Describe all the apparatus in the "Super Pumper" system.
2. What was a major change in U. S. fire departments operations in the past decade?
3. What was unique in the operations of the Wenatchee Fire Department?
4. How did the Memphis "Multi-Master" operate?
5. Describe the Los Angeles "Manifold" companies.
6. Describe the Laconia reel operation.

Discussion:

1. Is it better to use big supply hose with its large coupling and adaptors then to retain the traditional operations with standard 2½-, 3-, or 3½-inch hose? Explain the advantages and disadvantages of each.
2. If you *had* to select only *one* large capacity monitor nozzle for all-purpose heavy stream work, which of these would you pick: a deck gun, permanently installed, or a ground monitor? Explain the tactical advantages and disadvantages of your selection.
3. What combinations of hose loads, handlines, nozzles and heavy stream equipment would you select for a 1,750 gpm pumper?
4. Sketch the chassis of a 1,250 gpm pumper, showing pump and tank location and where you would place 2½-inch discharge outlets.
5. What size piping would you require from pump to outlets? Why?
6. Which is more efficient (1) a front-mount or midship pump; (2) a pump operator's panel at the side of the apparatus, or a panel located midship, behind the driver's compartment? Explain.

Looking over the shoulders of driver and company officer in normal response situation.

Chapter 12

Safety in the Engine Company

In all fire department operations the safety of fire fighting personnel should receive maximum priority. Because engine companies are apt to be the most active group within the department; it follows that much of the efficiency of fireground operations depends upon the teamwork and overall safe performance of each engine company. Yet, many studies have shown that injury and fatality rates among engine company personnel are higher than any other fire companies. Of course, there are more fire fighters in engine companies than in ladder or platform companies, rescue squads, service companies or any other group. They see more action and thus are apt to be exposed to more injury causes.

But the level of safety, the professional performance, the drive, the initiative, and the teamwork of any fire company depends on its leadership; the important quality that distinguishes a top fire officer from the average. In following safe practices and in all other work, the fire company responds to the individual actions and command performance of its company officer. The members will be more inclined to imitate his positive actions of movement, decision and self-protection, than they will be listening to his shouted commands and observing his disregard of common-sense safe practices. Each company officer carries a great responsibility

Unless he is careful, hydrant man can be injured when he wraps hose around hydrant and pumper moves away. (Photo by Charles A. Tuck, Jr.)

in commanding and leading the personnel under his leadership to perform their difficult tasks with a maximum of self-protection and efficiency. If he lacks the initiative to protect his men through application of his best judgment, he should not be an officer.

Here is a brief summary of safety principles he should consider for his engine company personnel:

Physical Conditioning. This is of maximum importance. Many fire departments are carrying out continual physical conditioning programs tied in with frequent medical examinations to spot a heart, respiratory, or other physical ailment in the early stages. If a fire department has such a program, company officers should be active participants and otherwise encourage men under their command to make the most of the program. Well-trained fire fighters usually are much more active and in better shape than many non-Fire Service persons, but there is a temptation to assume that the rigorous demands of emergency response and action can be met through normal physical routines. This is not so. The best, most capable fire fighter is one whose muscular and nervous system, metabolic responses, and entire physiologic patterns have been prepared for the extremes of danger and tension, temperature, and physical and emotional shock. The preparations for all of these require thorough training and top-notch physical conditioning. This is the first requirement for safety on the fireground.

Response in Apparatus. Well-designed pumpers include seats for assigned personnel, all enclosed under cab or canopy, seat belts and/or harnesses for security against crash or other impact, hand grips or bars, careful placement and attachment of tools and equipment that may be needed immediately by the officer or operator, good lighting, and other sensible arrangements. At time of this writing, Federal regulations are requiring air cushion restraint systems or other emergency protection for passenger cars; it is likely that fire apparatus and other emergency vehicles will be subject to similar requirements in the future.

For the company officer, such safety equipment is of prime importance and he must require the men under his command to use it as directed in departmental general orders. The tragic toll of injuries and fatalities in apparatus accidents is sufficient to underscore the common sense of this protection. In summary: each man riding in a pumper should be seated, should have his helmet and protective clothing fully donned and fastened, should be strapped in his seat by belt or harness, should be holding a hand rail or bar, and be fully alert to the possibility of traffic accidents.

Gloves are basic protection against cuts, bruises and burns especially when working with tools or handling hose couplings.

Coming into the Fireground. Here are some common accidents that occur when engine companies pull in to take a hydrant or some other fireground position: Leg sprains, broken bones, hernias, scrapes and bruises, all caused by someone jumping off the vehicle while it is still in motion; landing on an object or rough ground, or worse, on some sharp, hard object. Most of these injuries result because the incoming crew is too excited or untrained; the professional or seasoned fire fighter will realize that the seconds saved by such hasty action are wiped out immediately if one or more men are injured by these simple, unwise actions. It is up to the company officer to keep the men on the vehicle until it is stopped completely.

Another avoidable accident: When a man is dropped at the hydrant he has to wrap the supply hose around the hydrant or otherwise secure it while the pumper drives away. If the officer is not watching this action, if the hydrant man is not trained, or if the driver moves the pumper too quickly, the hydrant man can get injured by the coupling or hose. This may be more possible if the department uses a ring or hook when taking the hydrant. Jammed fingers or hands can occur if the hydrant is not secured quickly and properly.

And obviously fire fighters coming into the scene of action should have their standard boots on, to protect against broken glass, nails, and other sharp objects, hot embers, falling objects and the usual debris. For the same reasons, helmets, gloves and full protective clothing are needed.

"Smoke inhalation" has been a leading cause of fire fighter casualties and the only solution to this problem is to require all officers and fire fighters to use breathing apparatus according to recommendations of NFPA Standard No. 19-B. This recommends self-contained breathing apparatus for all fire fighters and officers who enter into fire-involved buildings. The company officer must maintain continual watch over his men to see that they use breathing equipment, work in pairs, maintain communications and otherwise follow safe practices. The officer should be the first to don protective breathing equipment and should keep using it as long as he requires his men to do so.

Lights. Handlights are among the most useful equipment for fires and night emergencies. Many departments provide all fire companies with sufficient lights so that each man entering a building can illuminate his immediate area. If there are not enough of these lights, company officers should try to have floodlights or other lighting units brought to the working area, because darkness, smoke and bad visibility are frequent contributors to accidents and injuries in fire control.

Operational Accidents. The department's training program usually includes lessons on the safest and best way to lift, drag or otherwise move tools, fire hose, equipment and injured persons. Yet, due to the urgency of some incidents, many fire officers and fire fighters have been seriously injured because they forgot or did not know how to use their muscles and physical frame in reaction to a weight or burden. To minimize these injuries, the company officer should (1) make sure that each company member knows the recommended methods of lifting, carrying, or otherwise moving the bulk and weights of objects normally encountered in emergencies; (2) make sure that strenuous efforts are undertaken in a calm slow manner, without the desperate urgency of undisciplined effort; (3) make sure that enough men are assigned to the task, especially if heavy nozzles, power tools, hose or other severe weights are to be moved.

In addition, each man should be wearing appropriate gloves to minimize the risk of cuts, splinters, a slipping handgrip, burns, acid and other hazards. Another practical form of protection are safety goggles to protect the eyes against smoke particles, dust, dirt and other harmful debris.

Exhaustion due to heat and sustained effort is another casualty-maker, and the company officer must be alert to the evidence of this strain. Salt pills and other prescribed medicine may be appropriate in summer months, but only on recommendations of the department medical officer, but even with such aids, a fire fighter can work himself to the point of collapse, if he is not relieved or otherwise helped in a tough, dangerous assignment. The company officer is apt to place himself in such a circumstance and, unless he realizes his predicament, or is being watched by someone in his company, or some other officer, he may become the principal casualty. Exhaustion is very common in fireground action and all fire officers must exert good leadership and sound tactics to keep the companies under their command working at the reasonable pace that minimizes the extremes of physical effort that lead to exhaustion.

Signals — by Hand or Light

Increase Pressure

Decrease Pressure

Report to Me

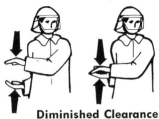

Diminished Clearance

Stop!

Left

Ahead or Back Up!

Right

Charge Line to Recommended Pressure

Shut Water Off in Line

Outside Fires. Most fire companies that have a lot of experience with outdoor fires have developed safe routines for moving apparatus and manpower for best tactical advantage. Even so, it seems that pumpers are the apparatus most frequently trapped, burned or otherwise damaged in these fires. And, if their companies are unfamiliar with the area or the burning possibilities of the fuel, injuries and fatalities can result.

Dump fires and grass, brush and forest fires, are the principal outdoor fires that might require engine company operations. Because of the location and scope of these fires, it is not likely that pumpers will be working from hydrant supply, but may instead be using water from their own tanks, or draft, or be supplied by tank trucks or other apparatus. This introduces an important limitation: there may not be enough water for protecting the truck and its crew if the fire flares back, or otherwise sweeps through the truck's position. Many fire fighters have been burned when a crown fire in high brush or a forest has suddenly dropped to ground cover and raced uphill. The obvious lesson is that the company officer should always be considering the possible vulnerability of his company's position, the capability of the pumper, the availability of water for self-protection, and the best escape routes if the fire situation turns bad.

There are certain hazards peculiar to outside fires and the downtown fire fighter may not be prepared for them if he responds to a fire beyond city limits. Dump fires and brush fires, for example, produce a lot of particulate matter in smoke which can be painfully irritating to the eyes. It usually is not practical for men to wear protective breathing equipment for these fires, but they should at least have the protection of goggles. (Standard issue in some departments.)

Dump fires are doubly treacherous: they may involve some highly toxic materials, or heavy smoke-producing items, like rubber tires, paints, chemicals; and they are likely to burn tunnels and pockets into the underground, so that unsuspecting fire fighters working above this area are suddenly dropped into a hot spot, or a flareup.

Grass, brush and forest fires can burn intensely and change direction very suddenly and fire fighters wearing full protective clothing have been badly burned, sometimes fatally, in these fires. The fire companies that are used to handling these fires treat them with respect and caution, making the best use of terrain, wind direction and communications as tactics develop. The big handicap is limited water supply, but when a fire company is called to one of these fires in unfamiliar territory, many command and control problems can develop and officers must be prepared for the unusual.

Pressures for Handlines and Nozzles. Among the serious accidents that occur on the fireground are those resulting from excessive pressures in hose lines. Too much pressure and flow can knock the nozzleman and his helpers off balance, or worse, cause him to lose his grasp so that the nozzle whips from his hands. Broken bones and other painful injuries can result when this happens. Another danger is the bursting of a hose line due to over pressure or a pressure surge. As mentioned in Chapter 3, hand signals and radio communications between the pump operator and men on the hose lines can keep pressures in proper limits, but the company officer should always be aware of the dangers of overpressure on lines and nozzles. The department's training program should develop the correct evolutions and pump operations to keep accidents at a minimum.

Winter Operations. Cold weather brings its own share of hazards and engine company personnel can expect greater risk of injuries during the winter months. Snow, ice and low temperatures are the principal hazards and all fire fighters must take sensible precautions in this season. Liners for helmets, facial covering, gloves, extra inside clothing and salve on exposed skin are some of the common sense measures for protecting against chill and frostbite. Cleats can be fastened on boots to cut down on ice slipping. Sand and dirt can be spread around an area where a crew might have to stand or work for a long period. Perhaps most important is the fact that men need to be relieved from their fire fighting, hose carrying, or other operations at intervals frequent enough to give them rest and otherwise improve the safety of their assignment. Particular attention should be given to the pump operator who may have to stand at the panel for hours to operate controls for the different requirements.

In Sausalito, California this attack unit was specially designed for the city's narrow roads and steep terrain. It includes a 4-inch manifold permanently mounted on the rear step, and attached to the pump by 3-inch piping. Here it drops part of its 3-inch supply hose which will be fed by a second pumper.

QUESTIONS

Chapter 12

Text:

1. What are three safety rules that a company officer should require men under his command to follow during response to alarms?
2. How can a man become an accident victim when he is "taking" a hydrant?
3. What are some hazards in controlling dump fires?
4. What is a reasonably safe nozzle pressure for a 1¼-inch tip supplied by a 2½-inch line?
5. How does an officer signal to a pump operator at night?

Discussion:

1. What is the best and safest maximum speed for fire apparatus?
2. If a pumper is hauling 500 gallons of water in its tank and is traveling at 50 miles per hour, how far will it move in three seconds?
3. How long would it take to brake this truck to a complete stop?
4. What is the best way to move a fully charged 3-inch hose line by manual effort?
5. Under what conditions should hose streams be directed against an angry mob of people?

Forest Grove, Oregon 1,000 gpm pumper supplies turret nozzle with two 3-inch lines, plus two 2½-inch lines feeding a ladder pipe, another 2½-inch handline and four 1½-inch lines, two from front discharge ports, two from cross-lay preconnects.

Chapter 13

Recording the Pumper's Work

Pumpers are the apparatus most frequently used by the average fire department. Yet when a pumper is backed into quarters upon return from a working fire, the work it has performed may not be adequately studied or evaluated. Yet, there is no better way to justify the purchase of new and improved pumping apparatus than to record the types of work that pumpers must do and to indicate where additional pumping capacity could have helped to control a fire. Such data also will help fire officers determine what methods and operations are most effective with the equipment available.

Let's say that a pumper has been in operation an hour or more. It may have supplied one line or several. If the fire streams were not fully effective, it may be that available pumpers and water supplies were not used to best advantage. It is not fair to blame "low water pressure" if there has been failure to operate pumpers correctly to make best use of available supplies. On the other hand, where there are water supply deficiencies, this information should be made part of the record and used to justify requests for larger mains and better hydrant distribution.

In every community, large or small, water should be piped to various sections in accordance with carefully made estimates of potential demand at the time that the mains were installed. In small communities particularly, the fire flow requirements for a given area form a major part of any estimate of water service requirements. Unfortunately, this is not always the case, particularly where rapid population and territorial expansion has been permitted to outstrip expansion of the water system. However, it is the job of fire department pumpers to take the water that is piped to hydrants and apply it effectively in fire control.

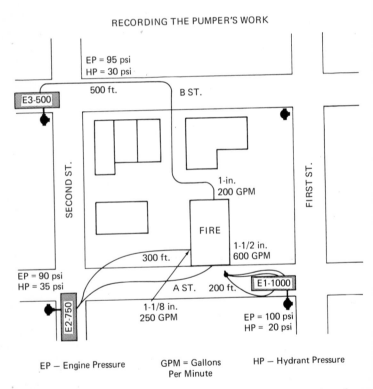

RECORDING THE PUMPER'S WORK

EP — Engine Pressure   GPM = Gallons   HP — Hydrant Pressure
                                Per Minute

Type of fireground layout that should be recorded so operations later can be analyzed. Of particular importance are long hose layouts and number of pumpers connected to single hydrants.

For best results pumpers should be placed at hydrants nearest the fire, unless it is known that these hydrants are on small water mains that cannot provide the needed flow of water and that more adequate supplies are available from other hydrants at a slightly greater distance. Pumpers must also be placed to provide a good distribution of streams on all sides of the fire. The further the pumper is from a fire, the more its power must be utilized to overcome resistance in the hose lines.

The question may be asked, "How can a fire department know whether it is getting the maximum efficiency out of its pumpers?" The answer is: keep a brief work sheet for each pumper covering the actual work performed at fires.

On this page is shown a typical pumper performance report with a diagram (left) showing the fire stream layout at the fire covered by this report. Separate sheets should be made out for each pumper in operation at the fire and this information can then be assembled to summarize the total performance of all the pumpers. In this typical case the tabulation shows that three pumpers having a total rated capacity of 2,250 gpm supplied six lines having a total discharge of 1,300 gpm. This was less than two-thirds the rated capacity of the pumps. A study of this data will show that it would have been possible to use somewhat larger nozzle tips and get a larger fire flow. Also, as shown by the diagram, No. 3 pumper could have been located nearer to the fire, permitting better performance, and still could have covered the rear of the fire.

Combined Report of Pumper Operation

Eng. Co.	Rated Capacity of Pumpers	Residual Hydrant Pressure	No. Lines	Supplying	Hose Layout	Nozzle Tips	Dischge Pressure	Nozzle Pressure	Total Dischge GPM
1	1000	20	3	Deluge Set	200'	1½″	100	80	600
2	750	35	2	Hand Lines	300'	2–1⅛″	90	45	500
3	500	30	1	Hand Lines	500'	1	95	45	200

Pawtuxet, Rhode Island Volunteer Fire Company pumper connects to three gated outlets of hydrant. It has 1400 feet of 2½-inch hose in split load, 200 feet of 1½-inch hose preconnected, and 200 feet of 1½-inch hose in skid load.

It is desirable for pump operators to record any changes in pumping conditions, together with the approximate time of the change. Change in the number of lines being supplied, change in discharge and intake pressures, and similar changes can be significant in the post-fire operation critique. For example, during the fire described in the preceding paragraph, hydrant pressures changed as each pump went into operation.

Here are some results that may be obtained by making studies of pump operation:

1. The fire department will know whether its pumping equipment is being used to maximum advantage. This information can be used in planning future fire fighting operations and in conducting drills.

2. The fire department will know what proportion of the actual rated capacities of its pumpers was delivered under fire ground conditions.

3. The fire department will have evidence to prove any need of greater pumping capacity to get the maximum from existing hydrant supplies.

4. Studies will show that, in many cases, greater efficiency could be obtained by having several companies run lines from the pumpers nearest to the fire, rather than by having late arriving pumpers supplying long lines with small nozzles.

5. The studies also will show when pumpers are being over-loaded in supplying too many streams. Where pumpers of small capacity and low engine power are required to operate for extensive periods, considerably beyond their rated capacity, serious damage may be done to the engine and other parts of the pumping equipment.

6. Such a check-up will show whether the proper size nozzle tips were used to provide the best streams possible with the length of line used.

7. The department will know whether or not it has delivered the maximum amount of water that was safe and practical when large flows were needed.

Another benefit comes to the fire department that keeps careful records of the work done by pumpers. Deficiencies in the water supply system will no longer be a matter of conjecture. The fire department will be able to point out actual cases where low water pressures, insufficient hydrants, dead-end or small water mains, or inadequate water storage facilities were responsible for failure to control a fire promptly.

Pirsch Model 41C, 1250 gpm one stage Hale QSMD Pump. Four door cab design with six man cab. Front 5″ inlet with operator control, rear preconnected discharges, full panel, 400 gallon tank.

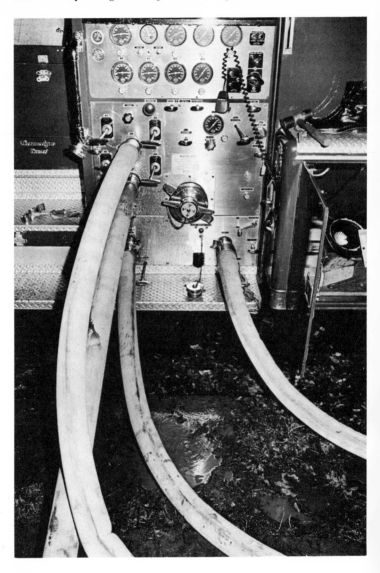

Typical supply and discharge lines at pump panel. Operator must know gage performance to be sure water supply is adequate.

QUESTIONS

Chapter 13

Text:

1. Why is it practical to record how a pumper is used at a fire?
2. Who is likely to use this information?
3. How can a pumper be overloaded?
4. What operational changes are significant in pump performance on the fireground?
5. How would you determine if a pumper was used to optimum capacity?

Discussion:

1. How do you determine the longest single 2½-inch supply line that should be employed for supplying a ladder pipe using a 1¼-inch tip?
2. What should be recorded concerning apparatus from other departments that respond on mutual aid? Identify fire items.
3. Would engine speed of a pumper be significant in a fireground operation? Explain.
4. What maximum operating conditions would you permit for a pumper? How would you keep within these limits?

*Pumper of Racine, Wisconsin Fire Department receiving annual mainte-
nance inspection.* (Racine Fire Department photo)

Chapter 14

Maintenance

The importance of fire department pumpers in control of fire emergencies cannot be emphasized too much. Apparatus that does not produce its full capabilities could permit a routine fire to reach major proportions. However, continuous top operation depends directly on the human element, and company officers must be aware of maintenance needs and of the tasks that must be performed regularly.

While the fire chief has general responsibility for the proper functioning of fire apparatus, this responsibility is usually delegated to subordinates and, through the chain of command to the engine company officer and then to the pump operator. The skill of the pump operator is probably the most important single factor in a good maintenance program.

There must be definite policy in every fire department specifying what constitutes normal maintenance, what constitutes apparatus repair, and who performs each function. In this book only normal maintenance is described. For example, it is rarely desirable to permit a pump operator to change the carburetor or to make distributor adjustments. It is essential that there be definite assignment, clearly understood, of preventive maintenance service. With the assignment of such responsibility should go authority to take steps necessary to correct any deficiencies.

When a fire truck is in need of repair, arrangements should be made to complete the repair without unavoidable delay. When parts need replacement they should be promptly secured from the supply source. Parts should be identified properly and ordered by the manufacturer's number. Every effort should be made to get fire apparatus back in service as quickly as possible and trucks out of service should be replaced by reserve or "covering" equipment.

Operator's Check When Coming on Duty

There are several items of primary importance in a fire pumper. Among these are the condition of the battery, the amount of fuel in the tank, the oil level in the engine, the amount of water in the radiator and in the booster tank, the air pressure in the tires, and similar items. The remedy is usually self-evident.

Keeping the apparatus fuel tank filled is the responsibility of the apparatus operator on duty. This is particularly important in the case of pumping apparatus since the engine often has to operate for several hours after it reaches a fire. Standard apparatus specifications require sufficient fuel capacity for uninterrupted operation for at least two hours without refueling. Of course the tank always should be full when an alarm is received. Each fire department must have arrangements for refueling vehicles at all time, day and night. Unless the fuel tank is checked when the driver comes on duty, and after each run, there is danger that the tank has been partly depleted, with the fuel supply inadequate for a big job. There have been instances of apparatus running out of gasoline at crucial times in fireground action.

When there are special assignments, such as long runs in response to mutual aid calls, provision should be made for carrying additional gasoline or diesel fuel safely. Because fire apparatus is used intermittently, fuel economy is seldom a factor, but good performance is an absolute must

When the oil gage, or dip stick, shows that the oil level is below the full mark, the required amount should be added. Oil in fire apparatus should be of good quality and of proper grade. Because of the nature of service, oil changes for fire apparatus should be on a calendar basis, rather than a mileage basis. The cheapest and most effective maintenance of fire apparatus involves regular changes of oil and periodic lubrication. Adding more oil if the level is low is not a good substitute for necessary regular oil changes. Unless the oil reservoir is regularly drained, flushed and refilled to the proper level with the required grade of oil, the life of the engine will be appreciably shortened by accumulations of sludge, sticking valves, friction and overheating. This will inevitably result in loss of power which can affect the pump. Oil should always be changed after any major pumping job. This will minimize costly repairs.

Road mileage has relatively little to do with the need for oil changes in fire apparatus. Much more important are the number of starts made by the engine and the "engine miles" involved in pumping. Oil dilution caused by condensation, or oil contamination by gasoline and other impurities, are of great importance in the maintenance program. Oil contamination can be minimized by running engines long enough to get them thoroughly warm each time they are started. This helps to vaporize contaminating products in the crank cases. At least every six months and preferably every three months, oil should be changed and the vehicle should be lubricated.

Another matter of importance is the lubrication of automatic transmissions. These are expensive and are quickly destroyed when not kept properly lubricated. The apparatus operator should make certain that proper level of lubrication is maintained.

The water level in the radiator should be checked, for the radiator should be full at all times. Any depletion of the water should be carefully investigated to determine the cause. Normally, antifreeze additives are not used in pumpers, for in normal operations the engine is kept running when the apparatus is out of quarters in subfreezing weather even when not pumping.

All lights should be checked by turning them on and making a visual examination. These include head lights, tail lights, spot lights, gage lights, and many others. Any that are burned out should be replaced. Keep spare bulbs on hand. Light failures due to loose connections or worn wiring should be promptly reported and corrected.

The condition of the battery, or batteries, should be checked with a hydrometer that measures the specific gravity of the liquid. This is done by drawing electrolyte from the battery into the glass tube by means of a rubber bulb. A weighted glass float will indicate the strength of the solution. When the float is low, the specific gravity is low.

A fully charged battery will have a specific gravity reading of 1280. (Note: This is actually 1.280, but in common usage the decimal point is forgotten and the reading is called "twelve-eighty.") As the battery discharges, the electrolyte solution becomes weaker. A reading of 1250 indicates a charge of about 75 per cent; while 1225 indicates a charge of about 50 per cent.

When testing the electrolyte in a battery with a hydrometer avoid spilling or dropping the solution, as it contains sulphuric acid. A small glass or rag can be used to catch drops from the tube inserted into the battery. Spilled acid can be neutralized by prompt use of bicarbonate of soda.

The hydrometer must be filled just enough to permit the float to be suspended without touching top or bottom. It must be held in a vertical position so the float does not touch the sides. The most accurate reading is obtained at eye level.

If the battery reading is 1225, or half charge, it should be immediately recharged, or replaced if the battery will not hold charge. It is better not to permit the battery to fall this low, especially in the winter when battery effectiveness is reduced by low temperature.

The fluid in the battery should be at the proper level to permit the liquid to expand when heated during charging. Use only distilled water. Do not fill with too much water so that the electrolyte overflows the cell opening, as the solution has a corrosive effect. The level should be the specified distance above the plates. The electrolyte level should not be permitted to fall below the top of the plates.

The oil pressure gage should be observed immediately after starting the motor and periodically during the entire time of operation. The reading on the oil gage does not indicate the quantity of oil in the engine; it only indicates there is some oil in the engine and that it is being pumped under some pressure. A shortage of oil should be indicated by a trouble light, or by the oil pressure gage reading rising and falling spasmodically. When this occurs, the engine should be stopped as soon as possible and the oil condition remedied. Every pumper operator should be thoroughly familiar with the normal oil pressure gage reading for his particular pumper.

Every time the engine is started the pump operator should be alert for any unusual noise. The cause should be determined immediately. Any unusual vehicle performance on the road or while pumping should be reported to the company officer at the first opportunity.

To assure that fire apparatus will function efficiently when needed, it is important to avoid practices which may be harmful, such as sudden, unnecessary opening and closing of valves or adjustments of engine speed when large quantities are being pumped, operating the pump with the engine in the wrong gear, racing the engine unnecessarily, "lugging" the engine by overload or using the wrong gear when driving, and using the clutch improperly.

All pumpers require a complete semi-annual inspection and an annual service test at draft of which records must be kept. Service pump tests are also required after any major repairs.

Other Inspections

In general, the same inspections are required after runs as are made periodically. Brakes that are not operating properly or brake drums that are too hot need immediate attention. Brake fade is dangerous and should be corrected. Tires should receive careful examination for nails or glass that may have been picked up in travel. Gasoline, oil and water levels are checked and brought up to a full condition if necessary. This *must* be done after every run and as necessary during prolonged operations.

If the pump has been operated from draft, it should be connected to a hydrant or other source of clean water and thoroughly flushed. This is especially important if salt water or dirty water was pumped.

Pump packing should be adjusted to permit only a slight drip. Packing and other possible points of leakage such as valves can be tested by filling the pump at ordinary domestic water pressure.

Hose gate valves should be cleared of sand or grit that may have been picked up. Gaskets in caps and connections should be replaced as needed.

Drain lines and valves clog readily with scale and other foreign matter from hydrants and should be flushed and kept clean.

The priming device should be examined to assure that it will function the next time it may be needed. If oil is used in the priming pump the oil reservoir should be checked and filled as necessary. Suction strainers should be checked to assure that they are not clogged.

Before returning to quarters from a fire, the driver and the company officer should make sure all equipment belonging on the truck is in place. On return to quarters all items that have been used should be checked for damage or readiness for future use. Any deficiencies should be corrected by replacement, sharpening, oiling, cleaning or recharging as the case may be. Nozzles and hose appliances should be examined for damage that could affect their operation. Any wet hose other than booster or suction hose should be replaced immediately with dry hose. If the pump is normally carried dry, drains should be opened to drain pump and piping, especially during cold weather.

Weekly Routine

Once a week fire apparatus should receive a complete and comprehensive checkup. Attention should be given to items that may reduce efficiency, such as corrosion, accumulations of sediment, or abrasive action.

The battery case and cable terminals should be kept clean. A weak solution of bicarbonate of soda can be used to wash corroded terminals and a good grade lubricant can then be used to inhibit corrosion. Check battery clamps to see if the battery is held securely.

If plain water is used in the booster tank it may be replaced with fresh water when necessary. Draining and flushing at periodic intervals will keep the accumulation of loose scale and rust to a minimum. If a wetting agent is used, or if a rust inhibitor is added to the booster tank, the weekly inspection may be just a visual examination of the liquid in the tank but tank strainers should be checked.

The transfer of "change-over" valve on multi-stage centrifugal pumps should be moved back and forth to the full extent of its travel and then left in the desired position (usually series or pressure position). Discharge gates should be opened and closed.

Careful visual examination should be made of the whole truck, including a close inspection of the underside of the chassis. Any suspicious condition should be a subject for further examination and immediate correction. Note signs of water leakage and request correction as necessary.

Tires should be studied to detect unusual signs of wear and presence of foreign articles in the tread or lodged between duals. A tire pressure gage will indicate whether the air pressure is within the recommended limits. If valve caps are missing they should be replaced. If chains are used in winter operations they should be examined for wear and proper adjustment.

The hood should be raised and the engine examined for any signs of leaks, looseness, chafing, or other defects. The engine should be wiped clean with a rag, for a spotless engine is usually a sign of good maintenance by the operator or department. Frequently, points of potential failure can be detected during this simple task of cleaning. Painting also helps to keep the engine clean. Fuel, oil or water leaks should be traced and repaired. Drip pans may be used, but should be kept clean. Many fire departments provide a creeper in each station so that the underside of the apparatus can be readily inspected. If extension lights are used they should be of the safety type with a proper guard.

Valves and levers on the pump should work easily and smoothly and should be in the proper position for quick emergency operation. Caps on the suction and discharge outlets should be in place and should not stick or bind. The threads should be cleaned with a brush, but flake graphite may be used as a lubricant when needed. This will usually correct sticking. Replace cracked or grooved gaskets and check relief valve or pressure governor for proper setting.

All tools, equipment and appliances should be securely fastened in their normal mountings. Attention should be given to nozzles and nozzle tips to assure that each size is in its proper place. No cleaning rags, gloves or other foreign materials should be allowed to remain stored in nozzles, suction hose, or in any other appliance where they may obstruct the flow of water. The condition of the suction hose lining should be checked, since a loose lining may block the hose when water is drafted. The condition of the hose load also deserves attention and any odor indicating mildew should be investigated immediately.

Routine After Every Run

Every time the apparatus engine is started the operator should pay close attention to the gages. The proper interpretation of the readings will give the pump operator a definite indication of the performance of the engine.

When the engine is running at more than idling speed the ammeter should show either a slight charge, or a zero reading. A discharge reading should be reported to the proper officer as soon as possible. When the engine is first started the ammeter may show an initial heavy charge but should drop back after a short period of operation. This indicates that the generator has restored the charge.

As mentioned before, after every run the apparatus should be refueled immediately and readied for further use.

One word of caution — engines should not be operated in confined quarters without adequate ventilation, because of the carbon monoxide hazard.

American LaFrance "Century" pumper includes large cab with wrap-around windshield, jump seats in back of driver's compartment, twin booster reels, large rear compartments and other features.

QUESTIONS

Chapter 14

Text:

1. What are eight items a pump driver/operator should check when coming on duty?
2. How can you minimize oil contamination in a pumper?
3. What is the function of a hydrometer?
4. How would you clean a pump of salt water residue?
5. What maintenance should be applied to coupling threads?

Discussion:

1. For fire apparatus, are diesel engines better than well-designed gasoline engines? Give reasons.
2. Is automatic transmissions on a pumper better than the standard shift type? Explain.
3. What engine capability would you require for a 1,000 gpm pumper? Why?
4. Standard No. 19 requires fire apparatus to pass road performance tests on level ground. What would be some reasonable tests on hills?
5. How long should fire apparatus be kept in service with good maintenance?

Unusual narrow roads and sharp turns in Bisbee, Arizona requires specially designed apparatus. Here a pumper negotiates a downhill turn.

Chapter 15

Buying a Pumper

Fire department pumping apparatus is used in many different tasks that usually are common to the locality or area protected by the department. Pumpers in cities probably operate from hydrants most of the time, and infrequently may be involved in relays, but it is unlikely that they will be used very often in drafting from static sources. Pumpers in small towns are liable to work from both sources, hydrants and static supply, and be used frequently in relays with tankers or other pumpers. In rural areas, pumpers most likely will have to obtain water by drafting or by relay, and, unlike city pumpers, may be designed and arranged to pump water while in motion — the "pump-and-roll" tactic can be very effective on grass and grain field fires.

These are only a few of the functions and needs that must be considered when a fire department is considering purchase of a new pumper. There are many more design and performance requirements that must be studied and evaluated carefully before commitment to purchase and acceptance of delivered apparatus is completed.

Most fire departments use NFPA Standard No. 1901 — *Automotive Fire Apparatus* — as a guide for determining the needed performance of a pumper, or any other apparatus. The standard, developed by the NFPA Committee on Fire Department Equipment, includes recommendations on performance, equipment and road tests and includes explanatory material in the appendix.

For regular fire department operations the standard requires a pump that meets one of these rated capacities: 500, 750, 1,000, 1,250, 1,500, 1,750 or 2,000 gpm. Any other permanently mounted pump of less than 500 gpm capacity is considered a booster pump. It is up to the purchasing fire department to define the needed pumps (standard and booster) and other requirements for the pumper. These would include: pump connections, controls, hose bed, tank size and layout, compartments, vehicle performance and configuration, basic equipment to be provided on delivery, and special items or needs. Most manufacturers are used to working within specifications developed from Standard No. 19 and can anticipate problems or adjustments that may result as a consequence of deviation from this standard, but are willing to meet reasonable purchase requirements of exceptional need, i.e., narrow width of chassis, high transmission, perhaps all bronze pump components, unusual hose bed layout, and similar items.

Pump performance must be completely adequate. The standard requires a pump to be able to draft from a static source (take suction) with a lift of ten feet in not more than thirty seconds and bring this water through twenty feet of suction hose to the pump. The suction hose is to be of the same size as the pump suction intake connection.

Next, the pump is required to be able to discharge water at the following pressures: 100 percent of capacity at 150 psi net pump pressure; 70 percent of capacity at 200 psi; and 50 per cent of capacity at 250 psi. For example, a 1,000 gpm pumper should deliver 1,000 gpm at 150 psi, 700 gpm at 200 psi, and 500 gpm at 250 psi and the same ratios would apply to other standard pumpers.

Suction inlets must be large enough to permit this capacity discharge at draft and the number and size of these inlets should be in the basic specifications. The following sizes are considered appropriate for standard capacities: 500 gpm, 4- or 4½-inch; 750 gpm, 4½- or 5-inch; 1,000 gpm, 5- or 6-inch; 1,250 gpm, 6-inch; and 1,500 gpm or larger, 6-inch or double suction lines. In addition, at least one gated suction inlet is needed, of 2½-inch or larger size, but if the pump is on a chassis with an aerial ladder, elevating platform, or water tower, an additional 2½-inch gated suction inlet is desirable. Of course, the purchasing fire department can specify any type and amount of intake and discharge connections, but as a practical matter the connections and all related piping should be designed and installed to gain optimum hydraulic performance to match the intended use of the pumper. For example, piping for discharge outlets are required in Standard No. 1901 to be the same size (or larger) as the nominal size of the valve. Piping from tank to pump and from the pump to outlets of preconnected lines or nozzles must be adequate for anticipated flow.

Number of 250 gpm Hose Streams Supplied by Pumpers of Different Rating

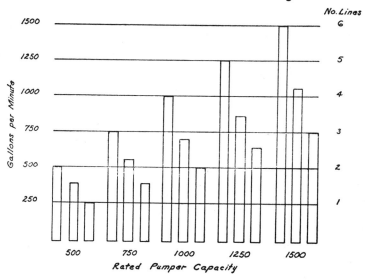

This chart shows simply what each size of Class A pumper can do at various test pressures. The column of figures at right represents the number of 250 gpm hose streams. The column at left shows the total flow of those hose streams. Figures at bottom indicate the rated gpm capacity of pumpers.

Vertical rectangles represent acceptance test pressures. For each size of pumper, tall column at left means 150 psi test pressure; middle column means 200 psi; and small column means 250 psi. For example, a pumper rated at 750 gpm, discharging at 200 psi pressure, will supply a little more than 250 gpm hose streams, or 525 gpm (70 percent of 750 gpm).

Pump Output at Various Discharge Pressures

Nominal Rating	25 Psi Hyd. Residual		At Draft		At Draft		25 Psi Hyd. Residual		At Draft	
Gpm — Psi	175 Psi	%	175 Psi	%	200 Psi	%	225 Psi	%	225 Psi	%
500 — 150	500	100	400	80	350	70	350	70	312	62
750 — 150	750	100	600	80	525	70	525	70	465	62
1000 — 150	1000	100	800	80	700	70	700	70	625	62
1250 — 150	1250	100	1000	80	870	70	870	70	775	62
1500 — 150	1500	100	1200	80	1050	70	1050	70	925	62

Note: Percentages shown are of rated capacity.

Because nozzle pressures in the 100 psi range are now common for fog and heavy stream nozzles, it may be helpful to think of the output of pumpers at 175 psi as well as at 150 psi. Notice the normal rating of each pumper and then the estimated output of these pumps at 175, 200 and 225 psi.

Thus, the pumper capable of 1,000 gpm at 150 psi becomes a 700 gpm pumper at 200 psi at draft. The 1,250 gpm pumper gives about 1,000 gpm at 175 psi and 775 gpm at 225 psi. The 1,500 gpm pumper will give over 1,000 gpm at 200 psi. Thus, if you need 1,000 gpm at pressures of 175 psi or 200 psi, you require the work potential of a 1,250 or 1,500 gpm pumper. These figures are approximations based upon equivalent work loads, and variations will be experienced.

While it is desirable to use 5- or 6-inch supply hose for 1,250 or 1,500 gpm pumpers, a 4½-inch soft suction may be used to supply these pumpers when working from a hydrant that can provide the desired flow with at least 10 psi residual pressure. If more water is needed a supplemental supply line can be run to the pump.

One important design feature concerns the venting of the tank on pumpers designed specifically for "fast attack." If a pre-connected deck gun, or a couple of preconnected 2½-inch lines are installed so that water in the tank might be pumped out quickly for fire attack, the location, venting and piping from the tank to pump must be such that the tank can be drained at the required rate.

For the majority of pumpers, the operator's position is at the side of the apparatus, where suction intakes, gages, controls and discharge outlets are located. There are exceptions: some manufacturers set up the pump panel and controls midship on the truck, just behind the driver's compartment, so that the operator does not have to step on the ground to get the pump into action. There are also front-end pumps, somewhat traditional in rural areas where a pumper must move right up to a pond or creek and drop a suction hose, with little alternative for taking another position to draft water.

With these exceptions, the average pump operator can expect that the panel board, with gages and controls, usually will be on the left side of the pumper, and from this position he must expect to maintain control over all operations involving this apparatus.

Purchasing specifications should be developed around the planned routines of the engine company — how initial attack will be supplied; how and when secondary supply will be obtained for more handline operations; and how heavy streams and relays will be maintained for extended fireground action. Pumps on modern fire apparatus can be designed and manufactured to perform specific fire control tasks and a purchasing fire department should be knowledgeable of the most recent methods of using pumpers for maximum efficiency.

Equipment. In normal purchasing, certain basic equipment is expected to be delivered with each new pumper, and must be included in the bid specifications by the fire department and described in detail in the purchase contract. Standard No. 1901 identifies equipment that must be carried on pumpers (and therefore included in original purchase specifications), such as the following: ground ladders, portable extinguishers, a pike pole or plaster hook, a pick-head axe and flat-head axe, two hand lights, swivel connections for suction hose, a suction strainer, and booster hose with a combination nozzle. These are essentials:

the standard recommends other equipment as desirable or optional and the purchasing department can decide which is most important for its planned operations.

Safety Features. At time of this writing there are indications that Federal safety requirements may have considerable influence on fire department specifications for apparatus because of new requirements for vehicle safety. In addition, there are a number of reasons for considering possible improvements beyond the basic design configurations of standard requirements. Seat belts, restraint harnesses, seating arrangements, enclosed compartments or canopies, special warning signals like backup alarms, and other positive safety improvements should be considered in addition to standard requirements. Much depends upon the department's attitude toward safe operations — how strongly regulations are enforced and how much hardship is displayed by company and chief officers. But obviously, certain accidents can be minimized through proper design of fire apparatus, and since pumpers are the most common and most utilized fire department vehicles, it follows that careful planning and specifying can help to minimize the more obvious hazards. (*Chapter* 15.)

Advisory Sources. When a fire department intends to purchase a new pumper, its principal advisors are the chiefs, master mechanics and other members of neighboring fire departments, all of whom have considerable experience and a variety of opinions about what type of apparatus is best for a given purpose. Most of these suggestions are helpful but usually the purchasing fire department must explore a number of different channels of information to get certain answers. Within each state there are several possible sources. For instance, some state fire marshals have detailed records of the apparatus and personnel of hundreds of fire departments, all with similar fire control problems. State training officers and insurance rating bureaus each can offer advice or assistance in the early stages of developing specifications. State fire chiefs' associations and representatives of apparatus manufacturers and fire equipment distributors are other sources.   The specifying and purchase of fire apparatus is a very difficult and important problem, and fire chiefs and everyone else involved should try to get help from all available sources including the NFPA.

Listing by UL. Since 1967 Underwriter's Laboratories, Inc., in Chicago, Illinois has provided pump certification for new fire department pumpers. Manufacturers deliver pumpers to the testing grounds, attesting to performance of the engine, transmission, gear ratio, pump and chassis features, wheel base, width, gross vehicle weight and distribution, loading on front and rear wheels, axle capacity and related details. Then the UL lab personnel test the pumper according to standard requirements, including rated capacity, overload performance, functions of controls, the fuel system, instruments and gages and pump connections. When a pumper meets each of the requirements, UL issues a certificate of inspection. This is a form of verification that the capabilities of the vehicle are dependable within the purpose of the original specifications, a feature that can be important in the evaluation of a community's fire protection. Tests include capacity performance at 150 psi for two hours; overload at 165 psi for ten minutes; 70 per cent rated capacity at 200 psi for thirty minutes; and 50 per cent rated capacity at 250 psi for thirty minutes.

Road Tests. Standard No. 1901 requires certain road performance which is not tested or verified by UL or any other testing laboratory, so it is up to the purchasing fire department to assure that the new vehicle can meet road performance requirements. The standard calls for the vehicle to be tested with full water tank and equipment and personnel allowances in two runs in opposite directions over the same route. From a standing start, the truck must reach a true speed of 35 miles per hour within 25 seconds, and from a steady speed of 15 mph, shall accelerate to 35 mph within 30 seconds, without movement of the gear selector. It must also reach a top speed of 50 mph and have braking capability of bringing the fully loaded vehicle to a complete stop within 30 feet from an initial speed of twenty mph. There are other general requirements, each of which must be evaluated by the chief and other members of the purchasing fire department.

It is generally true that modern pumpers have less difficulty meeting specified pumping requirements than they do in meeting road tests. Steep hills, lack of paved streets, sudden starts with cold engines, frequent response to distant alarms, traffic congestion, heavy loading of apparatus and winter road conditions are some of the factors that handicap over-the-road performance.

Fire apparatus should be capable of rapid acceleration, rather than of obtaining a high top speed. Standard No. 19 requires a top speed of only 50 mph.

Manner of Transportation

Manufacturers recommend that gasoline engines be run at controlled speeds during the initial "break-in" period. This is to assure that moving parts seat themselves without undue wear from friction that may be caused by the high temperatures produced during high speed operation of new engines.

Engines for fire apparatus should be no exception, whether built by a manufacturer specifically for fire service, or whether the engine is that of a regular commercial truck chassis. It should be the responsibility of the manufacturer to supervise and complete the delivery of a new pumper from the assembly point. If the pumper is driven overland or shipped by common carrier, the driving or unloading should be in charge of a representative of the manufacturer.

Placing Pumper in Service

On completion of the required acceptance and road tests the pumper should be carefully examined for any condition that may be below standard. Evidence of leaks, unusual wear, loose or missing bolts, nuts or cotter pins, rubbing or grating noises, or failure of some parts to function properly are some items that should be corrected before the pumper is placed in service at the fire station. All grease fittings should be lubricated and the oil in the motor changed. The presence of excessive carbon or metallic particles in drained oil should be investigated.

In the interest of efficiency, all company officers and driver/operators should have a good understanding of the manner in which a pumper is operated. There must be clear regulations governing the department policy for pumper operators and their duties. Assistance in testing driving ability may be gained from the Department of Public Safety in some states or from other agencies that have the necessary driver's testing equipment.

When a new pumper is purchased it should be outfitted with required appliances, and there should be basic equipment that comes with the apparatus. Other items may be specified or purchased or transferred from old apparatus. However, consideration should be given to providing the complete inventory of appliances needed with the new apparatus. It is well to look into the possibility of standardizing the placement of equipment and appliances on each pumper. It is an advantage to have all ladders, suction hose, axes, extinguishers, nozzles and other items located uniformly on each type of apparatus. Items of related usage should be placed together.

QUESTIONS

Chapter 15

Text:

1. What road performance is required of a pumper?
2. Describe the UL pump certification tests.
3. What, exactly, is an overload test?
4. What basic safety features are required in a pumper?
5. What minimum size booster tank is needed on a pumper?

Discussion:

1. Who in the fire department should help develop apparatus purchase specifications?
2. Who should attend and have opportunity to express opinion on acceptance tests?
3. What is the most efficient maximum capacity of a pumper that can be used by your fire department? Why?
4. Should the company officer and fire fighters don breathing apparatus during response to alarms?
5. What new and unusual equipment would you suggest for a pumper?

This operation at major fire in Boston, Massachusetts shows why fire officers and pump operators must understand the application of basic hydraulics to fireground work. (Boston Fire Department photo by G. E. Murphy)

Chapter 16

Hydraulics

Mathematical formulas used to calculate hydraulics on the fireground are intended only for approximate results; variances or differences must be expected if exact analyses and formulas are applied to fireground situations. Obviously, the many possibilities for inaccuracies in pumper operations, hose and nozzle use, coupling and gasket differences, water main and hydrant variances, and other factors influence fireground calculations of actual flows and pressures.

The difference of $\frac{1}{16}$th of an inch in the diameter of a 2½-inch hose can change pressure loss by ten per cent, a significant amount if a hose layout covers 1,000 feet or more. Similarly, considering the variety of operations undertaken by the average engine or ladder company, it cannot be expected that fireground estimates of volumes and pressures can be any better than approximate, because there are few opportunities for gage correction or other verification of operational results.

Certainly fire officers, pump operators and fire fighters must understand the fundamentals of hydraulics — the physical laws that apply to fluids at rest and in motion; without such knowledge the breakdown of apparatus and other disastrous consequences on the fireground would indicate the need for training and education.

As mentioned previously, trends in equipment development are diminishing the need for empirical calculations on the fireground — constant flow valves, water additives, nozzle controllers and other modifiers can simplify calculations of the pump operator or engine company officer. Even so, it is important for all fire officers to understand the principles of hydraulics and the physical formulas or factors that might affect the flow and use of water on the fireground.

This chapter identifies some of the recognized measurements and properties of water within accepted terminology of modern science and fire protection. For more extensive explanation refer to the NFPA *Fire Protection Handbook*, from which some of the following data are taken.

Weights and Measures

One U. S. gallon of water occupies 231 cubic inches, (.133 cubic feet), and weighs 8.34 pounds. It equals 0.8327 Imperial gallons, or 3.785 (metric) liters. An Imperial gallon equals 1.201 U. S. gallons.

Hydraulic Properties of Water

The density of water varies with temperature. At maximum density, occurring at 39.2 degrees Fahrenheit, fresh water weighs 62.425 pounds per cubic foot in vacuum, or 62.35 pounds per cubic foot in air. It weighs 62.400 pounds per cubic foot at 52.72 degrees F in vacuum. For ordinary calculations, the approximate value of 62.4 pounds per cubic feet is used. Average sea water weighs 64.1 pounds per cubic feet.

The following units are based on water at 62.4 pounds per cubic feet. One cubic foot of water equals 7.48 gallons.

250	gallons	of	water	occupy	57,750	cubic	inches;	33.42 cubic feet.
500	gallons	of	water	occupy	115,500	cubic	inches;	66.84 cubic feet.
750	gallons	of	water	occupy	173,250	cubic	inches;	100.26 cubic feet.
1,000	gallons	of	water	occupy	231,000	cubic	inches;	133.68 cubic feet.
1,250	gallons	of	water	occupy	288,750	cubic	inches;	167.10 cubic feet.
1,500	gallons	of	water	occupy	346,500	cubic	inches;	200.52 cubic feet.
2,000	gallons	of	water	occupy	462,000	cubic	inches;	267.36 cubic feet.

Tank Sizes and Capacities

Gallons	Cubic Feet	Weight
250	33.42	2,082.50 pounds (1 ton, plus 82.50 pounds)
300	40.10	2,499 pounds (1 ton, plus 499 pounds)
500	66.84	4,165 pounds (2 tons, plus 165 pounds)
750	100.26	6,247.50 pounds (3 tons, plus 247.50 pounds)
1,000	133.68	8,330 pounds (4 tons, plus 330 pounds)
1,500	200.52	12,495 pounds (6 tons, plus 495 pounds)
2,000	267.36	16,660 pounds (8 tons, plus 660 pounds)

Hose and Nozzles

Hose Diameter (Inches)	Cross Sectional Area square inches	Nozzle Tip Size	Area square inches
¾	.44179	1	.7854
1	.7854	1⅛	.9940
1½	1.7671	1¼	1.2272
1¾	2.4053	1⅜	1.4849
2	3.1416	1½	1.7671
2½	4.9087	1⅝	2.0739
2¾	5.9396	1¾	2.4053
3	7.0686	2	3.1416
3½	9.6211		
4	12.566		
4½	15.904		
5	19.635		
6	28.274		

Discharge Rates

50 gpm equals 416.5	pounds per minute	
100 gpm equals 833.00	pounds per minutes	
200 gpm equals 1,666	pounds per minute	
250 gpm equals 2,082.50	pounds per minute (one ton)	
500 gpm equals 4,165	pounds per minute (two tons)	
1,000 gpm equals 8,330	pounds per minute (four tons)	

Capacity

Volume of Rectangular Tank

Multiply length by width by depth

Volume of Circular Tank

Multiply depth (height) by end diameter squared, by .7854. (H times D^2 times 0.7854)

Pressure Head: The force exerted by water, neglecting any effects of motion or velocity, on a unit area is known as "static pressure," "static head," or "pressure head." Head (h) is customarily measured in feet, and pressure (p) in pounds per square inch (psi). The pressure produced by a column of water one foot high will be $\frac{62.4 \text{ (pounds)}}{144 \text{ (square inches)}} = 0.4333$ psi, represented by W in the formula $P = Wh = 0.433h$. The head (h) corresponding to a pressure P (psi) will be $h = \frac{P}{W} = \frac{P}{0.433} = 2.31P$.

Pressure Head Equivalents in Feet of Elevation

Psi.	43.4	100	120	150	175	200	225
Ft. Head	100	231	277	346	404	462	520

A 1-inch head of mercury gives a pressure of 0.491 psi, equal to a 1.134-foot head of water.

Normal atmospheric pressure, 14.70 psi, is equivalent to a head of water of 33.96 feet and a head of mercury of 29.94 inches.

Horsepower

One water horsepower will lift 33,000 pounds of water one foot or a lesser quantity of water proportionally to a higher elevation.

British Thermal Unit

The heat given off by various fuels and absorbed by cooling agents such as water is measured in British thermal units commonly known as Btu. One Btu is the amount of heat required to raise the temperature of one pound of water one degree Fahrenheit.

Fuels of different types when burned give off a certain Btu per pound and sufficient water must be employed to absorb this heat.

Each U.S. gallon of water occupies 231 cubic inches of space and must pass through the pump and hose. Unless waterways are sufficiently large excessive pressure losses result and efficiency will be low compared with the horsepower expended. In addition, a given number of cubic feet of water when heated to form steam will expand at a ratio of approximately 1,650 to 1 to displace heated smoke and gases purging the atmosphere and helping to smother the fire. Therefore, the more cubic feet of water properly utilized, the greater cubic volume of fire-smothering steam can be produced. (*This subject is covered in greater detail in Chief Lloyd Layman's book, "Attacking and Extinguishing Interior Fires," published by NFPA. — Ed.*)

Velocity Head or Velocity Pressure

The velocity (v) produced in a mass of water by pressure acting upon it is the same as if the mass falls freely, starting from rest, through a distance equivalent to the pressure head in feet. This relation is represented by $v = \sqrt{2gh}$, v being the velocity in feet per second, g representing the force of gravity and h the head in feet. This is a reversible relation because not only can a pressure head produce velocity, but velocity can be converted to an equivalent pressure head. This relation is

$_{hv}$ (velocity head) $= \dfrac{v^2}{2g}$ (ft.). Because $Pv = 0.433\ _{hv}$, the velocity

pressure $pv = 0.433\ \dfrac{v^2}{2g} = $ (psi)

Velocity head or velocity pressure may be calculated by formulae involving velocity (rate of flow) and pipe diameter.

$$h_v = \frac{v^2}{64.4} \text{ or } p_v + \frac{.433v^2}{64.4} + \frac{v^2}{149}.$$

Hazen-Williams Formula

One of the well-known formulas used in fire protection is the Hazen-Williams expression $p = \dfrac{452.4\ Q^{1.85}}{c^{1.85}\ d^{4.87}}$

$Q = $ U.S. gallons per minute.
$c = $ the constant given below.
$d = $ the actual internal diameter of pipe in inches.
$p = $ friction loss (FL) pounds per square inch per 100 feet of pipe.

Calculations with this formula can be made by logarithms or from appropriate tables. Numbers to the 1.85 power and to the 4.87 power are on page 267.

The formula can be arranged in terms of Q instead of p

$$Q = \frac{Cd^{2.63}p^{0.54}}{27.19}$$

Thus Q is directly proportional to C or to $p^{0.54}$ and for a given pipe with p contant, the greater the value of C the greater the flow for the same friction loss. Similarly, when C is constant, Q is directly proportional to $p^{0.54}$ or approximately to $\sqrt{p}$.

Determining Friction Loss, Pump Pressure

A number of quick formulas are used by pumper operators for determining proper pump pressures. One popular method, the "fraction system," is quick and easy to use. It is accurate enough for fire ground conditions where solid stream tips are employed.

The "fraction method" simply requires that a fraction be remembered for each size of tip. The desired nozzle pressure for each tip (whether high or low), when multiplied by the fraction will give the approximate friction loss per 100 feet of 2½-inch line.

Fractions Used for Nozzle Tips

Tip Size	¾	⅞	1	1⅛	1¼
Fraction	½₂	⅙	¼	⅓	½

To show how well this works we show a table (*next page*) with three or four different problems for each size of nozzle tip commonly used on 2½-inch hose. These problems include both long and short lines and high and low nozzle pressures. The first column shows the tip size and the fraction used in determining friction loss. The second gives the desired nozzle pressure. The third shows how much water the stream will throw in gallons per minute. The fourth shows the friction loss figure obtained by multiplying the nozzle pressure by the fraction. The fifth gives the length of line in feet. The sixth gives the friction loss determined from the formula. This added to the nozzle pressure gives the required pump pressure as shown in column 7. The last column gives a friction loss figure for the same layout obtained from more accurate methods. In a number of cases the answers are identical.

An advantage of this method is that the pumper operator knows very quickly whether the desired nozzle pressure is within the performance range of his pump. For example, assume that it is desired to supply two 800-foot lines with 1-inch tips at 60 psi pressure from a 500 gpm pumper operating at 200 psi. The operator knows from experience that at about 180 psi he must place his changeover or transfer valve in pressure position with a reduction in volume discharged. Without waiting to see if the layout will work he can determine whether his pump can give the desired nozzle pressure, as follows:

Fraction Method for Determining Friction Losses and Pump Pressures for 2½-in. Hose
(Typical Problems)

1	2	3	4	5	6	7	8
Nozzle Tip Size and Fractional Formula	Desired Nozzle Pressure in Lbs.	Gallons per Minute	Friction Loss per 100 Ft. 2½-in. Hose	No. Ft. of Hose in Line	Total Friction Loss in Line	Required Pump Pressure *	A More Accurate Friction Loss Figure
¾ in. (1/12 nozzle pressure per 100 ft.)	45	112	4	1000	40	85	33
	60	130	5	800	40	100	36
	75	145	6	600	36	111	33
	100	167	8	500	40	140	36
⅞ in. (⅛ nozzle pressure per 100 ft.)	40	144	5	1000	50	90	55
	60	176	7½	800	60	120	64
	80	205	10	500	50	130	53
1 in. (¼ nozzle pressure per 100 ft.)	40	187	10	600	60	100	54
	60	230	15	400	60	120	52
	80	265	20	300	60	140	51
1⅛ in. (½ nozzle pressure per 100 ft.)	45	248	15	500	75	120	75
	60	291	20	300	60	120	60
	75	325	25	300	75	150	74
1¼ in. (½ nozzle pressure per 100 ft.)	40	295	20	400	80	120	82
	60	360	30	300	90	150	90
	80	415	40	200	80	160	80

*Pump pressure will help to indicate position of change-over valve.

Multiply the 60 psi nozzle pressure by ¼ which shows 15 psi friction loss per 100 feet; 15 times 8 gives 120 psi loss in 800 feet. Add 60 psi nozzle pressure. Pump pressure required is 180 psi.

This indicates that the layout is the maximum at which the pump can work in volume or capacity position. The pump presumably can do the job, particularly if it is a centrifugal pump working from a fair hydrant. On the other hand, if the pump was at draft and pumping up a hill, about 50 to 55 psi nozzle pressure might be about all that could be expected with the two lines.

In this case, the operator knew that the delivery of each stream would be about 230 gpm so that the pump could easily handle the two lines in volume or capacity operation, or could supply one line in pressure operation. This type of problem should make it possible for every fireman to estimate the desired pump pressure for any layout of 2½-inch hose.

Another practical use is in determining whether it is possible to increase the nozzle pressure with any layout. For example:

Assume a 400-foot line of 2½-inch hose with 1¼-inch tip working outside at 50 psi nozzle pressure (discharging 326 gpm). This is supplied by 150 psi pump pressure. What pump pressure will be required to give 70 psi at the nozzle (discharging 386 gpm)?

Multiply the 70 psi nozzle pressure by ½ and multiply the resulting 35 psi friction loss per 100 feet by 4 to get 140 psi friction loss in the 400-foot line. Add the 70 psi nozzle pressure. Required pump pressure would be 210 psi. A 500 gpm pumper could supply this stream if working from hydrant with 25 to 30 psi residual pressure.

In the average hose stream layout a difference of 5 psi friction loss or pump pressure would mean a change of only one or two pounds nozzle pressure. There may be a greater variation of pressure between different makes of hose or due to slight differences in elevation between pump and nozzle.

Formulas for Calculating Discharge Volumes, Hydrant Pressures, and Nozzle Pressures

$$Q = k \sqrt{P} \qquad P = p\,(AB + 1) \qquad p = \frac{P}{AB + 1}$$

Q = Discharge, gpm

p = Nozzle (Pitot) pressure, psi

P = Hydrant pressure, psi

k = Constant for discharge

A = Constant for size of nozzle

B = Constant for length of hose

Nozzle Size (in.)	k^*	A	Length of 2½-in. C.R.L. Hose (ft)	B
1	29.1	.024	50	4.9
$1\frac{1}{16}$	32.8	.031	100	8.8
$1\frac{1}{8}$	36.8	.039	150	12.8
$1\frac{3}{16}$	41.0	.048	200	16.7
$1\frac{1}{4}$	45.4	.059	250	20.6
$1\frac{5}{16}$	50.1	.072	300	24.5
$1\frac{3}{8}$	54.9	.087	350	28.4
$1\frac{7}{16}$	60.0	.104	400	32.4
$1\frac{1}{2}$	65.4	.123	450	35.3
—	—	—	500	40.2
$1\frac{5}{16}$	70.9	.145	—	—
$1\frac{5}{8}$	76.8	.170	550	44.1
$1\frac{11}{16}$	82.8	.197	600	48.1
$1\frac{3}{4}$	89.0	.228	650	52.1
—	—	—	70	55.9
$1\frac{13}{16}$	95.5	.262	750	58.8
$1\frac{7}{8}$	102.0	.300	—	—
$1\frac{15}{16}$	109.0	.343	800	63.8
2	116.0	.389	850	67.7
—	—	—	900	71.6
—	—	—	950	75.5
—	—	—	1000	79.4

*The k values are based on 0.97 nozzle coefficients, and may be corrected to other coefficient values by direct proportion.

To obtain approximate figures for friction loss in different hose sizes for the same quantity of water flowing, multiply friction loss in 2½-inch hose by the factors given in this table.

Conversion Factors for Various Sizes of Rubber-Lined Fire Hose

Single Lines					
2¾-in. (3-in. couplings)	3-in. (2½-in. couplings)	3½-in.	4-in.	4½-in.	5-in.
.60	.43	.17	.09	.05	.03

Siamesed Lines of Equal Length				
2-2½-in.	3-2½-in.	2-3-in. (2½-in. couplings)	3-3-in. (2½-in. couplings)	1-3-in. 1-2½-in.
.29	.13	.11	.06	.17

Siamesed Lines

Approximate pressure loss in other sizes for the same quantity flowing can be calculated by dividing friction loss in 2½-inch hose by the factors listed under the following sizes. For example, 280 gpm flow causes 18.7 psi loss in 2½-inch hose. In 3-inch hose the loss at this flow would be 18.7 divided by 2.6, or 7.3 psi, as shown in the table on page 260.

Single Lines					
2¾-in.	3-in.	3½-in.	4-in.	4½-in.	5-in.
1.66	2.6	5.8	11.0	19.5	32.0

Siamesed Lined of Equal Length				
2-2½-in.	3-2½-in.	2-3-in.	3-3-in.	1-3-in. 1-2½-in.
3.6	7.75	9.35	20.4	6.1

Friction losses in these tables are based on tests of good quality rubber-lined fire hose. Diameters of hose as measured under 75 psi working pressure were as follows: For nominal 2½-inch, 2.575, or about 2⁹⁄₁₆ inch; for nominal 3 inch, 3.125 or 3⅛ inch; for nominal 3½ inch, 3.685, or about 3¹¹⁄₁₆ inch.

Friction losses in these tables are based on tests of good quality rubber-lined fire hose. Diameters of hose as measured under 75 psi working pressure were as follows: For nominal 2½-inch, 2.575, or about 2$\frac{9}{16}$ inch; for nominal 3 inch, 3.125 or 3$\frac{1}{8}$ inch; for nominal 3½ inch, 3.685, or about 3$\frac{11}{16}$ inch.

Nozzle Discharge

The following empirical formulas may be used in the field to determine the volume of discharge, hydrant pressure, or pressure for nozzles with different lengths of 2½-inch rubber lined hose when one factor is unknown. Within limits of ordinary practice these formulas should give the same results as John R. Freeman's Fire Stream Tables.

Nozzle Discharge Factors

The following factors, multiplied by the square root of the discharge pressure in pounds per square inch will give the discharge of the nozzle sizes listed below in gpm. These are based upon $Q = 29.8cd^2\sqrt{p}$ for fresh water and $Q = 29.5cd^2\sqrt{p}$ for sea water, with the same assumed coefficients of discharge used in the Nozzle Discharge Tables.

Nozzle Size	Fresh Water	Sea Water	Nozzle Size	Fresh Water	Sea Water
¼	1.81	1.78	1½	66.3	65.6
⅜	4.11	4.06	1⅝	77.9	77.0
½	7.30	7.22	1¾	90.3	89.5
⅝	11.4	11.3	1⅞	104.	103.
¾	16.6	16.4	2	118.	117.
⅞	22.4	22.2	2¼	150.	148.
1	29.5	29.2	2½	184.	182.
1⅛	37.4	37.0	2¾	223.	221.
1¼	46.1	45.6	3	266.	263.
1⅜	55.8	55.2	3½	36.1	35.7

Variations in roughness and exact internal diameter may increase or decrease losses as much as 25 per cent.

First stages of a major building fire in San Francisco. (Photo by Chet Born)

Chapter 17

Fire Stream Tables

Effective Range of Solid Fire Streams

Showing the distance in feet from the nozzle at which streams will do effective work with a moderate wind blowing. With a strong wind, the reach is greatly reduced. Vertical distances are with nozzle elevated 60° to 75°; horizontal distances with nozzle elevated 30° to 35°.

Pressure at Nozzle.	SIZE OF NOZZLE									
	1-In.		1⅛-In.		1¼-In.		1⅜-In.		1½-In.	
	Vertical Distance, Ft	Horizontal Distance, Ft	Vertical Distance, Ft	Horizontal Distance, Ft	Vertical Distance, Ft	Horizontal Distance, Ft	Vertical Distance, Ft	Horizontal Distance, Ft	Vertical Distance, Ft	Horizontal Distance, Ft
20	35	37	36	38	36	39	36	40	37	42
25	43	42	44	44	45	46	45	47	46	49
30	51	47	52	50	52	52	53	54	54	56
35	58	51	59	54	59	58	60	59	62	62
40	64	55	65	59	65	62	66	64	69	66
45	69	58	70	63	70	66	72	68	74	71
50	73	61	75	66	75	69	77	72	79	75
55	76	64	79	69	80	72	81	75	83	78
60	79	67	83	72	84	75	85	77	87	80
65	82	70	86	75	87	78	88	79	90	82
70	85	72	88	77	90	80	91	82	92	84
75	87	74	90	79	92	82	93	84	94	86
80	89	76	92	81	94	84	95	86	96	88
85	91	78	94	83	96	87	97	88	98	90
90	92	80	96	85	98	89	99	90	100	91

Note: Nozzle pressures are as indicated by Pitot tube. The horizontal and vertical distances are based on experiments by John R. Freeman. *Transactions Am. Soc. C. E. Vol. XXI.*

Nozzle Reaction at Different Pressures

Nozzle Pressure Lbs. per sq. in.	Nozzle Tip Diameter								
	½"	¾"	1"	1⅛"	1¼"	1½"	1¾"	2"	2½"
25	10	22	39	50	61	88	120	157	246
30	12	26	47	60	74	106	144	189	284
35	14	31	55	70	86	124	168	220	344
40	16	35	63	79	98	142	192	252	393
45	18	40	71	89	110	159	217	283	442
50	20	44	79	99	122	177	241	315	491
55	22	49	86	110	135	194	265	346	540
60	24	53	94	119	147	212	288	377	589
65	25	57	102	129	159	230	312	409	639
70	27	62	110	139	172	247	336	440	688
75	29	66	118	149	184	265	361	472	737
80	31	71	126	159	196	282	385	502	785
90	35	80	141	179	221	318	432	566	883
100	39	88	167	198	245	353	481	629	981
125	49	111	196	248	307	442	601	786	1228
150	59	132	236	298	368	530	721	942	1474
175	: :	: :	: :	: :	: :	618	832	1100	1698
200	:	:	:	:	:	708	961	1258	1964
225	:	:	:	:	:	796	1082	1416	2210
250	:	:	:	:	:	883	1204	1573	2460

Nozzle Pressures Required for Given Flows

	(Tip Diameter in Inches)					
GPM	1	1⅛	1¼	1½	1¾	2
100	11	7	5	3	2	1
200	45	28	19	9	5	3
300	100	63	41	20	11	7
400		112	73	35	19	12
500			114	55	30	18
600			167	80	43	25
700				109	59	35
800				142	77	45
900				179	97	57
1000					120	70
1100					145	85

Relative Discharge Capacities of Nozzles

(Tip Size in Inches)

Number of Nozzles												
1	⅝	¾	⅞	1	1⅛	1¼	1⅜	1½	1⅝	1¾	1⅞	2
2	⅞	1 1/16	1¼	1⅜	1⅝	1¾	1 15/16	2⅛	2 5/16	2½	2⅝	2 13/16
3	1 1/16	1 5/16	1½	1¾	1 15/16	2 3/16	2⅜	2⅝	2 13/16	3	3¼	3½
4	1¼	1½	1¾	2	2¼	2½	2¾	3	3¼	3½	3¾	4
5	1⅜	1 11/16	2	2¼	2½	2¾	3 1/16	3⅜	3⅝	3 15/16	4 3/16	
6	1½	1 13/16	2⅛	2 7/16	2¾	3 1/16	3⅜	3 11/16	4			
7	1⅝	2	2 5/16	2⅝	3	3 5/16	3⅝	3				
8	1¾	2⅛	2½	2 15/16	3 3/16	3 9/16	3⅞					
9	1⅞	2¼	2⅝	3	3⅜	3¾	4⅛					
10	2	2⅜	2¾	3 3/16	3 9/16	4						
11	2 1/16	2½	2⅞	3 5/16	3¾							
12	2 3/16	2⅝	3	3½	3 15/16							

Example — To find which size nozzle equals two 1⅛-inch nozzles: On the line marked 2 in the left column, the size nozzle (1⅝) in the 1⅛ column will be the answer. Check also: four 1⅝-inch tips equal one 3¼-inch tip; four 2-inch tips equal one 4-inch tip.

Pressure Losses in Rubber-Lined Hose
(PSI Loss per 100 Feet of Hose)

U.S. Gallons per Minute	2½-inch	2¾-inch (3-inch couplings)	3-inch (2½-inch couplings)	3-inch
100	2.5	1.7	1.2	1.2
110	3.2	2.1	1.4	1.4
120	3.9	2.4	1.6	1.6
130	4.5	2.8	1.9	1.8
140	5.2	3.1	2.1	2.0
150	5.8	3.6	2.5	2.3
160	6.6	4.0	2.9	2.6
170	7.4	4.5	3.2	2.9
180	8.3	5.0	3.6	3.2
190	9.2	5.6	3.8	3.5
200	10.1	6.1	4.0	3.8
210	11.1	6.7	4.4	4.2
220	12.0	7.2	4.5	4.6
230	13.0	7.8	5.3	5.0
240	14.1	8.5	5.8	5.4
250	15.3	9.2	6.2	5.9
260	16.4	9.9	6.8	6.3
270	17.5	10.5	7.3	6.7

U.S. Gallons per Minute	2½-inch	2¾-inch (3-inch couplings)	3-inch (2½-inch couplings)	3-inch
290	19.9	11.9	8.4	7.7
300	21.2	12.7	9.0	8.2
310	22.5	13.5	9.7	8.7
320	23.8	14.3	10.3	9.3
330	25.3	15.2	10.9	9.9
340	26.9	16.2	11.6	10.5
350	28.4	17.1	12.3	11.0
360	30.0	18.0	13.0	11.5
370	31.5	18.9	13.7	12.2
380	33.0	19.8	14.4	12.8
390	34.6	20.7	15.2	13.4
400	36.2	21.7	16.0	14.1
420	39.9	24.0	17.7	15.4
440	43.2	25.9	19.4	16.8
460	46.8	28.1	21.3	18.2
480	50.8	30.5	23.1	19.7
500	55.1	33.1	25.0	21.2

Pressure Losses per 100 Feet in Rubber-Lined Fire Hose

(Large Hose or Siamesed Lines)

Flows in Gals. per Minute	2 Lines of 2½-in. Siamesed	2½-in. and 3-in. Siamesed	2 Lines of 3-in. Siamesed	3 Lines of 2½-in. Siamesed	3-in.* 3-in½. Hose	3½-in. 3½-in. Hose
400	10.1	5.9	3.9	4.7	14.1	6.3
420	11.1	6.5	4.2	5.2	15.4	6.9
440	12.0	7.1	4.6	5.6	16.8	7.5
460	13.0	7.7	5.0	6.1	18.2	8.1
480	14.1	8.3	5.4	6.6	19.7	8.8
500	15.2	9.0	5.9	7.1	21.2	9.5
520	16.4	9.6	6.3	7.7	22.7	10.3
540	17.5	10.4	6.7	8.3	24.3	11.1
560	18.7	11.1	7.2	8.9	26.0	11.9
580	19.9	11.9	7.7	9.5	27.9	12.7
600	21.2	12.7	8.2	10.1	29.8	13.4
620	22.5	13.5	8.7	10.7	31.6	14.2
640	23.8	14.2	9.3	11.4	33.5	15.0
660	25.3	15.1	9.9	12.0	35.5	15.9
680	26.9	15.9	10.5	12.7	37.5	16.8
700	28.3	16.8	11.0	13.4	39.6	17.7
720	29.9	17.7	11.6	14.1	41.7	18.7
740	31.5	18.6	12.2	14.8	43.8	19.7
760	33.0	19.5	12.8	15.6	45.9	21.7
780	34.6	20.4	13.4	16.4	48.0	21.7
800	36.2	21.5	14.1	17.2	50.1	22.7
820	38.0	22.5	22.5	18.0	....	23.8
840	39.9	23.6	15.5	18.7	....	24.9
860	41.5	24.5	16.1	19.5	....	26.0
880	43.2	25.6	16.8	20.4	....	27.1
900	45.0	26.7	17.5	21.2	....	28.2
925	47.2	28.1	18.4	22.3	....	29.7
950	49.6	29.5	19.3	23.4	....	31.2
975	52.3	30.9	20.2	24.5	....	32.7
1000	55.1	32.4	21.2	25.8	....	34.3
1100	....	38.5	25.2	31.0	....	41.0

Hose Diameters and Areas

Internal Diameter	Area	Percentage of Next Larger Size
¾	.44179	56%
1	.7854	44%
1½	1.7671	34%
2½ (actually 2⁹⁄₁₆)	5.1573	73%
3	7.0686	73%
3½	9.6211	—

GPM Flow 100 lb. Fog Nozzle	Equivalent Flow 50 lb. Solid Stream Tips	Approximate FL with 1½-inch Hose*
50	½	10
80	⅝	20
100	¾	30

*In most cases actual friction loss will be somewhat less.

Discharge from Heavy Stream Nozzle Tips

Nozzle Diam. In Inches	No. Lines*	Nozzle Pressure in Pounds							
		64		81		100		121	
		GPM	Friction Loss	GPM	Friction Loss	GPM	Friction Loss	GPM	Friction Loss
1¼		369	(9)	415	(11)	461	(13)	509	(16)
1⅜	2–2½	445	(12)	503	(15)	560	(19)	615	(22)
1½		533	(17)	600	(21)	667	(26)	733	(15)
1⅝		627	(23)	704	(14)	783	(17)	861	(20)
1¾	3–2½	727	(14)	818	(18)	909	(22)	1000	(15)
2		951	(23)	1069	(17)	1189	(21)	1308	(25)
2¼	4–2½	1206	(21)	1355	(27)	1506	(32)	1656	(38)

*Number of lines shown will keep friction loss to not over 25 pounds per 100 feet of hose line with flows up to 1300 gpm.

Diameters, Squares of Diameters and Areas of Circles

Diameter		Square of Diam.	Area
1/16	.0625	.003906	.00307
1/8	.1250	.01563	.01227
3/16	.1875	.03516	.02761
1/4	.2500	.0625	.04909
5/16	.3125	.09766	.07670
3/8	.3750	.1406	.11045
7/16	.4375	.1914	.15033
1/2	.5000	.2500	.19635
9/16	.5625	.3164	.24850
5/8	.6250	.3906	.30680
11/16	.6875	.4727	.37122
3/4	.7500	.5625	.44179
13/16	.8125	.6601	.51849
7/8	.8750	.7656	.60132
15/16	.9375	.8789	.69029
1	1.0000	1.000	.7854
1 1/16	1.0625	1.1289	.8866
1 1/8	1.1250	1.2656	.9940
1 3/16	1.1875	1.4102	1.1075
1 1/4	1.2500	1.5625	1.2272
1 5/16	1.3125	1.7227	1.3530
1 3/8	1.3750	1.8906	1.4849
1 7/16	1.4375	2.0664	1.6230
1 1/2	1.5000	2.2500	1.7671
1 9/16	1.5625	2.4414	1.9175
1 5/8	1.6250	2.6406	2.0739
1 11/16	1.6875	2.8477	2.2365
1 3/4	1.7500	3.0625	2.4053
1 13/16	1.8125	3.2852	2.5802
1 7/8	1.8750	3.5156	2.7612
1 15/16	1.9375	3.7539	2.9483
2	2.0000	4.000	3.1416
2 1/16	2.0625	4.2539	3.3410
2 1/8	2.1250	4.5156	3.5466
2 3/16	2.1875	4.7852	3.7583
2 1/4	2.2500	5.0625	3.9761
2 5/16	2.3125	5.3477	4.2000
2 3/8	2.3750	5.6406	4.4301
2 7/16	2.4375	5.9414	4.6664
2 1/2	2.5000	6.2500	4.9087
2 9/16	2.5625	6.5664	5.1573
2 5/8	2.6250	6.8906	5.4119
2 11/16	2.6875	7.2227	5.6727
2 3/4	2.7500	7.5625	5.9396
2 13/16	2.8125	7.9102	6.2127
2 7/8	2.8750	8.2656	6.4918
2 15/16	2.9375	8.6289	6.7771
3	3.0000	9.0000	7.0686

Dia.	Sq. of Diam.	Area
3.5	12.25	9.6211
4.0	16.00	12.566
4.5	20.25	15.904
5.0	25.00	19.635
5.5	30.25	23.758
6.0	36.00	28.274
6.5	42.25	33.183
7.0	49.00	38.485
7.5	56.25	44.179
8.0	64.00	50.265
8.5	72.25	56.745
9.0	81.00	63.617
9.5	90.25	70.882
10.0	100.00	78.540
10.5	110.25	86.590
11.0	121.00	95.033
11.5	132.25	103.87
12.0	144.00	113.10
13	169	132.73
14	196	153.94
15	225	176.71
16	256	201.06
17	289	226.98
18	324	254.47
19	361	283.53
20	400	314.16
21	441	346.36
22	484	380.13
23	529	415.48
24	576	452.39
25	625	490.87
26	676	530.93
27	729	572.56
28	784	615.25
29	841	660.52
30	900	706.86
31	961	754.77
32	1024	804.25
33	1089	855.30
34	1156	907.92
35	1225	962.11
36	1296	1017.9
37	1369	1075.2
38	1444	1134.1
39	1521	1194.6
40	1600	1256.6
41	1681	1320.3
42	1764	1385.4
43	1849	1452.2
44	1936	1520.5
45	2025	1590.4
46	2116	1661.9
47	2209	1734.9

Dia.	Sq. of Diam.	Area
48	2304	1809.6
49	2401	1885.7
50	2500	1963.5
51	2601	2042.8
52	2704	2123.7
53	2809	2206.2
54	2916	2290.2
55	3025	2375.8
56	3136	2463.0
57	3249	2551.8
58	3364	2642.1
59	3481	2734.0
60	3600	2827.4
61	3721	2922.5
62	3844	3019.1
63	3969	3117.2
64	4096	3217.0
65	4225	3318.3
66	4356	3421.2
67	4489	3525.7
68	4624	3631.7
69	4761	3739.3
70	4900	3848.5
71	5041	3959.2
72	5184	4071.5
73	5329	4185.4
74	5476	4300.8
75	5625	4417.9
76	5776	4536.5
77	5929	4656.6
78	6084	4778.4
79	6241	4901.7
80	6400	5026.5
81	6561	5153.0
82	6724	5281.0
83	6889	5410.6
84	7056	5541.8
85	7225	5674.5
86	7396	5808.8
87	7569	5944.7
88	7744	6082.1
89	7921	6221.1
90	8100	6361.7
91	8281	6503.9
92	8464	6647.6
93	8649	6792.9
94	8836	6939.8
95	9025	7088.2
96	9216	7238.2
97	9409	7389.8
98	9604	7543.0
99	9801	7696.9
100	10000	7854.0

Approximate Discharge of Straight Stream Nozzles

Nozzle Pressure PSI	√NP	% of Flow at 100 PSI	¼	⅜	½	⅝	¾	⅞	1	1⅛	1¼	1⅜	1½	1⅝	1¾	2	2¼
									Nozzle Diameter in Inches								
25	5	50	9.1	20	37	57	83	112	148	187	230	280	333	391	454	594	753
30	5.5	55	10.0	23	40	63	91	123	162	204	254	308	367	431	500	654	828
36	6	60	10.9	25	44	68	99	134	177	223	277	336	400	470	545	713	904
42	6.5	65	11.8	27	47	74	107	146	192	242	300	364	434	509	591	773	979
49	7	70	12.7	29	51	80	116	157	207	261	323	392	467	548	636	832	1053
56	7.5	75	13.6	31	55	86	124	168	221	280	346	420	500	587	682	892	1129
64	8	80	14.5	33	58	91	132	179	236	299	369	448	534	626	727	951	1204
72	8.5	85	15.4	35	62	97	140	190	251	318	392	475	567	666	773	1010	1279
81	9	90	16.3	37	66	103	149	202	266	337	415	504	600	705	818	1070	1354
90	9.5	95	17.3	39	70	108	157	213	280	356	438	532	634	744	863	1130	1430
100	10	100	18.2	41	73	114	165	224	295	374	461	560	667	783	909	1187	1506
111	10.5	105	19.1	43	76	120	173	235	310	393	484	588	700	822	954	1247	1581
121	11	110	20.0	45	80	125	182	246	325	411	507	616	734	861	999	1306	1657
132	11.5	115	20.9	47	84	131	190	258	339	430	530	644	767	900	1045	1366	1732
144	12	120	21.8	49	87	137	198	269	354	449	553	672	800	940	1090	1425	1807
156	12.5	125	22.7	51	91	143	206	280	369	467	576	700	834	979	1136	1485	1883
Approximate change in gpm caused by increase or decrease of √NP by one.			2	4	7	11	16.5	22	29.5	37	46	56	67	78	91	119	150

Nozzle Flows Related to Square Root of Nozzle Pressure

Nozzle Pressure (Pounds)	1	4	9	16	25	36	49	64	81	100	121	144
Square Root of Nozzle Pressure	1	2	3	4	5	6	7	8	9	10	11	12
Tip Diameter (Inches)						Flows in gallons per minute						
¼	1.8	3.6	5.4	7.2	9.1	10.9	12.7	14.5	16.3	18.2	20	21.8
⅜	4.1	8.2	12.3	16.4	20.5	24.6	28.7	32.8	36.9	41.1	45.2	49.3
½	7.3	14.6	21.9	29.2	36.5	43.8	51.1	58.4	65.7	73.0	80.3	87.6
⅝	11.4	22.8	34.2	45.6	57.0	68.4	79.8	91.2	103	114	125	137
¾	16.5	33.0	49.5	66.0	82.5	98.0	114	131	148	165	181	198
⅞	22.4	44.8	67.2	89.6	112	135	157	179	202	224	246	269
15/16	25.9	51.8	77.7	104	129	155	181	207	233	259	285	311
1	29.5	59.0	88.5	118	147	177	207	237	265	295	324	354
1⅛	37.4	74.8	112	150	187	224	262	299	337	374	411	449
1¼	46.1	92.2	138	184	230	277	323	369	415	461	507	553
1⅜	56.0	112	168	224	280	336	392	448	504	560	616	672
1½	66.7	133	200	267	333	400	467	533	600	667	733	800
1⅝	78.3	157	235	313	391	470	548	626	705	783	861	940
1¾	90.9	182	273	363	454	545	635	727	818	909	1000	1091
2	119	238	357	476	595	713	832	951	1070	1189	1308	1427
2¼	150	301	452	603	754	905	1055	1205	1355	1506	1657	1807

Psi Loss Per 1000 Feet of Pipe
Ordinary Wrought Iron and Cast Iron

U. S. Gallons		Pipe Diameter in Inches								
Per Minute	Per Day	6″	8″	10″	12″	14″	16″	18″	20″	24″
25	36,000	0.1	…	…	…	…	…	…	…	…
50	72,000	0.2	0.1	…	…	…	…	…	…	…
100	144,000	0.8	0.2	0.1	…	…	…	…	…	…
200	288,000	2.6	0.6	0.2	0.1	…	…	…	…	…
300	432,000	5.6	1.4	0.5	0.2	0.1	…	…	…	…
400	576,000	9.6	2.4	0.8	0.3	0.2	0.1	…	…	…
500	720,000	15.0	3.5	1.2	0.5	0.2	0.1	0.1	…	…
1,000	1,440,000	52.0	12.8	4.3	1.8	0.8	0.4	0.2	0.1	…
1,500	2,160,000	111.0	27.0	9.1	3.8	1.8	0.9	0.5	0.3	0.1
2,000	2,880,000	190.0	46.2	15.6	6.4	3.0	1.6	0.9	0.5	0.2
2,500	3,600,000	287.0	71.0	23.5	9.7	4.6	2.4	1.3	0.8	0.3
3,000	4,320,000	…	99.0	33.0	13.6	6.4	3.3	1.9	1.1	0.5
3,500	5,040,000	…	132.0	44.0	18.3	8.6	4.6	2.5	1.5	0.6
4,000	5,760,000	…	166.0	56.0	23.1	11.0	5.7	3.2	1.9	0.8
4,500	6,480,000	…	208.0	70.0	29.0	13.7	7.1	4.0	2.4	1.0
5,000	1,200,000	…	252.0	86.0	34.9	16.5	8.6	4.9	2.9	1.2

Based on Hazen and Williams' formula with C = 100.

Common Conversions to Metric System
Accurate to Six Significant Figures

Symbol	When You Know	Multiply by	To Find	Symbol
in	inches	[A]25.4	[B]millimeters	mm
ft	feet	[A]0.3048	meters	m
yd	yards	[A]0.9144	meters	m
mi	miles	1.609 34	kilometers	km
yd^2	square yards	0.836 127	square meters	m^2
	acres	0.404 686	[C]hectares	ha
yd^3	cubic yards	0.764 555	cubic meters	m^3
qt	quarts (lq)	0.946 353	[D]liters	l
gal	gallons (lq)	3.785	[D]liters	l
oz	ounces (avdp)	28.349 5	grams	g
lb	pounds (avdp)	0.453 592	kilograms	kg
°F	Fahrenheit temperature	[A]5 9(after subtracing 32)	Celsius temperature	°C
mm	millimeters	0.039 370 1	inches	in
m	meters	3.280 84	feet	ft
m	meters	1.093 61	yards	yd
km	kilometers	0.621 371	miles	mi
m^2	square meters	1.195 99	square yards	yd^2
ha	[C]hectares	2.471 05	acres	
m^3	cubic meters	1.307 95	cubic yards	yd^3
l	[D]liters	1.056 69	quarts (lq)	qt
g	grams	0.035 274 0	ounces (avdp)	oz
kg	kilograms	2.204 62	pounds (avdp)	lb
°C	Celsius temperature	[A]9/5 (then add 32)	Fahrenheit temperature	°F

[A]Exact

[B]for example: 1 in = 25 4 mm, so 3 inches would be

$$(3 \text{ in}) (25 4 \tfrac{\text{mm}}{\text{in}}) = 76.2 \text{ mm}$$

[C]hectare is a common name for 10,000 square meters

[D]liter is a common name for fluid volume of 0.001 cubic meter

(lq) = liquid

(avdp) = avoirdupois

Note: Most symbols are written with lower case letters; exceptions are units named after persons for which the symbols are capitalized. Periods are not used with any symbols.

Reference Publications

As mentioned previously in this book, manufacturers' manuals and representatives should be consulted for information on the capability, performance and special characteristics of their elevating platforms and water towers. For related information on fire control tactics and other operations, the reader is referred to the following publications, available from the National Fire Protection Association, 470 Atlantic Avenue, Boston, Massachusetts 02210.

FPH 1476	Fire Protection Handbook
FSP-1	Fire Attack 1
FSP-2	Fire Attack 2
FSP-5	Handling Hose and Ladders
FSP-7A	Operating Aerial Ladders
FSP-27A	Fire Apparatus Maintenance
FSP-34	How to Judge Your Fire Department
FSP-35	Communications for Fire Attack
FSP-39	Elevating Platforms and Aerial Towers

Glossary

ADAPTORS. Devices used for connecting hose couplings of different screw threads, pitch and diameters, such as in handlines or pumper intakes and outlets. Adaptors may also be reducers, used for connecting a larger coupling to a smaller size.

ADJUSTABLE FOG NOZZLE. A nozzle that provides a variable stream pattern from straight stream to ninety degree spray or water fog. It is usually adjusted by rotating a nozzle sleeve that changes the shape and size of the discharge opening.

ATMOSPHERIC PRESSURE. Pressure of the air or atmosphere at sea level, approximately 14.7 pounds per square inch — equivalent to a 33.9 foot head of water. On pumpers, pressures below atmospheric are usually indicated by gages calibrated in inches of mercury.

ATTACK UNIT. Specially designed and equipped pumper capable of quick discharge of its full capacity through handlines and heavy stream nozzles. These units need to be supplied promptly by other apparatus after initial operations on the fireground.

AQUEOUS FILM FORMING FOAM (AFFF). A fluorinated foaming agent that creates a film that floats on flammable liquids or water to exclude oxygen and thus smother the flames.

AVAILABLE FLOW. Usually the estimated amount of water available within the immediate area of fireground operations. Sometimes this term refers to the amount available from a single hydrant, or from a static source.

AWWA. American Water Works Association.

BAROMETER. Instrument for measuring pressure of the atmosphere.

BLITZ. Slang term intended to define quick, full attack capability of a pumper that can discharge its tank contents through preconnected handlines and/or a monitor nozzle.

BONNET. Top part of hydrant that encloses end of stem. Turning the stem with a hydrant wrench opens valve permitting water to flow from the underground main to hydrant outlets.

BOOSTER TANK. Term sometimes used to designate tank on a standard pumper. Originally, it referred to the small water tanks on chemical wagons in the early 1900s.

BURY. Portion of a hydrant below ground level.

CAPS. Threaded fittings attached to hydrant outlets when the hydrant is not in use. Caps are usually chained to minimize chance of losing them in the haste of fireground action or through vandalism.

CAVITATION. A condition that occurs when an operating pump begins to exceed its water supply. Cavitation can occur during drafting or when operating from a hydrant. Air cavities are formed within the pump and water hammer may develop and cause serious damage to pump impellers and other parts.

CENTRIFUGAL PUMP. A pump with one or more impellers that rotate on a shaft, taking water into the eye of the impeller and discharging through the volutes. Centrifugal pumps may be single- or multi-stage.

CLAPPER VALVES. A hinged valve that permits flow of water in only one direction, i.e., a clapper valve in a siamese connection which closes to prevent escape of water through an unused inlet.

DEAD-END MAIN. A water main supplied from only one direction. "Dead-end" also refers to a hydrant or other fire protection equipment served by such a main.

DECK GUN. A large capacity monitor nozzle usually mounted mid-ship on a pumper or hose wagon. Also referred to as a monitor nozzle or "turret." Some deck guns are permanently fixed in place; others can be removed to be used as portable monitors on the ground.

DISTRIBUTION GRID. Layout of water main and hydrants protecting a certain locality.

DRAFTING. The process of drawing water from a static source into a pump. This is accomplished by removing air from the pump chamber and allowing atmospheric pressure to push water through a suction hose up to the pump.

DRY BARREL. A type of hydrant used in communities where temperatures below freezing occur. The hydrant valve must be opened by turning the stem, permitting water to flow up to the outlets.

DUMP VALVE. A quick-opening valve used for emptying water rapidly from a tank, such as when a tank truck is filling a portable container from which a pumper can draft water.

EDUCTOR PUMPING. Method of using the flow of water and the venturi effect to induce or educt water or some other fire extinguishing agent into a hose line or nozzle. Eductor nozzles are sometimes used to pick up a foaming agent from a container. Eductor pumping can also be used at heights which are too great for drafting.

ELEVATED STREAMS. Usually large capacity streams discharged by ladder pipes or monitor nozzles on elevating platforms. The term may also refer to handlines or monitor nozzles positioned at some high level on a building but supplied by pumping apparatus at a lower level.

ENGINE COMPANY. The personnel and apparatus designated to carry out pumping operations. An engine company may have a single pumper or may be a two-piece company with a pumper and hose wagon or a pumper and some other apparatus. Standard manning for an engine company includes officer, a pump operator and at least four other fire fighters.

FEEDER LINES. A hose line from a source of water supply to pumping apparatus. The term may refer to one or more lines from the hydrant, or supply lines from one pumper to another, as contrasted with hand lines used for fire fighting.

FIRST-IN. The first arriving apparatus and manpower on the fireground.

FLUOROPROTEIN. Foam concentrate extinguishing agents similar to protein foam concentrates but with a synthetic fluorinated surfactant additive. In addition to forming an air-excluding foam blanket the fluoroprotein foam may also deposit a vaporization-preventing film on the surface of a liquid fuel. These agents are diluted with water to form three percent to six percent solutions, depending on the type.

FLOW TEST. The procedure of opening a hydrant valve and outlet to measure the pressure and quantity of water discharged by the hydrant under certain conditions. The flow test may be applied to an individual hydrant or to a group of hydrants simultaneously. It is best to take flow test measurements from two or more hydrants simultaneously to estimate the effect of pumpers using that same hydrant supply for fire fighting purposes.

FRICTION LOSS. Term commonly applied to loss of pressure in fire hose, pipe or fittings due to friction, turbulence, gravity, amount of water flow and other effects. Friction loss normally is measured in psi (per hundred feet).

FULL CAPACITY. The total amount of water that can be discharged by a pumper under certain conditions. For example, a 1,000 gpm pumper, operating from draft, should be able to discharge its full 1,000 gpm capacity. However, when operating from a good hydrant, the same pumper may be able to move as much as 1,250 or 1,300 gpm of water. (See rated capacity.)

GATED INLETS. Intake connections on pumpers, monitor nozzles or other devices which have a gated control valve for each inlet.

GOVERNOR. A device used to regulate the engine and thus control the speed of the pump. The governor is said to permit a certain maximum pressure and slows down engine speed when nozzles are shut down quickly. Thus, it keeps pressure on other lines within safe limits.

GROUND MONITOR. A portable monitor nozzle moved manually into position on the ground. For prolonged fires, some fire departments permit these monitors to be operated unattended, once they are fastened into position. This also can be a safe and effective operation for cooling tanks, tank trucks, railroad cars, or other units containing hazardous material that may be explosive or otherwise injurious to fire fighting personnel.

HIGH PRESSURE HYDRANTS. Baltimore, Boston, New York, San Francisco, Chicago and a number of other major cities have used separate Fire Service water mains providing large flows at high pressures for the high value downtown districts. Pressures in a normal public water system usually are below 100 psi, even though hydrant fittings are designed for maximum working pressures of 150 psi. A high pressure system might provide 150 psi or greater pressure at hydrants.

HIGH VALUE DISTRICTS. This term formerly applied only to the downtown business areas of cities but in recent years, when shopping centers, industrial parks and other large concentrations have been developed in smaller communities, the term "high value" has broader application. Obviously, greater water supply is needed for concentrations of business and industrial properties than for residential districts and less congested areas.

HYDRANT GAGE. A gage that can be attached to a hydrant outlet to measure residual pressure.

IMPELLERS. The slotted, disc-like pump components that turn on the impeller shaft. As the impeller rotates, water is drawn into the impeller eye, then is discharged by centrifugal force through the impeller volute.

LARGE DIAMETER HOSE. Hand lines normally used from pumpers usually are from 1- to 2½-inch size but a few fire departments have used 2¾-inch or 3-inch hand lines. Large diameter hose, used principally for supply purposes, would be from 3-inch to 6-inch diameter.

LIFT. Distance in feet of elevation between a static source of water and the suction chamber of a drafting fire department pumper.

LINE RELIEF VALVE. A small valve that can be inserted into a hose line to discharge water when pressure in the line rises to a certain level. These relief valves sometimes are used on the intake side of a pump to prevent damage from excess pressure.

MANIFOLD COMPANIES. Engine company operating especially designed apparatus that requires attachment of a number of hose lines into a manifold. Los Angeles, Chicago, Memphis and other major fire departments have used special apparatus companies.

MONITOR NOZZLE. A large heavy stream nozzle, usually controlled by wheel operated gears. They may be equipped with 2-inch or 2½-inch tips or larger to discharge 1,000 gpm or more.

NOZZLE PRESSURE. The amount of pressure in pounds per square inch (psi) measured at tip of discharging nozzle. A Pitot gage can be used to record this pressure.

OUTLETS. Threaded discharge connections of pumpers, hydrants, sprinkler and standpipe systems and other connections requiring attachment of couplings. National Standard Thread is recommended for such couplings.

OUTSIDE SPRINKLERS. A sprinkler system with especially designed sprinkler heads installed to protect a structure and window openings against a severe exposure hazard.

PITOT GAGE. A curved tube attached to a pressure gage. The open end of the tube is inserted into the center of a discharging stream and pressure is recorded on the gage. Flow from the discharge opening can be determined from published tables.

PRE-CONNECTED. Hose lines or heavy stream nozzles attached and ready for operation before apparatus responds to alarms. Many fire departments have at least one 2½-inch line and one or more 1½-inch lines preconnected on first line pumpers. Some departments have deck guns preconnected.

PRIMING. Filling a pump with water prior to drafting.

PROTEINFOAM. Proteinfoam concentrates consist primarily of products from a protein hydrolysate, plus stabilizing additives and inhibitors to prevent freezing, corrosion and bacterial decomposition and to control velocity and otherwise insure readiness for use under emergency conditions. These agents are diluted with water to form three percent to six percent solutions, depending upon the type.

RATED CAPACITY. The standard requirements for pump performance are: 100 percent rated capacity at 150 psi net pump pressure; 70 percent rated capacity at 200 psi net pump pressure; and 50 percent rated capacity at 250 psi net pump pressure.

RELAY PUMPING. Use of two or more fire department pumpers to move water distances which would require excessive pressure to overcome friction loss if only one pump was employed at the source. In general, pumps are required for relays where the nozzle is not over 2500 feet from the water supply and three pumps are needed for longer relay. For maximum performance in series operation, supply pumps at relay should be operated at 200 psi with the pump nearest to the fire adjusting for nozzle pressure. For supplying volume, fire pumps may be limited to about 150 psi net pump pressure.

RELIEF VALVE. A pressure controlling device which bypasses water at a fire department pump to prevent excessive pressures when nozzles are shut down. (See line relief valve.)

RESIDUAL PRESSURE. Pressure remaining on inlet side of a fire department pumper while water is being discharged from the pump outlets. The amount of residual pressure compared with the static pressure before pump discharge is started will indicate the relative volume of water that can be taken from a hydrant or from a pumper relay.

SECOND-DUE. The fire company designated to respond second at a given alarm site.

SERIES. Operation of a multi-stage pump so that water passes through each impeller consecutively to build up pressure rather than simultaneously to provide volume in parallel operation.

SIAMESE CONNECTION. Double or triple intake to a monitor nozzle, sprinkler system or other device. Also a hose fitting for combining the flow from two or more lines of hose into a single line.

SPLIT HOSE BED. Hose bed on a pumper or hose wagon divided into a compartment for carrying different sizes and amounts of fire hose.

SPRINKER STOPPERS. Devices for stopping the flow of water from individual sprinkler heads.

STANDPIPE SYSTEMS. A vertical water pipe riser used to supply fire hose outlets in buildings. Standpipes usually supply 1½- or 1¼-inch hose line in domestic or private water pressure that must be supplemented by fire department pumpers.

STATIC PRESSURE. Water pressure available at a specific location with no fire flow being used so that no pressure losses due to friction are being encountered. Static pressure is recorded on a pumper inlet gage before any water is taken from the hydrant.

STATIC WATER SOURCE. A supply of water at rest which does not provide a pressure head for fire fighting but may be used as a suction source for fire pump.

STEM. The vertical center shaft of a hydrant which usually has a pentagonal nut on top on which a hydrant wrench can be placed. Turning the stem opens or closes the hydrant valve at the base.

STRAINER. Wire or metal guard used to keep suction hose or pump free from clogging.

SUCTION HOSE. A stiff, reinforced hose or a soft hose used to connect pump to water supply. Hard suction hose is used for drafting from suction source and may also be used on hydrants. Soft suction hose, from 2½-inch size upward, is used for hydrant supply and pumper relay.

SUPER PUMPER. Large capacity, specially designed pumper used by New York City Fire Department.

SUPPLEMENTAL PUMPING. Technique of using pumpers to relay water from two or more hydrants into other hydrants closer to the fireground.

SUPPLY LINE. Hose line between water source and pumper or between pumpers.

SYNTHETIC FOAM. Extinguishing foam concentrate usually derived from hydrocarbon surface active agents, sometimes listed as wetting agents or as foaming agents.

TANKER SHUTTLE. A procedure for moving water supply in tank truck from a static or hydrant source to portable containers from which pumpers can draft.

TORQUE. The force that tends to twist or to produce rotation. In measuring useful engine power at the shaft the torque can be calculated by the following formula:

$$\text{Torque} = \frac{\text{HP} \times 5252}{\text{RPM}}$$

TRANSFER VALVE. A control valve for placing a multi-stage pump in volume or pressure operation.

TWO PIECE COMPANY. A fire company regularly operating and responding with two motor driven fire apparatus.

VACUUM GAGE. Gage for measuring pressure below atmospheric.

WET BARREL. Type of hydrant used in California and other warm weather climate areas.

WHEEL CHOCKS. A rubber, wooden, or synthetic material triangular block that can be placed under fire apparatus wheels to prevent movement of the vehicle.

WYEING. Using a hose connection with two outlets to permit two hose lines to be supplied by one. For example, a 2½-inch wye permits supplying two 2½-inch lines from a single 2½-inch or 3-inch line having 2½-inch couplings. Reducing wyes are also available to permit smaller diameter lines from a large line.

Index